Mission to Tokyo

Mission to Tokyo

The American Airmen Who Took the War to the Heart of Japan

Robert F. Dorr

ZENITH PRESS

First published in 2012 by Zenith Press, an imprint of MBI Publishing Company, 400 First Avenue North, Suite 400, Minneapolis, MN 55401 USA

Zenith Press titles are also available at discounts in bulk quantity for industrial or sales-promotional use. For details write to Special Sales Manager at MBI Publishing Company, 400 First Avenue North, Suite 400, Minneapolis, MN 55401 USA.

To find out more about our books, join us online at www.zenithpress.com.

Library of Congress Cataloging-in-Publication Data

Dorr, Robert F.
 Mission to Tokyo : the American airmen who took the war to the heart of Japan / Robert F. Dorr.
   p. cm.
 Includes bibliographical references and index.
 Summary: "An overview of the bombing campaign against Tokyo in World War II as well as a detailed account of a specific bombing mission from a Pacific island airfield on Tinian to Tokyo and back, told in the veterans' words, including pilots and other aircrew, groundcrew, and escort fighters that accompanied the B-29 bombers on their perilous mission"--Provided by publisher.
 ISBN 978-0-7603-4122-3
 1. World War, 1939-1945--Campaigns--Japan--Tokyo. 2. World War, 1939-1945--Aerial operations, American. 3. Tokyo (Japan)--History--Bombardment, 1945. 4. Flight crews--United States--Biography. 5. United States. Army Air Forces--Biography. 6. B-29 (Bomber) I. Title.
 D767.25.T6D67 2012
 940.54'252135--dc23
                         2012017849

Editor: Scott Pearson
Design Manager: James Kegley
Cover design: Simon Larkin
Layout: Helena Shrimizu

On the front cover: B-29s over Mount Fuji. *U.S. Air Force*
On the back cover: A B-29 flies high above an unidentified city. *Terry Tucker Rhodes*
B-29 schematics by Onno Van Braam

Printed in the United States of America
10 9 8 7 6 5 4 3

Ten thousand Americans had roles in the air assault on the Empire on March 9–10, 1945. This book is dedicated to four of them:

Sam P. Bakshas, mission leader on the B-29 Tall in the Saddle

William J. "Reb" Carter, gunner on the B-29 God's Will

Hubert L. Kordsmeier, airplane commander of an unnamed B-29

Percy Usher Tucker, airplane commander of the B-29 Lady Annabelle

Of the four, two survived.

Contents

BOEING B-29 SUPERFORTRESS

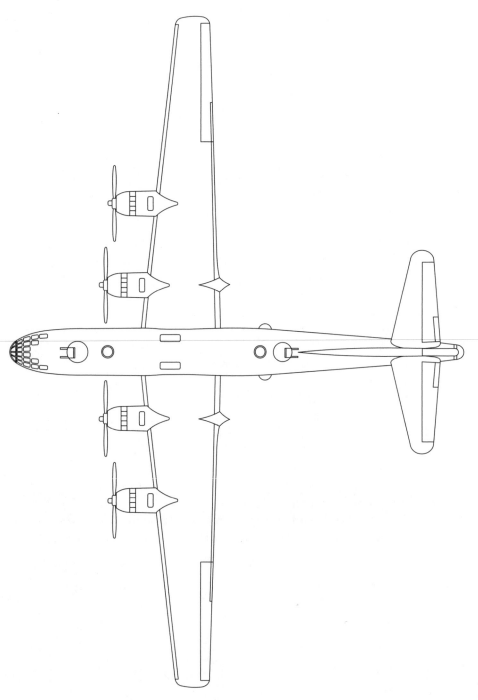

CHAPTER 1

Wake-Up

Mission to Tokyo

March 9, 1945, 10:00 a.m.–4:45 p.m.

MAJOR SAM P. BAKSHAS woke up that morning with the secrets in his head.

Bakshas was one of the men flying B-29 Superfortress bombers from three Pacific islands—Guam, Saipan, and Tinian. A writer dubbed these men "the thousand kids." There were actually several thousand, and they were giving heart and soul to bombing the Japanese home islands—what they called "the Empire"—with no success. They were dropping bombs from high altitude and not hitting much. The precision daylight bombing that worked so well in Europe was not working here, not at all. The air campaign against Japan was failing.

Bakshas believed the situation could be turned around.

Bakshas was thirty-four. He was older and bigger than the Superfortress crewmembers around him. He was six foot one and almost two hundred pounds. He was from Fergus County, smack in the center of Montana, had courted his wife Aldora with the gift of an airplane ride, and was piloting biplanes with the National Guard in the previous decade. Today, Bakshas commanded the 93rd Bombardment Squadron, a component of the 19th Bombardment Group.

He'd been sleeping on a cot with an air mattress inside a partitioned Quonset hut. Awake now, on the day the secrets were unraveling around him as he prepared to bomb Japan that night, Bakshas needed to take care of a routine chore.

"I need a haircut," he said to a fellow officer.

He was on the island of Guam (code name: Stevedore), the American territory that had recently been wrested back from its Japanese occupiers. Guam was farther south than Saipan and Tinian, and was the only island among the three considered to be fully tropical, with palm trees, high mountains and great jungles full of towering mahogany trees.

The temperature was in the eighties with a constant parade of showers carried through by high Pacific trade winds. Naval officer Lt. James N. Sussex, a medical officer on the seaplane tender USS *Bering Strait* (AVP 34) who was destined to be very busy today, wrote home about Guam after its liberation from the Japanese. "It rains nearly every day and the mud is thick," Sussex said in a letter composed on a military typewriter called an MC-88 that wrote only in capital letters. "The Guam natives, called Chamorros, are glad to see the Americans. They were treated to various forms of torture when their Japanese occupiers were here. If a Chamorro picked up an American propaganda bulletin dropped from a plane he would be beheaded in front of his family. Others lost arms and legs. Yet they are a friendly people, made gracious by the warmth and the sun."

In Guam's affable climate, many B-29 crewmembers had taken scissors to their long khaki trousers to create frayed and sloppy-looking shorts. Not Bakshas. Sammy Bakshas—always Sammy, never Sam—did not understand sloppy. Bakshas was wearing long khakis and low quarters as he stepped through a series of tents until he found the right one.

Bakshas would be one tall guy among many in the plane he'd fly today. The B-29 was named *Tall in the Saddle* because no one in its regular crew was less than six feet in height. Bakshas was not a regular crewmember but would command *Tall in the Saddle* today, relegating airplane commander Capt. Gordon L. Muster to copilot duty. Bakshas had come a long way as a first-generation American, the son of Lithuanian immigrants who toiled the land in Montana.

"As a squadron commander, Bakshas knew things other crewmembers didn't know," said a 19th group veteran. "By the time we got up that morning, a lot of us knew we would be going to Tokyo that evening, but we didn't yet know the two key secrets— that we'd be attacking at low altitude and that we'd be told to leave our guns behind. Sammy knew we were going to introduce a new kind of warfare on this date. The rest of us found out from gossip and babble before our afternoon briefing and evening takeoff. If Sammy was going to help introduce a new way of flying B-29 missions, I guess he wanted to look right."

"There was a wonderful urgency and an exhilarating secrecy about the B-29 outfits in the Marianas," wrote St. Clair McKelway in a perspective. Even after others began learning the two key secrets—low level, no guns—Bakshas kept them locked up, much like his buttoned-up expression, as the morning unfolded.

Bakshas found the tent marked "Blinn's Clip Joint," raised a flap, and stepped inside. Private First Class Earl P. Blinn was cutting hair. Bakshas sat next to another airman on an empty bomb crate, pulled out a letter from home—probably from his wife of eight years, Aldora, who lived in Ridgefield, Montana, with their four-year-old son, Jerome—and started reading.

Blinn finished with a customer and said, "Next." Others, deferring to Bakshas's rank, beckoned him to take the barber's chair—a rebuilt ammunition box. Bakshas waved them off. He got his haircut, but only after the men who'd been waiting ahead of him. *It was 10:30 a.m. Chamorro Standard Time, March 9, 1945.*

Also on Guam was a young 1st Lt. Robert "Bud" McDonald, from Michigan, a lookalike for Hollywood personality Bert Parks. McDonald would soon go into battle as an airplane commander, responsible for a bomber crew at the ripe age of twenty-three, but today he wasn't scheduled to fly. McDonald would later say that he was a witness to history.

It was the morning of the great firebomb mission to Tokyo. They would launch in early evening and arrive over the Japanese capital in tomorrow's early hours. It was the mission for which XXI Bomber Command boss Maj. Gen. Curtis E. LeMay changed tactics in hope of changing the war against Japan. It was the mission on which many B-29 Superfortress crewmembers were certain LeMay was going to get them killed.

Mature leaders like Sammy Bakshas would take the B-29 crewmembers into battle. But while Bakshas was getting his hair cut, some of the thousand kids on Guam, Saipan, and Tinian were writing what they feared were their last letters home. Among them were Staff Sgt. Carl Barthold, a radio operator on Saipan, and Staff Sgt. LeRoy "Trip" Triplett, a radar operator on Tinian.

The Face of Fear

Paul Didier, the right blister gunner on Carl Barthold's bomber crew, was certain that none of them would return from the Tokyo mission because of the shift to low altitude. Barthold observed Didier engaged in frenetic activity in their Quonset on the island of Saipan (code name: Tattersalls) just after they awakened in mid-morning.

As for Saipan itself, it was "an attractive island," naval officer Sussex wrote. "It is not very tropical. It has a few palms but mostly the usual type of temperate plants. Doves are common and other birds are just beginning to come back after the scare they had last summer." This was a reference to the furious battle for the island, now finished. "The hills are rolling, some fairly high, with deep, fairly steep, shaded valleys. The most striking topographical features of Saipan are two—the bluff at the north end, over which the Jap remnants jumped last summer, and the lovely jewel of Magicienne Bay on the east side of the island. The bay is too shallow for an anchorage and I'm almost glad. Its loveliness is too rare to spoil with a fleet."

There was loveliness around Barthold's Quonset that morning, but no one was savoring the view. The men in the hut were the enlisted men who would fly a plane called *Star Duster* today, and all of them thought Didier was overdoing it: the gunner stuffed almost everything he owned into his B-4 bag, the multipocketed, fabric-covered equivalent of a travel suitcase, and left all of his belongings tidily packed atop the center of his cot. If he did not return to occupy the cot, others would know what to do with his personal effects. "He said something about how he was looking at his stuff for the last time," recalled Barthold.

"THE DISCRETE ELITE: EXCLUSIVE PERSONNEL" read an elaborate black sign with gold lettering in front of Barthold's Quonset hut near the ocean on Saipan. Barthold, a radio operator with the 870th Bombardment Squadron, 497th Bombardment Group—a rail-thin, twenty-one-year-old Missouri boy at five-ten and a lightweight 142 pounds—thought it amusing that someone had posted the sign next to the vegetable garden the men were cultivating in front of the Quonset. "The purpose of the sign was to tell everybody we weren't afraid," said Barthold, "even though we were scared stiff."

Clad in underwear and clogs and carrying soap and a towel, Barthold jogged back from the shower, a hundred yards uphill from his Quonset. While outdoors he had a spectacular view of Aslito airfield, now renamed for Navy Commander Robert H. Isely, who'd been killed almost a year earlier while strafing the place when it was in Japanese hands. Isely's name was spelled wrong when the name was bestowed and the airfield was now named Isley Field. Its two 8,500-foot parallel runways were straddled by parking spots for about a hundred aircraft, looking like giant silvery cigars with wings and surrounded by men making preparations. While crewmembers like Barthold had been sleeping, ground crews had bloated the Superfortresses with fuel and bombs and now the great bombers basked and waited.

"That guy worries me," Barthold said aloud when he looked at the B-4 atop the cot. He meant Didier. That's how it would have looked if the gunner had gone to heaven, but as far as Barthold knew he had only gone to chow.

Two months earlier, Barthold had had a bombardier die in his arms high over the Empire. On this mild morning, the secrets were rapidly unraveling within Barthold's bomb group. The night before, Barthold and the rest of the crew of his B-29 Superfortress had gotten a casual heads-up from their airplane commander, Capt. James M. Campbell. Like most airplane commanders, he had been told the secrets—low level, no guns. While crewmembers learned about this in different ways on each of the three islands and from one bomb group to another, Barthold and his crew now knew it all,

all the secrets that most hadn't known twenty-four hours earlier: they would take off early this evening, climb into the night, but not as much as usual, and they would assault Tokyo not from the usual height of around 28,000 feet—from which their bombing hadn't been especially accurate—but at around 8,000. They were being told to leave guns, gunners, and ammunition behind.

Barthold shared the general concern that this might be a catastrophic mistake by the big brass—meaning LeMay—that would get a lot of men killed. Unlike his right blister gunner, however, Barthold believed he would survive this evening's mission. Barthold walked out of the Quonset on this warm, balmy morning in the Mariana Islands sucking in a soothing tropical breeze that swept over Saipan. He talked briefly to a member of his B-29 crew.

"That guy has me spooked," said the crewmember, referring to Didier's packed B-4 bag. "Maybe we're all dead, just like he thinks."

"Well, I'm a little uncomfortable with this," Barthold confessed.

The other man was a gunner. While LeMay had ordered airplane commanders to leave their guns and gunners behind, Campbell had instructed the gunner to ignore the order, come on the mission, and bring ammunition. "Some guys are more than uncomfortable," said the gunner. "This is going to be a very bad mission."

"I think this is going to be the mission we've heard all the rumors about," Barthold said to another airman.

In fairness to Didier, it must be said that in making preparations for his own death he was being prudent. Although his precautions disturbed others, Didier was preparing not only to die but, first, to go out to his plane, climb aboard, and do his job. In this narrative, other B-29 crewmembers will be encountered who couldn't do that because the fear made them dysfunctional. In two important ways the war in the Pacific was different from the war fought by B-17 Flying Fortress crews in Europe. Crews were less cohesive, with officers and enlisted men often worlds apart even when working together aboard same aircraft. And incidences of fear, real fear strong enough to impair one's ability to function, were more common in the Pacific—perhaps because, in Europe, bomber crews returned to civilization and comfort at the end of a mission. There were few comforts on the Pacific Islands.

The men had never liked Saipan, despite its semitropical charm. It was a beautiful island where savagery had been commonplace during a bloody invasion by U.S. Marines, an island transformed now into a B-29 Superfortress base by Seabees and combat engineers. "We turned that place into a livable garden of sorts," Barthold remembered, years later. "I don't know that we ever felt at home there."

Saipan, with its tall cliffs from which so many Japanese flung themselves in suicide leaps while the Marines were securing the island, was a place of raw beauty with deep blue, wave-capped ocean readily visible on all sides. It was a place where Barthold never felt quite right. It was a place from which a B-29 Superfortress could plummet down toward the sea after leaving the runway's end, taking a pronounced dip before gaining sufficient power to climb aloft—or, instead, go smashing into an ocean that could crumple the big plane into pieces and swallow it up.

It was 11:30 a.m., Chamorro Standard Time, March 9, 1945, still hours before the planned afternoon briefing of his bomb group, and Saipan was the place from which Carl Barthold and his B-29 would attack the Japanese Empire tonight, if they could take off without going into the drink and if they could fly to the Japanese Empire's home islands without crashing or being shot down. At the moment, Barthold's expectations were more prosaic: before the briefing, he was going to catch some chow and check over his radios. He was uneasy, but believed he was in control of himself.

Trepidation on Tinian
The noon meal proffered by mess sergeant Sgt. Jim Thompson consisted of fried Spam. Having eaten more of it than he may have needed, LeRoy "Trip" Triplett stepped out of the mess hall into the glaring sun and pulled the bill of his cap a few degrees lower over his peeling nose. A hundred yards to Triplett's right and two hundred feet down the jungle-covered cliffs, the Pacific Ocean rolled westward until it merged with the pale, heat-hazy sky. Out there somewhere, Triplett thought, lay the Philippines and the China coast. Across the chalky white, coral-covered road in front of him, his squadron's Quonset huts squatted shimmering in the sun. The huts were corrugated tin shells shaped like loaves of bread.

This was Tinian (code name: Tearaway)—thirty-eight square miles of coral rock, dust, jungle, and cane fields, crowded with B-29 hardstands, Quonset huts, and docks. Tinian was a little green flat slab formed by prehistoric volcanoes and dead coral animals. It lay 125 miles northeast of Guam and just 3 miles southwest of Saipan with its clearly visible harbor of ships and its high mountains. Tinian boasted two airfields, including North Field with its three crushed-coral runways 8,500-feet long and 200-feet wide running parallel, with a fourth soon to be added and with parking revetments for 265 Superfortresses between the runways, making it the largest and busiest airport in the world.

It was 12:30 p.m. Chamorro Standard Time, March 9, 1945. Triplett—who later in life would shorten his first name to Le—was a radar navigator on a B-29 Superfortress of the 421st Bombardment Squadron, 504th Bombardment Group. Triplett and his buddies had been flying out of Guam, Saipan, and Tinian for several months, carrying the war to the Japanese homeland with what Triplett believed were imperfect results. Others wondered if there was any success at all in the troubled journey B-29s and their crews had made to the western Pacific. Just as they were trained to do, they were bombing from high altitude in daylight, but their bombs were often ineffectual. "We weren't hitting anything," Triplett remembered later. Aborts were common because engines overheated in the process of climbing to altitude. As Triplett viewed it, bad weather over Japan, poor target maps, too few planes, and formidable Japanese opposition were "creating a situation where precision bombing from altitude just wasn't working."

Triplett was an Oklahoma farm boy with Cherokee heritage who'd played shortstop and third base in high school. With his parents' permission, he'd become an aviation cadet at age seventeen. Now, Triplett was fully nineteen years of age.

In an unpublished memoir, Triplett wrote, "Up the hill to my left, nestled under some pawpaw trees was the squadron shack and the bulletin board. Might as well get the latest poop from group, I mused to myself and set a course in that direction.

"As I approached the board, questioning murmurs from the knot of men clustering around told me that something hot was on the griddle. I considered the various possibilities. It was the wrong time of the month for promotions to be posted. We hadn't been overseas long enough to even think of leave. USO shows never created a stir. Maybe it was another order like the one that forbade us to cut our suntans off at the knees, or the one that ordered all GIs to steer clear of the Navy nurses' beach area, or the one that ordered all nudes painted on our planes to be removed or properly clothed.

"Elbowing nearer the board, I quickly scanned the brief notice. 'All airplane commanders, pilots, navigators, bombardiers, radio operators, radar operators, right and left gunners will report for briefing at 1600 hours.' That was all. It was an odd time of day for briefing. More odd was the fact that command gunners and tail gunners had been omitted from the order."

Percy Usher Tucker Crew

Also on Tinian, but at a different location south of the parallel runways on North Field, flight engineer-pilot 1st Lt. George "Laddie" Wale—on his birth certificate, it read Elmer G. Wale—was making his own preparations for a mission that would begin in early evening. Others on his B-29 (named *Lady Annabelle*) called Wale a "patrician," or, as one put it, "a college professor in uniform." In civilian life Wale was neither an aristocrat nor an academic; he simply had a look of propriety about him.

In casual banter at their wing intelligence shop, Wale and *Lady Annabelle*'s airplane commander, Capt. Percy Usher Tucker, had learned most of the secrets, which were now making the rounds on the Tinian. "We're supposed to leave guns and ammunition behind," Tucker repeated, as if a crazy person had imparted this tidbit of information to him. It struck Laddie Wale that, in repeating the obvious, Tucker had just uttered one of the longest sentences of his life.

Tucker and his crew belonged to the 40th Bombardment Squadron, 6th Bombardment Group on Tinian. Like Bakshas, Tucker was six foot one, although in photos, which show him with a mustache and a grin, he looks smaller. He absolutely hated the name Percy and sometimes envied the first name given his brother Lee, who was a cavalry officer in the Army. He was not the kind of man who begged, but he begged people not to call him Percy. The officers in the front of his aircraft—bombardier Flight Officer

Joseph Krogman, pilot 1st Lt. John T. "Gummy" Kearney, navigator 1st Lt. Edwin J. Koniusky, and engineer Wale—all addressed him as "Tuck" when enlisted men weren't listening and the conversation wasn't too serious. Tucker was often jovial, but when things *were* serious he left no doubt that he was in charge.

The men of Tucker's crew respected him. His fellow officers in the crew were friendly. Tuck didn't talk much about stuff that didn't matter (his own daughter never learned from him that he hated cats), but he really was very much in charge. One acquaintance called him both terse and "exquisitely restrained." He was a man of few words. A typical crew spent days or weeks haggling over a name for its B-29. Not Tucker's. They were assigned a bomber and Tucker told everyone it would be named *Lady Annabelle*. (The source of the name was Tucker's wife, the former Annabelle Jossman.) "There will be no further discussion," Tucker said, a favorite expression.

There wasn't going to be much discussion about today's order either. But there was a little, and tail gunner Staff Sgt. Joe Majeski was listening in. Tucker used few words but he sometimes repeated himself.

"I'm not leaving guns behind," said Tucker.

"I'm not sure what General LeMay is thinking," said Wale.

"I'm not leaving guns behind."

"He says we're supposed to."

"Actually, the order says something about leaving the ammunition behind."

"Well?"

"It ain't his ass," said Tucker. "It's our ass."

Wale later wrote in his journal—the rules forbade a diary but not a journal, which amounted to the same thing—that he'd never seen Tucker so talkative. Majeski later said the same thing. Wale didn't know it yet, but among the thousand kids manning B-29s at Guam, Saipan and Tinian, many were reacting just as he and Tucker were. The history books would later report that guns and ammunition were left at home for today's mission. It was only partly true. In some crew manifests, gunners' names were missing but the men and their weapons were not. Tucker's group commander believed, as Tucker did, that if you were going against the heavily defended capital of an Axis enemy, you had damn well better go armed.

Krogman, the bombardier on Tucker's *Lady Annabelle*, customarily radiated good cheer, as inseparable from his Remsen, Iowa, farm upbringing as his habit of cussing up a storm. He was a ladies' man. His best friend from back home, 2nd Lt. Richard Treinen, who was in pilot training, had sent him a handwritten letter in which he wrote about Joe "making out with the women." "He liked women and they liked him," a family member said. Joe Krogman's voice was a very deep bass with a little nasal. He was sturdy, with great upper-body strength. Treinen seemed to view him as some sort of superman with the opposite gender, while his crewmates saw him as a virtuoso with the Norden bombsight.

The good cheer was missing now. On the same day he received Treinen's letter, Krogman received news of Treinen's death in an air crash in Oregon. Because Krogman was already overseas, an officer who didn't know Treinen escorted his remains back to Remsen.

Krogman had difficulty with the concept of death. "He told me that his way of coping with the ongoing threat of death was to already think of himself as a dead man," said a family member. "I think he shared that with many of his fellow fliers. I also think that this played a large part in their off-duty actions, including heavy drinking. When sober, he was a fun loving, easygoing individual who made friends easily and granted favors readily. However . . . with a few drinks under his belt he would be a surly drunk with a hair-trigger temper."

Today, preparing to bomb Tokyo, Krogman was as sober as a stone. And he was unduly serious. Wale remembered him uttering two words, referring to today's changed tactics:

"We're dead," Krogman said.

The Fling Crew

Also at North Field, Tinian, but in a different group—the 9th Bombardment Group—normally cordial airplane commander Capt. Dean Fling had a little of the stern, all-business bearing of Tucker. Fling was uncharacteristically abrupt with crewmembers of his B-29, named *God's Will*.

"No guns," said Fling.

"No guns?" someone said. "This cannot be right."

"It is."

Listening intently, left blister gunner Sgt. William J. "Reb" Carter (usually addressed by buddies using the short form for "Rebel") had good reason to ponder the circuitous path he'd followed from urban Atlanta to this tropical paradise that wasn't a paradise. Carter, twenty-one, had once briefly worked to become a pilot but had been halted in his tracks by the odd situation that prevailed the previous autumn, when the Army found itself with too many of them. Carter had been a local yo-yo champion back home before getting into all this. A tall, toothy, eager Georgia boy delivered at birth by a doctor who arrived at his house via horse and buggy, Carter been born with no sense of smell. Now he wondered if he'd also been born with no sense of hearing. "We can't have escort fighters to protect us at night," Carter thought. Despite his disability, he smelled trouble.

Not everybody in LeMay's command was going to heed today's battle order, but the Fling crew in *God's Will* was going to follow it to the letter. "It looks like we're going to Tokyo unarmed," Carter said. "I hope the big brass know something we don't."

Target for Tonight

Tokyo (code name: Meetinghouse) was more than people, houses of wood and paper, and an objective in LeMay's crosshairs: it was Japan's largest city.

Tokyo is built along the edge of a big, gently curving bay. The city's two important rivers, the Sumida and the Arakawa, come almost to a point northeast of the Imperial Palace and bend apart as they wind down to the bay. The congested lowland between these rivers is shaped like a squat arrowhead. Crisscrossed by a network of canals, the crowded Japanese capital in 1945 had overgrown the site of the original Tokyo, the nucleus of Japan's population. The previous year, two governments, those of Tokyo Prefecture and Tokyo City, had merged to form Tokyo Metropolis or Tokyo-to.

Tokyo was a legitimate military target. It was the center of Japanese life. For symbolic reasons, the Americans planned not to bomb the Imperial Palace where Hirohito held court, but the rest of the city was fair game with its military assembly plants and vehicle factories. Moreover, it was home to a cottage industry in which tens of thousands of Japanese families manufactured small parts for the military. The wood and paper houses that would fall beneath LeMay's firebombs were also factories.

About six million people lived in Tokyo on the eve of the B-29 Superfortress bombing campaign that would kill many inhabitants, send many more fleeing to the countryside, and reduce the city's population by fully half. Rather astonishingly, the city had only a token fire department and almost no civil dense or shelter infrastructure. LeMay was very much mindful of Tokyo's closely packed wooden homes and buildings. It was a city of wood and paper, of fragile houses with sliding shoji screens, floored wooden *roka*, or passageways, and *fusuma*, or partitions of wood and paper. It was no accident that the Americans were coming to Tokyo with fire.

On tonight's bombing mission, the primary weapons, E-46 chemical incendiary bombs, would rain down on Japan like giant firecrackers. They came in bunches of forty-seven small bomblets called M69s—the more widely recognized term—strapped together inside a metal cylinder that was fused to break open at 2,000 feet or 2,500 feet, depending on bombing altitude, and scatter the individual bombs. Three to five seconds after the big firecrackers hit, they would go off. An explosive charge would violently eject a sack full of gel that would burn intensely. The sack held the gel in one spot, thereby igniting a hotter fire. Other weapons that would be employed today were the E-28 incendiary cluster bomb and the M47, a petroleum-based bomb that would be carried by the lead B-29s—including the one piloted by the in-air commander of the mission, Brig. Gen. Thomas Power—and would penetrate buildings and scatter gel in all directions to burn out the insides.

Bakshas on Guam, Barthold on Saipan, and Triplett on Tinian had not yet reached their B-29 Superfortresses. The afternoon had begun and soon there would be briefings, and then preparations for flight. Meanwhile, ground crews were just about finished preparing the bombers for the mission. Flight engineer Laddie Wale went out to the hardstand to take an early look at *Lady Annabelle. It was 1:00 p.m. Chamorro Standard Time, March 9, 1945.*

Some B-29s were going to Tokyo with guns and gunners, whether LeMay liked it or not. *Lady Annabelle* stood on the concrete surface of its revetment between parallel runways at Tinian, fueled, bombed, and loaded with ammunition. Its guns were stowed off the horizontal, the signal that they were loaded and hot. The .50-caliber ammunition belts were each twenty-seven feet in length, according to lore the source of the term "the whole nine yards."

Wale paced around the *Lady Annabelle*, making a superficial look for any exterior sign of damage or difficulty. He was overreacting, he told himself. Nothing was wrong. The crew chief and the rest of the ground crew simply wouldn't allow anything to be wrong. The plane wouldn't fail on them. It wouldn't dare. "Get me home," Wale said to the B-29.

"It was my job to be at the plane first and to make everything work," Wale explained. A B-29 flight engineer had more responsibility than engineers on other types of aircraft. The instruments and flight controls, when all was said and done, belonged to him. If Wale didn't do his job right, it wouldn't matter what the pilots did.

So it was time for a second inspection, this time closer up. Slowly, studiously, with ground crew watching him, Wale inspected the entire B-29, beginning at the nose wheel, examining the wheels, tires, struts, wheel well, and all visible wring and tubing. He walked beneath the right wing and inspected the number three and four engines, their cowlings, nacelles, propeller blades, and hubs. Wale did not see any damage. The guys on the ground kept this ship in fine working condition—and clean.

Wale scrutinized the trailing edge of the wing, the flight surfaces and landing flaps, and the wing lines that ran along the back of the wing spar. He liked the way this work distracted him from worries about tonight and whether he would have a tomorrow. "It was comforting to do the preflight check," he said. At the main landing gear, Wale examined the wheels, tires, brakes, and all the tubing and fittings in the wheel well. Next, he looked into the aft bomb bay (where the canisters of fire were neatly packed inside bomb shapes) and the right aft fuselage, sighting blisters, aft entry door, stabilizers, rudder, elevators, tailskid, tail gunner's hatch, and the tail navigation light.

Wale discovered no flaws, no scratches, no dirt. *Lady Annabelle* was primed for the journey awaiting her this evening. He was

overreacting, he repeated to himself, no question about it. He repeated his right-side inspection on the left side, but Wale knew he wouldn't find anything. He turned his back to the B-29 and hitched a ride on a truck that would take him back to group headquarters. He didn't want to miss this afternoon's briefing.

In the terminology of Field Order No. 43, issued at 8:00 a.m. on March 8, 1945, by XXI Bomber Command, Tokyo's city center was "the urban area of Meetinghouse"—a code word that was more of a convenience than an attempt to disguise the identity of the target. In the written order, the geographical coordinates—3541N-13948E—followed the term "Meetinghouse."

This was the order Sammy Bakshas knew about when he woke up. It was the order whose contents were already known to many B-29 crewmembers, but only became known to Gordon Muster, Carl Barthold, and Trip Triplett as this morning of March 9 progressed.

This was the order that tasked men like Bakshas on Guam (in the 314th Bomb Wing) to attack at 5,000–5,800 feet, men like Triplett and Carter on Tinian (313th Bomb Wing) to also strike at 5,000–5,800 feet, and those like Barthold on Saipan (73rd Bomb Wing) to bomb at 7,000–7,800 feet. Nothing like this had ever been done before. No armada of warplanes had ever been launched in such numbers without flying in formation. No American heavy bomber had ever flown so low on a mission against a major target. No bomber crews had ever before been dispatched into battle using methods that were totally untried and untested. Historian William Wolf wrote that the advantages offered by a low-level attack were:

1) The elimination of flying formation and climbing to very high altitude, which consumed large volumes of fuel, meant that bomb loads could be greatly increased.
2) There were fewer aborts and other losses when flying at lower altitude, as the engines endured less stress and strain, and consequently there were more effective aircraft over the target for each mission.
3) Although the low altitude missions involved the increased risk of heavier [antiaircraft] fire, it was felt that the advantages of surprise and the weak enemy night fighter strength would outweigh this disadvantage.

The order to attack "Meetinghouse" included Paragraph 3x4: "*No ammunition will be carried.*" Low altitude and no ammunition: it had never been tried before. Many airplane commanders on Guam, Saipan, and Tinian, like Tucker, decided to ignore this order.

The first bombing of Tokyo, the Doolittle Raid of April 18, 1942, by carrier-launched B-25 Mitchells, was more symbolic than destructive. Following a long gap and using high-altitude precision bombing techniques that had worked well in Europe but were not working at all here, B-29s had struck Tokyo on February 18, February 25, and March 4, 1945. These missions had done little to alter the size or shape of Tokyo or to interrupt the bustle of life in the city. Partly because of the jetstream (the furious winds high over Japan), partly because of weather, and partly because of mechanical issues, the Americans weren't hitting their targets. "We might as well fly around in circles," said one bombardier. B-29 crews desperately needed to do something differently but hardly anyone believed LeMay had the answer. "When you're going into the valley of the shadow of death," said flight engineer Wale, "you want more than change for the sake of change."

"I don't like this," Laddie Wale said to someone in the Tucker crew when he rejoined them. *It was 4:45 p.m. Chamorro Standard Time, March 9, 1945.*

"I don't like this at all."

CHAPTER 2

Starting

American Bombers against Japan, December 7,

1941–February 18, 1943

Most OF THE AMERICANS who flew B-29 Superfortresses against the Japanese home islands were young in years, but matured by experience.

Many were still boys and hadn't ever set foot inside an airplane when Japan attacked the United States on December 7, 1941. Some had never even seen an airplane. When they learned about the surprise attack that brought them into the war, some of them did not know where Pearl Harbor was. They were "the thousand kids" in the apt phrase of St. Clair McKelway, but they grew up fast. Like their elders—men like Sam P. Bakshas, who was already a mature officer when the United States was drawn into the war—the kids had to adjust quickly and grow rapidly.

Carl Barthold, age eighteen, the rail-thin Missouri boy who later became a radio operator, went to an ROTC dance at the St. Louis Armory on Saturday, December 6. A freshman at Washington

University, Barthold was up to date on his schoolwork and could afford to sleep in on Sunday morning. That afternoon, Barthold drove his father's year-old Chevrolet to church for a meeting of the Epworth League, also called the Methodist Youth Fellowship. "I was on my way to church," Barthold said. "I came up to a stop sign. A guy was hawking papers: EXTRA! EXTRA! PEARL HARBOR BOMBED. I wasn't sure what that meant but I bought a paper."

At the Salem United Methodist Church on King's Highway and Cote Brilliant, Barthold unfolded the paper in a small meeting room surrounded by other young people. Barthold was considered good-looking by the girls, but was never certain whether their attentions were lured by his handsome features or by his access to an automobile. One of his friends was a Roosevelt High School cheerleader, Jenny Grant. Not yet fully aware of the significance of the news report—no one in the room owned a radio—Barthold said, "This is about a naval base in the Pacific."

Carl passed the newspaper around. Each looked at it in turn. Jenny's hand went up to her mouth. She uttered a couple of words. It might have been, "Oh, my God!"

Barthold would remember the expression on her face for the rest of his life. "Jenny?" he said. And again: "Jenny?"

"My brother is in the Navy. He's on the battleship *Arizona*. It says here they bombed the *Arizona*."

She knew. Her eyes, her face, and her expression—she knew. It would be a couple of weeks before she and her family would have official confirmation, but in that late afternoon get-together in St. Louis on December 7, 1941, Jenny Grant was already certain.

Seaman 3rd Class Lawrence Everett Grant from Missouri was one of the 1,177 sailors aboard the USS *Arizona* (BB 39) who died when a Japanese bomb sent the warship to the bottom of the harbor. The ship accounted for almost half of the 2,402 Americans killed by Japanese carrier planes on what President Franklin D. Roosevelt called "a date which will live in infamy."

For Carl Barthold, the date was a new beginning. He was thin and lightweight, but there was a power behind his expression now: he was mad as hell. Like so many other Americans, Barthold hoped he could get into the fight that beckoned to his countrymen. "I want to be there when this ends," he told his friends.

Milburn P. Sanders would one day be a young sailor aboard a seaplane tender tasked with rescuing B-29 crewmembers during a great Tokyo firebomb mission. A 1940 graduate of Herndon High School in Virginia, near the nation's capital, Sanders was a clerk in the Navy's Bureau of Ships in Washington. He wrote the following:

> On December 7, 1941, one brother took me with him to the country and we rode around the foothills of the Blue Ridge Mountains in his 1932 Plymouth couple, and then returned to Washington at the end of the day. Since his car did not have a radio, we were unaware of the attack on Pearl Harbor. We were surprised to find an Army command car, armed with a machine gun, Guarding Key Bridge [which crossed the Potomac River into Washington]. Then we got the news. Subsequently, Pearl Harbor created work for me. I mailed the reports of damage to ships in the Pearl Harbor attack to the naval shipyards.

On December 7, 1941, Trip Triplett, a future B-29 radar operator on Tinian, was a sophomore in high school and living just nine miles east of Holdenville, Oklahoma (population 6,000) —"with an old country church on one corner and a filling station on the other." Said Triplett: "After church, some of us boys would go over to the store and play checkers and dominos and listen to the radio. We got the news. I remember the sun shining on the corn stalks across the way on the field. It was a sunny afternoon. We knew we were in for it then. We didn't have a clue where Pearl Harbor was, but we absolutely knew this meant war with Japan. On Monday in the school gymnasium we listened to Roosevelt's address. I felt a mixture of emotions—anger, dread. I figured we'd end up in the middle of it."

In a two story, all-brick house elevated on a hill and looking down at a residential, middle-class Atlanta neighborhood from a huge bay window, Reb Carter listened to the radio. Carter would become the left blister gunner on *God's Will*, commanded by Dean Fling, but on this day Carter was best known as the local whiz in yo-yo competitions. Carter was in the eleventh grade and had just turned eighteen, a little old for his level in high school and ten months older than a distant relative—Jimmy, living down southwest in Plains—who would one day become president. Right now, the president was named Roosevelt, and like Triplett, Carter would be hearing *his* voice the next day, Monday.

On this Sunday afternoon, Carter was listening to the family's favorite afternoon radio show, *Top Tunes* on Atlanta station WATL, with his parents, William and Anne, and his fourteen-year-old brother Pete. Carter was consuming the last of the cake from his birthday party four days earlier. The cake's vanilla icing was a special favorite of his.

A few minutes after 2:30 p.m. Eastern Standard Time, a Mutual Broadcasting System bulletin interrupted *Top Tunes*. The news was about a place called Pearl Harbor, and the words were going to change the Carter family's world. "Turn the sound up," Carter's mother said.

"This is an outrage," said his father. Carter looked at his dad, who was an accountant, and saw a furrow in his brow, his face flushed with anger. There was no accounting for what they were hearing. "The Japanese have attacked us and we are going to be in some kind of war," the older man said. He gave his sons a special look. They were a loving family. "I'm glad this thing won't last long enough for either of you to be in it."

Romance in the Air

When the Japanese attacked Pearl Harbor, Sammy and Aldora Bakshas and their ten-month-old infant, Jerry, were living in a trailer in Ridgefield, Washington, but were visiting her parents' house in Scappoose. Aldora's parents were happy that their daughter, a teacher, had married this handsome and dashing pilot. But even they didn't know all the details of the couple's touching love story.

Sam Bakshas grew to be a strapping young man on his father's farm in Kendal, a small community in Montana. The family raised small animals and his father worked in coal mines in the area. Sam left high school to make money to pursue his love of flying. He began taking lessons when he turned eighteen on October 8, 1928.

After teaching flying in Alaska, Bakshas returned and went to work welding a center slab of iron in the Fort Peck Dam in northeastern Montana. There he met Earl A. Wood, another welder, and they became fast friends. Both had great senses of humor and enjoyed writing back and forth to one another. They discussed politics, and both were great kidders and enjoyed the usual antics of two single young men. Sammy liked to listen to Big Band music, but he didn't like to dance. He was a thirty-second-degree Mason and was liked by everyone. Many people referred to him as "a fine man."

Sam took Earl in his small plane to see his family. On the return flight, they encountered a very bad storm in the mountains. The turbulence caused the small plane to lose altitude and they crashed. Earl was sitting behind the pilot's seat and was unhurt. Sam, sitting in the front seat, received a broken wrist. The plane was demolished, but they both walked away from the crash.

One day in the mid-1930s, amid the Great Depression, a girlfriend of schoolteacher Anna Aldora Wood, Earl's sister, was bubbly with excitement. The friend planned to catch an automobile a ride out to a nearby farm and meet a pilot who had offered her a plane ride. The girls in the region knew this pilot, Sammy, and thought he cut a dashing figure with his leather jacket, scarf, and helmet. Aldora knew of him from her brother. She'd never actually seen him, but she wanted to.

Aldora created a distraction to divert the girlfriend and reached the farmer's field first. She became the woman to whom Sammy gave the ride. "I hadn't been in a plane before," Aldora remembered. Sammy piloted Douglas O-38 observation planes in the military and flew a variety of Stinsons, Stearmans, and Wacos in civilian life. Soon after meeting Aldora, he acquired a canvas-covered, high-wing Taylorcraft, a close cousin of the Piper Cub, and began giving Aldora rides in it. He clearly loved to fly, and Aldora thought he was "a fine-looking young man who could be serious but was gifted with a happy disposition."

They were married in Glendive, Montana, on May 8, 1938, and settled down in Fort Peck after a three-day honeymoon. Their new home had a living room, a dresser, and a bedroom. Aldora cooked, and even baked, out of doors.

"I was teaching school when I met him," Aldora said. "He was training people to fly. He was in the service and soon we were traveling around the country. He was a wonderful person."

Traveling between Sammy's base and his in-laws' home, Sammy and Aldora often used the Narrows Bridge at Tacoma, better known as "Galloping Gertie." Sammy remarked at how much the bridge seemed to sway in the wind. The bridge was very familiar to them, but fortunately they weren't around on November 7, 1940, when, in one of the most spectacular accidents in the region up to that time, Galloping Gertie shook herself apart and collapsed in pieces. Sammy and Aldora saw the extraordinary film footage in a movie newsreel soon after.

At his in-laws' house on December 7, 1941, Sammy Bakshas listened to the radio intently. In many American households on that Sunday, "Pearl Harbor" was a new and unfamiliar term, but in this house the handsome lieutenant, the schoolteacher, and her parents all knew that the United States fleet was moored at the huge naval base on the American territory in the far Pacific. All recognized instantly that the United States was at war. Sammy borrowed the in-laws' phone to call his military outfit, the 116th Observation Squadron at Felts Field near Spokane, 293 miles away. It was a long-distance call, a cumbersome process, but Sammy got through. "We were notified to get back home and report for duty," Aldora said.

The United States declared war on Japan following President Franklin D. Roosevelt's December 8, 1941, speech. Germany broke diplomatic relations and declared war on the United States on December 11. The United States responded in kind later that day.

While Americans were experiencing defeat at Pearl Harbor, in the Philippines, and in Java—where a handful of U.S. four-engined bombers were hopelessly outnumbered—the Army Air Forces (AAF) arrived in England in early 1942. On a very modest scale, the military outfit that would become the Eighth Air Force began tentative bombing missions to targets in occupied France. Americans believed in the big, four-engined heavy bomber, and now they were out to prove that airpower could be a decisive force in battle.

The Doolittle Raid

To retaliate for Pearl Harbor, the United States planned an extraordinary assault on the Japanese home islands to be mounted by Army medium bombers launched from a Navy aircraft carrier. The most experienced pilot in the United States, Lt. Col. James H. "Jimmy" Doolittle, formed the medium bomber strike force, trained the men, and readied a batch of B-25 Mitchell medium bombers. The war's first mission to Tokyo was flown not by the B-29 Superfortress—which, so far, hadn't even achieved its maiden flight—but by B-25s.

Twenty-five Mitchells were modified for the mission. Of these, twenty-two made it to the West Coast, where Doolittle's hand-picked raider force went aboard the aircraft carrier USS *Hornet* (CV 8) at Alameda, California. As planned in advance, Doolittle trimmed the force by six aircraft and crews. This meant that thirty men made it all the way to the finish line without participating in the raid.

One of these was 2nd Lt. Samuel N. Slater, a navigator. Like so many Americans, Slater wanted to strike back at the Japanese. Slater did not get his chance this time, but a another opportunity was in the cards for him.

On April 18, 1942, on the noisy wooden deck of the *Hornet*, Joe Evon was one of the nervous sailors watching as sixteen twin-engined Mitchells, each with a five-man crew, prepared to launch from a spot in the ocean where the only other naval forces in the region were Japanese.

"There was a lot of scrambling around," said Evon, an SBD Dauntless gunner whose own aircraft was stowed below decks. "I can't say they were hasty or frantic, but they were moving quickly. As we watched them prepare to get into the air, we all felt that they had know what they were doing, or we wouldn't be out here in enemy waters." Evon, wearing ordinary sailor attire and goggles, is barely visible in a photo taken from Vultures' Row, the spot on the island of the carrier that looked down at the bombers. Evon did not know that a Japanese picket boat had spotted *Hornet*, and that the bombers were launching 170 nautical miles farther from the Japanese home islands than planned.

A superbly skilled pilot and engineer who was thought to have little chance for promotion because of his status as a reserve officer, the short, personable Doolittle was the driving force behind the raid. President Franklin D. Roosevelt picked Doolittle over more senior officers and Doolittle assembled his force—the Doolittle Raiders—at Eglin Army Air Field in the Florida panhandle. Doolittle proved that the powerful B-25 could take off in less than five hundred feet.

At first, some of the Doolittle Raiders did not know why they were practicing short takeoffs. Slater, the navigator who was later cut at the last minute, was one of these. But the purpose was fairly obvious, and the Doolittle Raiders, without actually being told, soon understood that they were practicing to fly takeoff from a carrier deck. No aircraft the size of a Mitchell had done so before. No one was certain it could be done under operational conditions. In *Thirty Seconds over Tokyo*, Capt. Ted Lawson wrote the following of preparing to take off:

> If a motor quit or caught fire, if a tire went flat, if the right wing badly scraped the island, if the left wheel went over the edge, we were to get out as quickly as we could and help the Navy shove our $150,000 plane overboard. It must not, under any circumstances, be permitted to block traffic. There would be no other way to clear the forward deck for the other planes to take off.

The first B-25, with Doolittle at the controls, roared down the carrier deck, dipped briefly from view as if heading into the water, and then reappeared in a slow climb. Weighing almost fifteen tons fully loaded with fuel and bombs, pulled aloft by a pair of Wright R-2600 radial-piston engines, the Mitchell banked and set course for Japan. Fifteen more followed. Each Mitchell carried four specially constructed 500-pound bombs. Three were high-explosive munitions and one was a bundle of incendiaries. The incendiaries were long tubes, wrapped together in order to be carried in the bomb bay but designed to separate and scatter over a wide area after release. The idea of using firebombs against Japan was not a new idea, even then.

Back home, citizens were reading newspaper headlines that told only of defeat at the hands of the Japanese—of the American fleet being smashed at Pearl Harbor and U.S. troops being routed in the Philippines. Java fell. Wake Island fell. Few Americans alive today remember the frustration and fury of being badly trounced by a superior enemy's war machine.

Americans wanted payback.

All sixteen B-25s got aloft, navigated the ocean vastness, made landfall at the Empire, and attacked their targets. The B-25s pressed separate attacks on Tokyo, Kobe, Nagoya, Osaka, Yokohama, and the Yokosuka navy yard. American doctrine favored precision bombing, and the Doolittle Raiders felt they put their bombs in the right places. Japanese fighters engaged one or two of the Mitchells. All encountered antiaircraft fire.

The symbolism of an assault on the Japanese homeland was important. The Doolittle Raid lifted American spirits. It also inflicted real damage. Japan was forced to withdraw a carrier group from the Indian Ocean to defend the homeland. The raid prompted decisions in Tokyo that led to the battle of Midway—Japan's first major defeat.

None of the B-25s landed safely in China as had been planned. Except for a crew interned in Russia, the men had to crash or bail out—some over Japanese-held areas of China. "We ran out of fuel and had to bail out in Japanese-occupied territory," said B-25 copilot Robert Hite, then a second lieutenant and later a retired lieutenant colonel. A wartime Japanese photograph shows Hite, blindfolded, tied, and wearing a fleece-lined flight jacket and wheel hat, being escorted by Japanese guards. He was one of the lucky ones. The Japanese shot and killed three captured Doolittle Raiders. A fourth died of malnutrition while in captivity.

Altogether, eleven B-25 crewmen were killed or captured. Still, the entire crews of thirteen of the sixteen medium bombers, and all but one of the fourteenth, recovered in friendly territory, were able with some difficulty to return to the United States. Doolittle initially believed the raid had been a failure but soon learned otherwise.

In later years, surviving Doolittle Raiders held reunions and established a tradition of raising silver goblets—eighty altogether, one for each crewmember—to toast their fallen comrades. In 2008, when only eight were able to attend the reunion, they decided to retire the goblets, each inscribed with a raider's name. All are now on display at the National Museum of the Air Force in Dayton, Ohio.

As navigator Chase Nielson, also a second lieutenant then and a retired lieutenant colonel now, and one of Hite's fellow prisoners, said of the Doolittle Raid: "I learned . . . how to appreciate mankind, our democracy and the beautiful wonderful world we live in."

Doolittle himself never held the rank of colonel. When Roosevelt presented him with the Medal of Honor for the Tokyo attack, the president promoted Doolittle from lieutenant colonel to brigadier general. *Hornet* was lost in waters near Guadalcanal in late 1942. The B-25 Mitchell went on to become one of the most successful bombers of World War II but was never in the same category as America's mighty four-engined heavy bombers, the B-17 Flying Fortress, the B-24 Liberator, and, eventually, the "very heavy" B-29 Superfortress.

Growing Bomber Force

While the United States and its allies were still losing battles in the Pacific, a bomber force began to assemble in England in 1942. B-17 crews began flying missions over the European continent. One of the most experienced B-17 pilots in those early days was Curt LeMay, who pioneered bomber tactics before the war and later commanded a bomb group, and then a wing, and then an air division during the air campaign in Europe. While LeMay was helping to shape the tactics used by B-17s and B-24s in Europe, work was proceeding on a bigger, better bomber. It would be a bomber in which men could fight in their shirtsleeves rather than electrically heated clothing. They would be comfortable rather than cold. They would not need oxygen masks. It was a superbomber and it was rushed through the various stages of design, development, and operation long before it was ready.

On August 17, 1942, just eighteen B-17E Flying Fortresses were led by Major Paul W. Tibbets on a bombing mission to railroad yards in France. Tibbets did not yet know about a superbomber that would dwarf his Flying Fortress, nor did he know that the United States would soon begin developing a new and very different kind of bomb. For now, Tibbets was living and flying in a world where U.S. commanders believed bombers could defend themselves. In Europe, it would soon be obvious that they couldn't and that they would need fighter escort.

If Tibbets was the embodiment of the American combat commander and LeMay was an important force behind American bomber tactics, AAF boss Lt. Gen. Henry H. "Hap" Arnold was the architect of American airpower. Arnold was pushing for a new superbomber when it was still expected that the plane would be used in Europe. "Our B-29 idea came to birth in those days when it appeared that England would go down in defeat and there'd be no place left to us in the European part of the globe where we might base our planes for future sorties against the Axis powers," LeMay wrote. He added his thoughts about the challenges confronting Arnold: "B-29s had as many bugs as the entomological department of the Smithsonian Institution. Fast as they got the bugs licked, new ones crawled out from under the cowling. . . . General Arnold had a dozen battles on his hands. He was fighting with the Joint Chiefs for resources; he was struggling to get an organizational setup for airpower in that war; he had to rassle against the Army and the Navy every minute." Largely because of the furious energy of the seemingly unstoppable, 210-pound Arnold, the B-29 Superfortress moved from drawing board to factory floor to flight. Arnold did not yet know that in the very near future his powerhouse personality would be taken down several notches by a series of heart attacks.

Painted in Army olive drab, which would not last long as the standard color for Superfortresses, the first B-29 in an initial batch of three taxied out for its maiden flight on September 21, 1942, with renowned test pilot Edmund T. "Eddie" Allen doing the honors. The location was Boeing Field in Seattle, a congested and relatively small airport sunk in a gully with a mere 5,200 feet of runway. Allen flew with a crew of six: copilot A. C. Reed (the term "pilot" was not yet being used for the second aviator on the flight deck); flight test engineer W. F. Milliken; assistant flight test engineer Edward J. Wersebe; flight engineer M. Hanson; radio operator A. Peterson; and observer K. J. Laplow. Allen took the aircraft up to 6,000 feet, performed a few gentle maneuvers, and tried a few power-off stalls. One hour and fifteen minutes later, the B-29's tires touched ground. Allen later wrote in his postflight report that the B-29 had "exceptionally good aerodynamic characteristics; aileron and rudder turns were satisfactory; stalling characteristics excellent; spiral stability and controls generally satisfactory; window arrangement affords good vision in attitudes of flight, particularly good in landing." That last point was an important one. No other aircraft built in large numbers had a flush forward fuselage like the B-29. It was important for the crew to be able to see out, especially the aircraft commander, whose seat was relatively far back in the plane.

The initial enthusiasm by Allen, Boeing engineering vice president Wellwood Beall, and others was misplaced. The B-29 was indeed a superbomber, bigger and better than any aircraft before it, but the B-29 was also a super headache. As early as September 30, 1942, technical problems with the Wright caused the B-29 to be grounded for ten days. There was more trouble to come.

By the time the second B-29 took to the air on December 30, 1942, the program was in trouble. There were repeated engine failures caused in part by a faulty carburetor design. There was a further grounding in January 1943. Mechanics and engineers were finding all kinds of problems and making fixes to the Wright R-3350 "corncob" engine, but the basic design was still flawed.

Moment in Michigan

In late 1942, a young pilot named Robert "Bud" McDonald was on furlough and visited his parents, two brothers, and sister in Jackson, Michigan. The family had playful fun together. In photographs, McDonald wears a mustache and bears a resemblance to actor Errol Flynn, or even more to the lesser-known celebrity Bert Parks, though he was neither so solemn as Flynn nor so trifling as Parks.

He did have a sense of humor. "Even back then, there were rules about riding more than one on a bicycle," said his sister Nancy. "As was usually his practice, he would play with me and my two other brothers before even going into the house to get out of his uniform. This one trip he got out his old bike and three of us rode down the street in front of the house, which at that time was considered a highway. A police car approached us, took one look, waved, and went on their way. . . . Other times when he would come home on leave he would play baseball or football, in his uniform, with all the kids in the neighborhood. He was a hero to all of us. The neighbor kids looked forward to his visits and were just as excited as the family. They would be over bright and early on the day of his arrival, so they could greet him."

Bud's father, John W. McDonald, was a World War I veteran; after Pearl Harbor a recruiter judged him too old, at age forty-six, to reenter the military. The older McDonald worked for the Fisher Body Division of General Motors—an aircraft manufacturer at that time—and was the company's liaison to a similarly named company, General Electric. The older McDonald was working on a new concept, a kind of gun that could be mounted aboard a military aircraft and operated remotely from some distance away. He wrote in a family document that he "was sent to the General Electric Aircraft Armament School, Schenectady, NY, where for a period of five weeks I received instruction in the theory, operation and maintenance of electrically operated and remote controlled machine gun turrets for aircraft." Until now, aerial gunners had always held their guns in their hands and operated them manually. Now, it would be different.

Everyone in the family (which remained in Jackson while Bud's father worked in Detroit) had known forever that young Bud wanted to be a pilot. Now, Bud was a flying cadet in the AAF, training to become one. His father wasn't supposed to talk about remotely operated guns or about the new aircraft they would be used on, but he did. When a conversation began about what aircraft Bud McDonald might request upon pinning on his military pilot's wings, his father dragged him aside. "Bud," he said, "I want to tell you about a new plane called the B-29."

Trouble after Takeoff

The U.S. bombing effort in Europe continued to grow while the B-29 continued to pose technical challenges. The Eighth Air Force in England, initially commanded by Maj. Gen. Carl "Tooey" Spaatz, would eventually number 350,000 men in forty combat groups. B-17 and B-24 bombers with fighter escort would fly deep into the Third Reich on missions with a thousand planes or more. In these early days, they were facing a determined German air arm, the Luftwaffe, which perfected the technique of attacking an American bomber head-on from a few degrees above centerline— twelve o'clock high—with the specific intent of killing the bomber's pilots. In early 1943, a B-17 or B-24 crew did not have excellent chances of surviving the required twenty-five missions, later raised to thirty. But all of that would change.

On December 1, 1942, Ira Eaker replaced Spaatz as commander of the Eighth Air Force and pinned on a second star. On December 20, 1942, 101 bombers attacked a Luftwaffe support installation at Romilly-sur-Seine. No fighters reached the target with them. Six

B-17s were lost. Thirty-one were damaged. The Americans claimed they shot down three German fighters, although more were written off while landing. It was a day filled with mediocrity for a target barely one hundred miles inside enemy territory. In the days and weeks that followed, the Eighth Air Force wasted considerable blood and treasure attacking German U-boat pens. This was a measure of how badly German submarines were mauling the Allies in the Battle of the Atlantic, but it was also mostly fruitless. The Fortresses and Liberators were exposing themselves to a formidable enemy fighter force to attack targets that were all but impervious to bombing.

It would turn out, ultimately, that the B-29 would not be ready for the war in Europe. While the program was still in its infancy, it was struck by tragedy.

Test pilot Allen was assigned to make another in a series of increasing troubled test flights in the second Superfortress prototype on February 18, 1943. Allen took off at the Superfortress's design gross weight of 105,000 pounds with full fuel tanks—6,803 U.S. gallons of volatile aviation fuel.

Allen's crew included copilot Roger Dansfield; flight test engineers Wersebe, Thomas Lankford, Charles Blaine, and Raymond Basel; flight engineer Fritz Mohn; instrument monitor Robert Maxfield; observer Barclay Henshaw; aerodynamicist Vincent North; and radio operator Harry Ralston.

Eight minutes after takeoff, climbing through 5,000 feet, someone reported a fire in the number one engine. Allen cut mixture and fuel to number one, feathered the propeller, closed cowl flaps, and discharged a fire extinguisher bottle. He began a descent toward Boeing Field. Since the fire appeared to have been extinguished and the bomber seemed to be under control, Allen planned a landing from the north on Runway 13, rather than making a downwind landing on the 5,200-foot runway with a heavy aircraft. The radio operator reported descending through an altitude at 1,500 feet at a point four miles northeast of the field. The bomber was on its downwind leg, starting a left turn onto base leg.

Two minutes later, ground witnesses heard an explosion. A piece of metal fell from the aircraft. Radio operator Ralston, who could see into the forward bomb bay and the wing center section front spar, said on an open microphone: "Allen, better get this thing down in a hurry. The wing spar is burning badly."

Aubrey Pebble, a Seattle resident who'd retired from Boeing recently, looked up at the dark, shuddering shape of the B-29. Pebble was no expert on the design of the secret new bomber, but he was pretty sure part of its wing leading edge was missing. Dirty little streaks of gray smoke trailed behind the number one engine nacelle.

"Is he in trouble?" a passerby asked. The aircraft was close enough for its sound to nearly drown the voice.

"He seems to have a problem, but the runway is right over there," someone else said.

Pebble felt a chill. "That airplane is not going to make the runway," he said.

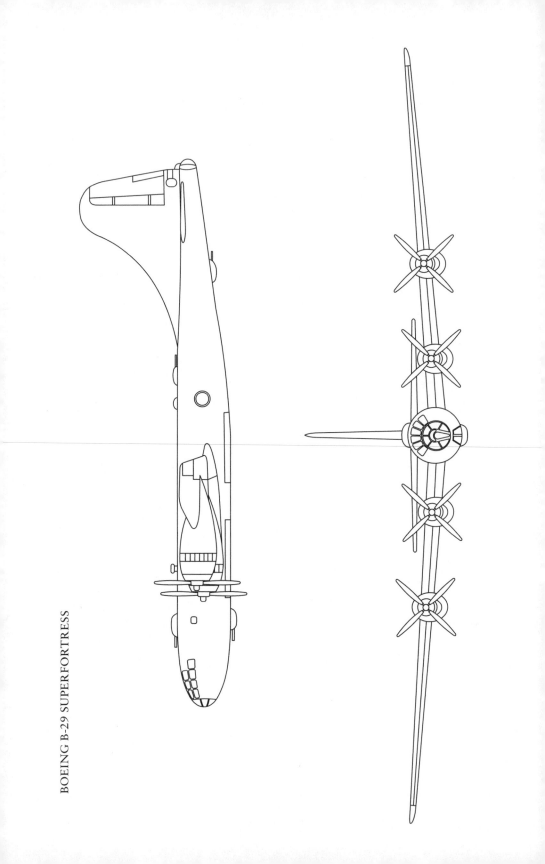

BOEING B-29 SUPERFORTRESS

CHAPTER 3

Warm-Up

Mission to Tokyo
March 9, 1945, 4:45 p.m.–6:30 p.m.

DEPENDING ON THE ISLAND—Guam, Saipan, or Tinian—
and depending on the bombardment group (a dozen in
all), the briefing for the March 9–10 mission to Tokyo was held
at different times throughout Friday March 9. Speakers placed
different emphases on what lay ahead for bomber crews, and the
crews reacted differently. Most B-29 crewmembers shuffled into
giant Quonset huts where crews sat together and stared up at maps
and charts. The group commander, the intelligence guy, and the
weather guy each took his turn to strut and fret on the stage, but by
now the secrets were out and the surprises were few.

The record isn't clear on who officiated at the briefing for
the 19th Bombardment Group on Guam. It may have been 93rd
squadron commander Sammy Bakshas. The airplane commander
with whom he would be flying, Muster, made it clear before the
briefing that the secrets in Sammy's head weren't secrets any longer.
Some kind of conversation with a bit of an edge took place between

the two men. A pilot like Muster was never completely comfortable when the boss, even a boss with whom he got along well, came along for the ride. It felt like being held in judgment. The climate around these men was tense with the knowledge that new tactics meant new risk. Today, we do not know what happened at this group's briefing or in that conversation between Bakshas and Muster, or whether there was tension between the two men, but it is was obvious that B-29 crewmembers were upset about the plan for tonight's journey to the Empire. The briefing room was pretty much the last place where any bitching could be done before going out to the aircraft. No airplane commander would tolerate disgruntlement after that.

At the 504th Bombardment Group on Tinian, where Trip Triplett, Percy U. Tucker, and Laddie Wale sat in a crude tin building to hear the briefing, almost everyone knew before arrival that they would be carrying firebombs and flying low, but they learned their destination only when the intel guy announced, "Your target tonight, gentlemen, is . . . Tokyo." They had already figured out most of the rest. "You will bomb from 7,500 feet dropping clusters that will open up at 1,500 feet." Each received a "flimsy," a mimeographed paper outlining what he needed to know about the mission. Each crew remained together and, at completion of the briefing, boarded a truck for the flight line after first having an opportunity, if wanted, for a final chat with 504th chaplain Earl Rait.

At the 497th Bombardment Group on Saipan, where Carl Barthold was a radio operator, the briefing was held inside a large concrete building the Americans had erected. The intelligence officer talked too long about Japanese antiaircraft guns, Japanese fighters, and Japanese treatment of prisoners. "We were impatient to find out what was going to happen to us," said Barthold, recalling crewmate Didier and the B-4 bag. "My plane was a pathfinder and we . . . felt this intel officer, who had never seen the Empire from the air, wasn't much help." Barthold was ready to go. "The ground crews had our gear already on the plane. All we needed was a web belt with a knife and a .45. Our Mae West and other gear was aboard the airplane."

Members of one bombardment group somewhere on Guam, Tinian, or Saipan were told that if they had to bail out, they should try to find their way to the emperor's palace. According to the intelligence briefer, the emperor was more humane than the police or the Army—a curious idea, apparently without any basis in fact. At another bombardment group, the intel guy claimed that the Japanese would give better treatment to officers than to enlisted men—again, a fanciful notion not based on actual knowledge. One sergeant spotted a flight jacket draped over a chair sporting colonel's eagles. He borrowed the insignia and wore them on every mission thereafter, a sergeant dressed as a colonel, without ever being forced to put the claim to the test.

The Briefing II

Late in the afternoon, amid caustic comments about the values and virtues of command and tail gunners, Trip Triplett and his crewmates shouldered their gear and prepared to plod up the hill to the briefing shack, called the war room. The war room of the 504th Bombardment Group on Tinian was a large, barnlike structure, gable roofed, vertically sided with knotty, unpainted 1x10 pine boards. The alternating blazing heat and drenching rains had already smeared the new boards with dark weathering streaks. Triplett thought to himself that everything and everybody aged quickly overseas in wartime.

Inside were rows of pine benches divided by a coral-covered aisle that led to a rough raised platform in front. On the wall behind the platform hung a map with a long, red yard string that pointed to the target. Triplett may have been one of the few who didn't know the target yet, and he couldn't see where the red yarn went.

Triplett crowded onto a bench with the rest of his crew and made quiet small talk and guesses about the target. "The usual banter was missing," Triplett recalled. "Something told us this was no ordinary mission.

"Someone called us to attention. We snapped to. Col. Glen W. Martin, group commander; Lt. Col. Robert Barrowclough, commander of the 421st squadron, my squadron; [and others] strode quickly down the aisle to the raised platform and their chairs.

"'At ease.' We sat.

"Colonel Martin stepped to the front of the platform. Quiet tenseness settled over the hot, muggy room. He got right to the point.

"'Men, all of you know that we have been hitting our targets in daylight with demolition bombs from between twenty and thirty thousand feet. You also know that the weather and cloud cover beneath us has kept us from getting enough bombs on target. The climb for altitude drinks up the fuel and cuts down on our payload of bombs.

"'This strike will be different. We are bombing tonight from eight to ten thousand feet. [The battle order called for altitudes from 5,500–8,500 feet.] By going in low, minus guns, ammo and two gunners we can carry less fuel and more bombs. This is a maximum effort. Every plane that we have that can fly will be airborne. If this raid is successful, it can set the pattern that can shorten the war by months. Here is your target. Good luck and I'll see you when you get back.' With his last words, he jerked the curtain to one side and jabbed a pointer to where the red string stopped. Tokyo!

"An involuntary tremor raced up the back of my neck. Major Kenim from G-2 [Intelligence] was speaking now. '. . . and there are 600 to 700 fighters in this area, as you already know. We don't know how many night fighters they have. We expect to know more about that when you get back'.

"Weather briefing, sea-rescue ditching points, and benediction from the chaplain followed anticlimactically. I thought to myself, 'This is suicide, pure and simple.'" *It was 4:30 p.m. Chamorro Standard Time, March 9, 1945.*

Triplett had plenty of company.

A great many of the thousand kids were wondering if today's mission to Tokyo was a pending disaster disguised as a bombing raid. A special concern was ditching. The forty-eight Superfortresses known to have put down in the Pacific thus far with normal crews would have carried 528 airmen; during that time, air-sea rescue had spotted 164 survivors and picked up every one of them. An elaborate system that made use of PBY Catalina and PBM Mariner aircraft, seaplane tenders, and submarines was taking shape, but B-29 crewmembers knew that the ocean was vast, and even a big bomber could be a tiny speck when viewed bobbing on the waves. It didn't help that crewmembers were sometimes their own worst enemies. Many B-29s were short of Mae West flashlights, invaluable when ditching at night, because crewmen borrowed them for use in their quarters and forgot to bring them along on combat missions.

When Laddie Wale's group completed its briefing, the men filed out, prepared to go to their planes—Wale had already visited *Lady Annabelle* and would return to the B-29 with the others. They all looked at each other. Tucker, their airplane commander, looked no more or less serious than usual, which was pretty serious. Although he wasn't talkative, crews usually walked out of the briefing engaged in lively chatter. Today, most were silent.

The Campbell Crew

In brighter light, the plane's silver surfaces would have gleamed, almost mirrorlike. It was a thing of beauty to some but simply a machine to most. The B-29 Superfortress had the mechanical look of a functional machine, its cigar-shaped fuselage confronting Barthold, its 141-foot wingspread in front of him with the four-bladed propellers ready to turn. Ground crewmembers were finishing their final checks, having spent many hours overnight since yesterday inspecting systems, loading bombs, loading fuel, and performing a hundred tasks to make the giant bomber ready. Barthold's B-29 was prepared to fly to Tokyo with its cargo of fire.

Barthold was part of a pathfinder crew that was scheduled to arrive over a night-shrouded Tokyo ahead of the main attack force. "There were twelve pathfinder planes in our group," Barthold said. "We were to take off a half hour before everybody else. We were to arrive first and put a big X across Tokyo for those coming behind us to see."

Some airplane commanders required a line-up inspection at planeside before climbing into the B-29. The airplane commander of a different crew was considered "a strutting martinet," as Barthold remembered him. The tiny tyrant didn't exactly conduct a white-glove exam, but he "made a very big deal out of that inspection while everyone stood in squad formation in front of the leading edge of the wing." In contrast, Barthold said, "our plane commander [Campbell] had confidence in us. We didn't hold a formal inspection. The ground crews had our gear, including our Mae West, already on the plane. All we needed was a web belt with a knife and a .45. Our plane commander considered us adults and let us behave like adults as we checked our own gear, climbed aboard, and prepared to take off."

With the rest of the crew, Barthold climbed aboard his B-29, entering the aircraft by climbing up into a dark space behind the nose wheel. Once seated in his radar compartment, he could hear the pilots and flight engineer talking on the interphone, running through the engine-start checklist. He thought they sounded more tense than usual, but he couldn't see them. "I was the radio operator," Barthold said. "I sat next to a bulkhead facing the right side of the plane. I had my radio, key, and codebooks. I was jammed in there. I was in a little chair that infringed on the upper and lower gun turrets and I was facing to the right. My head pressed up against the four .50-caliber machine guns in the upper turret and they always used to rattle in my head. Across from me was the navigator [Gerald A. "Jerry" Rau], who faced forward. In front of me but separated by a partition was the flight engineer [Charles Francis], who faced to the rear. Were we all a little more nervous than usual that evening because we were going to Tokyo at low altitude? Yes. Yes, we were." Barthold's B-29 trembled and the noise level went up as the engine start procedure began. *It was 5:15 p.m. Chamorro Standard Time, March 9, 1945.*

The Fling Crew
At North Field, Tinian, following the briefing and a quick, mild, late-afternoon thunderstorm typical of these islands, left blister gunner Reb Carter dismounted from a boxy, 4x4 weapons carrier at the hardstand and started toward a B-29 with his crewmates, including airplane commander Dean Fling.

The only southerner on his crew, Carter was more or less middle class. He was a six-foot, eager-looking, toothy son of a successful accountant so close to his father that he hoped to study accounting if there was to be a future for him after this. The trappings of his childhood were gone now; he'd once been preoccupied with spinning a yo-yo with greater speed and dexterity than anyone else, but he'd left his modest collection of yo-yos behind in his house in Atlanta, not far from where Bell Aircraft was one of several companies manufacturing B-29s.

Carter's B-29 today was slotted at the cutting edge of the air assault being mounted on the Japanese capital. It would be the seventh aircraft from their group over target; the first six would carry M47 incendiaries and use their fiery bombload to mark the "urban area of Meetinghouse" for those to follow. The rest of the group would follow with larger, 500-pound E-46 bombs.

Carter had no idea that tonight his crew would become hopelessly lost. He had no guns to fire if Japanese night fighters found them later that night, but his role as a scanner, tipping off the flight-deck crew about engine operations and events around the aircraft, would never be more important.

Some B-29 crews, ignoring orders, were preparing for the mission with a full load of guns, gunners, and ammunition. Some were following the battle order to the letter and leaving both guns and gunners behind. In Carter's 9th Bombardment Group, airplane commanders like Fling had found a middle ground: they would take every gunner, and use every gunner as an extra pair of eyes, but they would travel to the Empire unarmed except for a tail gun in the case of some crews. Tonight, Fling's tail gunner would not be armed, either. Seeing Carter without his gear, a member of the line crew who may have been new to the job asked Carter which plane he was heading for.

"It's *God's Will*," said Carter.

It was 5:20 p.m. Chamorro Standard Time, March 9, 1945.

Men and Bombers

Not everyone on Guam, Saipan, and Tinian was in the habit of talking to an airplane, but most of the thousand kids had superstitions, lucky charms, and a tendency to think of their aircraft as a living creature. Jo Haney, the daughter of one of those B-29 Superfortress crew chiefs, Sgt. Philip N. Phillipson, was mystified by the relationship between men and aircraft. In his famous quote, author Ernest Hemingway was writing about fighters but could just as easily have meant bombers: "You love a lot of things if you live around them, but there isn't any woman and there isn't any horse, nor any before nor any after, that is as lovely as a great airplane, and men who love them are faithful to them even though they leave them for others. A man has only one virginity to lose . . . and if it is a lovely plane he loses it to, there his heart will ever be."

Haney wondered how anyone could put his heart into a B-29. The plane, said Haney, "was prone to breakdown. It was put into production way too soon. The engines constantly overheated. It was planned for high altitude, yet height was at times the cause of engine failure. And at high altitude, bomb runs weren't all that successful. So why did men love this plane so much?"

The B-29 was an untidy, barely functional collection of sheet metal, rivets, wires, joints, engines, and, yes, guns and bombs. Haney remembered her father saying the B-29 "always had 'bugs in her jugs.' So, I asked him, 'What's a jug?' He told me that it was a cylinder, that the engines each had eighteen cylinders each, and that those damn cylinders were always leaking oil and fowling the spark plugs."

The unlikely love affair between men and machine began in the Pacific Northwest. Seattle-based Boeing's success with its B-17 Flying Fortress still lay mostly in the future in October 1938, when Army Air Corps chief of staff Maj. Gen. Oscar Westover established a requirement for a superbomber. The designation B-29 was assigned. The B-29 Superfortress won out over other designs, although the Army turned to Consolidated to develop a backup aircraft, which became the B-32 Dominator.

The B-29 became the first fully pressurized bomber to be produced in large numbers. When everything was working right, the crew could work in shirtsleeves, without heated clothing or oxygen masks. It became the first warplane to regularly fly high enough to encounter the furious winds known as the jetstream, which, at great heights, were often a greater enemy to the big bomber than the Japanese. Those violent winds were also one of many reasons bombs dropped from high altitude weren't hitting their targets.

A four-engine, midwing, "very heavy" bomber with a crew of eleven, the B-29 was powered by 2,200-horsepower Wright R-3350 Duplex Cyclone 18, twin-row, turbocharged, radial-pistol engines— jugs, bugs, and all. The engine took far too long to develop and was seen by many as a threat to the success of the plane it pulled through the air.

The R-3350 almost seemed to enjoy overheating, swallowing valves, and even catching fire in flight. Hoping to eke out greater horsepower, Boeing delivered the Superfortress with a crankcase made of magnesium, a very light, very strong metal that unfortunately was also flammable. When the crankcase problem was combined with the difficulties of a fuel induction system, which tended to catch fire and burn long enough to catch the magnesium afire, it became a very serious situation. Shortsighted treatments such as air baffles to direct more air to the rear row of cylinders and propeller cuffs to force more air through the engine only helped temporarily.

The wing of the B-29 spanned 141 feet 3 inches. It was an innovative design, a long and narrow, high-aspect ratio wing equipped with large Fowler-type flaps. The unusual shape and configuration of the wing enabled the B-29 to fly very fast at high altitudes without having unmanageable flight characteristics during the slower speeds required for landing and takeoff.

More revolutionary was the size and sophistication of the pressurized sections of the fuselage: the flight deck forward of the wing, the gunner's compartment aft of the wing, and the tail gunner's station. Crewmembers traveled from nose to tail in the B-29 through a padded "personnel tunnel" above the bomb bay. The tunnel was an innovative answer to the obvious question: how could you pressurize an aircraft with huge bomb bay doors that had to be opened over the target?

In fact, the B-29 had two tandem bomb bays and was usually flown with both bays equally loaded for balance. Boeing's answer was to pressurize both ends of the fuselage plus the linking tunnel, but not the bay itself. There were also other sections of the fuselage, not where crew stations were located, that were not pressurized.

Superfortress Crew

The thousand kids had basically about a dozen jobs to perform, from handling yoke and throttle to firing machine guns. The composition of a B-29 crew varied slightly from one plane to another according to the mission, but it typically included eleven men. Moving from nose to tail, those crewmembers located forward of the bomb bay and the tunnel above the bomb bay were:

- The *bombardier* sat farthest forward in the B-29 and also acted as nose gunner. The bombardier had primary control of the upper and lower forward turrets when he was not bomb aiming; gun sight was stowed to his right and could be released to pivot about 120 degrees when in use. Joe Krogman of the Tucker crew was typical.

- The *airplane commander* (the pilot), Sammy Bakshas, Gordon Muster, Percy Usher Tucker, and Dean Fling being examples, occupied the front left seat on the flight deck.
- The *pilot* (on a B-29, this was the official term for the *copilot*), who flew the aircraft from the right seat. This was a less experienced pilot, sometimes a recent flight school graduate. First Lieutenant Harold L. "Pete" Peterson of the Dean Fling crew was one of these men.
- The *flight engineer*, Laddie Wale on the Tucker crew being an example, sat behind the pilot facing an instrument panel and monitoring engine performance. Unlike the engineer on earlier bombers, he was not trained as a gunner. The B-29 was the only bomber on which the pilots did not have a complete set of instruments or controls. The flight engineer was in actual control of the mechanical function of the aircraft.
- The *navigator* sat to the left of the forward turret behind the two pilots. He had a window, which didn't amount to much; "a day or night indicator," one navigator called it. He had to crawl into the tunnel above the bomb bay to use the astrodome when performing celestial navigation. In the B-29 the bombardier and navigator were almost always military occupational specialty 1036, navigator-bombardier, meaning they were dual trained. In practice they almost always specialized in one duty or the other.
- The *radio operator*, someone like Carl Barthold on the Campbell crew, sat behind the top turret with no window in a very narrow, confined space. He was the bomber crew's communications link to the outside world, including the other bombers in the strike force.

Crewmembers situated aft of the bomb bay and the tunnel above the bomb bay were:

- The *left blister gunner* was also the left scanner and fired guns from a remote control in the left blister. Reb Carter of the Dean Fling crew (and later the George Bertagnoli crew) was one of these gunners.

- The *right blister gunner* (Didier in the Campbell crew was one of them) scanned and operated guns from the right blister.
- The *central fire control gunner* or "ring gunner" rode in a barber chair or "ring seat," looked out from atop the fuselage, and coordinated the firing of the remotely controlled guns by various gunners.
- The *radar operator*—men like Trip Triplett or Richard "Bake" Baker of the Fling crew—sat in an enclosed compartment in the back and had no windows. The navigator and the radar operator each had a six-inch screen operated by the same radar transmitter and relying on the same power source.
- The *tail gunner* rode facing to the rear and manned the tail guns. Joe Majeski of the Tucker crew was one of these.

Preparing to Fly

Now bomber crewmembers coped with one of the aspects of their duty they dread most. Takeoff was always a tense time. Takeoff in a B-29 fully loaded with fuel, bombs, and ammo was always a very dangerous proposition. Almost everyone on Guam, Saipan, and Tinian had seen at least one crash. If you lost an engine past the halfway mark of the takeoff run, you probably wouldn't be able to stop before the end of the runway and the plane would crash off the cliff or go into the water and explode. It is a tribute to the skill of the mechanics, the pilots, and the flight engineers that it did not happen more often.

But as Barthold was well aware, on Saipan at least there was a margin of safety if it was used correctly. As bombardier William C. Atkinson wrote,

At Isley Field it was common on takeoff for the pilot of a fully loaded B-29 to hold the wheels to the runway until the final few hundred feet (the last two percent of the runway's length), hauling back at the last possible instant to lurch over the road along the cliff edge; then diving full throttle for the sea far below, gaining airspeed while retracting the wheels; and finally beginning the long takeoff climb as the belly of the plane virtually skimmed the water. More than one of the crews failed at this maneuver, especially at night.

Said B-29 pilot Jim Farrell, "I believe the drop off the Saipan runway was over two hundred feet and often saved our butts. Taking off on twin runways—1 minute behind the plane on your runway but only thirty seconds behind a plane on the other—often found us in prop-wash and at that low speed. Many times I felt we wouldn't have made it without that dip."

The pathfinders were in the air, with dusk approaching, while crewmembers of the remainder of the attack force of 334 B-29s on three islands were still arriving at their planes, climbing aboard, and beginning preflight checks. Because Guam was farther from Japan, B-29s from Guam were already taxiing out, lining up, watching their intervals, and going into the takeoff roll.

Closely observing the noisy, busy preparations for takeoff was the boss, Major General LeMay. He was gruff, tough, yet more articulate than they gave him credit for. LeMay himself used the word "gamble" for what he was doing today—sending men at low altitude against a heavily defended target. In later years some would view him as inhuman, willing to burn human beings into cinders to win a war, but LeMay was too complex to be cruel. Still, to St. Clair McKelway, there was "something deeply, bottomlessly disturbing in this stocky, plain-looking new commanding general of the Twenty-First Bomber Command." LeMay perceived that his job was to erode Japan's ability to wage war, and he knew that the tactics used thus far by the B-29 force were not working. He was only one of many who had thought of using firebombs to ignite Japanese urban areas, but he alone bore responsibility for ordering his men to attack at low level and to leave their ammunition behind.

McKelway, who was the military public relations officer on Guam and who wrote about the thousand kids and their war against the Empire for the *New Yorker*, worried about LeMay. "'My God,' I think I was saying soundlessly to myself," McKelway wrote, "if this LeMay turns out to be another great young Air Forces general, I will desert. I will run up into the hills and hide, like the Navy radio operator who stayed up there all those months the Japanese were on Guam. Couldn't I have a lousy, easygoing, mediocre general for just a few weeks, a few days? I want to relax! I've got to relax!"

LeMay was about as easygoing as a stroke. But he was no strutting warlord, either. Though he spoke in a stern, commanding voice, it was never really loud enough for others to hear, even in a small room. As author Barrett Tillman pointed out, LeMay lived for an extended period in a tent, in vivid contrast to Guam's admirals, who entertained him in hilltop houses and even on a yacht. His headquarters was in an unadorned Quonset hut. LeMay maintained a lean staff, shunned most creature comforts, and did his best to hide his frustration that his boss, Hap Arnold, would not allow him to pilot a Superfortress over Japan.

LeMay wasn't at the controls of a B-29 today or any other day because Arnold had made him part of a small inner circle who knew about a supersecret U.S. program to create a new weapon. No one with knowledge of that weapon—it was being developed in the high desert of New Mexico by a LeMay acquaintance, Maj. Gen. Leslie Groves—could be permitted to risk falling into Japanese hands. LeMay must have been frustrated at being clued in on the new weapon: it was not available. It would not improve his results in the bombing campaign today. It would not help with LeMay's immediate chore, which was to reduce Japan's warfighting ability with the weapons he possessed.

LeMay and his chief of staff, Brig. Gen. August Kissner, were in a Jeep at North Field, Guam, as late afternoon blended into evening. The pathfinders were in the air and on their way. LeMay's command was committed to the mission. Now, LeMay and Kissner watched as Brig. Gen. Thomas S. Power led the first B-29s into the sky. *It was 5:36 p.m., Chamorro Standard Time, March 9, 1945.*

Power, 39, had been tested in battle in the Mediterranean Theater and was perhaps the most trusted of LeMay's lieutenants, even though Tillman deemed him "almost totally lacking in people skills." Tommy Power was not universally loved, in part because of a propensity to linger overhead while bombing a target, risking his crew in order to gather intelligence. But whatever else he was, as his Superfortress vaulted skyward, Tommy Power today was the on-scene air commander of the mission to Tokyo.

Tall in the Saddle, with Sammy Bakshas in the airplane commander's seat and Gordon Muster alongside him, made a smooth takeoff from North Field at Guam not far behind Tommy

Power. They climbed into the early evening sky while B-29s were still warming up on Saipan and Tinian. Bakshas and Muster were now among the most experienced of the B-29 pilots, and when teamed with their flight engineer 2nd Lt. Leland P. Fishback, they could make the huge, cigar-shaped bomber perform miracles. This was a B-29 crew at the top of its game, its skills enhanced by Bakshas's presence and the aircraft itself a testament to the perfection maintenance crews could achieve.

Tall in the Saddle, climbing, was in fine shape. Not a nick or scratch spoiled the smooth, natural metal skin of the Superfortress. *Tall in the Saddle*'s four R-3350 engines, treated lovingly by the ground crew assigned to Gordon Muster, were purring smoothly—something the trouble-prone R-3350 did not always do. The electrical system, which had been cantankerous on earlier models of the B-29, was functioning to perfection.

Japanese fighters and flak had thus far never touched *Tall in the Saddle*. The bomber typified a B-29 performing at the top of its game with a calm and capable crew taking her up. Sadly, no photo of the *Tall in the Saddle* appears to have been taken in the weeks leading up to the evening of this mission. But whether or not it was preserved on film for posterity, the bomber was on her way up into the night and northwest toward the Empire and was in perfect working order. *It was 6:05 p.m., Chamorro Standard Time, March 9, 1945.*

CHAPTER 4

Struggling

American Bombers against Japan,
February 18, 1943–April 4, 1944

THE VOICE OF TEST PILOT Eddie Allen was businesslike but ice cold as he spoke to Boeing Radio while descending over Seattle on February 18, 1943, in a prototype B-29 Superfortress that was afire and was spraying pieces of itself in all directions.

"Have fire equipment ready," said Allen. "Am coming in with a wing on fire." Watched by numerous Seattle residents, including Boeing retiree Aubrey Pebble, Allen's bomber turned south on an oblique final approach in a desperate effort to reach Boeing Field only three or four miles away. Allen was at an altitude of less than 250 feet.

Witnesses said part of the wing leading edge was missing. On the ground beneath the bomber's flight path during its next mile, a passerby found the flight engineer's data sheet. In the course of that mile, three of the forward compartment crewmembers leaped from the aircraft—too low for their parachutes to open. Radio operator Harry Ralston hit a high-tension wire. His parachute snagged. He was strung over the wire. Recovery workers had to climb up to the wire to retrieve his remains.

At 12:26 p.m., three scant miles from Boeing Field, the Superfortress crashed into the Frye Meat Packing Plant at 2203 Airport Way South. The bomber collided with a building that was dedicated to the slaughter of pigs and the manufacture of, among other products, Frye's big buckets of Wild Rose Lard. Passersby heard the surreal agony of squealing pigs in the first sounds that followed the explosion.

Among the dead were pilots Allen, Dansfield, and the other crewmembers. The crash and resulting fire also killed twenty Frye employees plus twenty-three-year-old fireman Luther Dean Bonner, who had been on the job just eighty-five days and who suffocated. Eighty pigs were lost. Very little was left of the plant or the aircraft. There was clear evidence that fire and dense smoke had gone through the bomb bay into the cockpit in the last moments before impact. Part of that evidence was the burns on the bodies and clothing of the three crewmembers who had bailed out.

About a mile down the flight path from the explosion, burned parts of a deicer valve, hose clamps, and instrumentation tubing were found later.

In the aftermath of the catastrophe, there was rampant confusion, as author William Wolf wrote:

Since the XB-29 was a top-secret project, news releases described the crashed airplane as a "four-engine bomber." Since the second B-29 was unpainted, unlike the first XB-29, the many witnesses either thought it was an airliner or assumed it to be a B-17. However, the Seattle City Transit Weekly, a newspaper for transit company employees, nearly exposed the secret bomber. A bus diver who had been near the crash had taken photos of the crashed aircraft before it completely burned, and submitted them to the Transit Weekly, which published them with its story of the crash. The FBI quickly investigated and confiscated all but a few of the 500 copies printed.

An obscure Missouri legislator, Senator Harry S Truman, chaired an investigative committee that looked into the problems of the rather complex Wright R-3350 engine. Truman's panel concluded that engine-maker Wright was at fault for quality-control failings. Equally at fault, according to the committee report, was the AAF, for putting too much pressure on Wright to accelerate R-3350 production. The R-3350 would continue to pose problems for AAF and for the B-29. However, contrary to myth, the R-3350 was not to blame for the Allen crash.

Author Stephan Wilkinson wrote that a "fire started that blew off a large part of the left wing's leading edge and rapidly spread throughout the wing. The accident investigation showed that the faulty fuel filter atop the wing could, in certain flight configurations, cause raw fuel to siphon down into the wing. On this day, it was ignited by a length of test-instrument manometer tubing that touched a hot exhaust manifold and created a slow-burning fuse. The B-29 became uncontrollable on final and crashed."

Entering into War

While politicians, pilots, and engineers were struggling to fix the B-29, the men who would eventually fly the great firebomb mission to Tokyo were experiencing military life and preparing to go overseas. In February 1943, none had yet seen or even heard of a B-29. The handsome, mature Sammy Bakshas was instructing student pilots and helping make policy in the AAF's rapidly expanding training command. Sammy was moving around a lot and Aldora and baby Jerry moved with him. They spent plenty of time in fleabag hotels and in their shiny '42 Buick, which Aldora recalls as being "several colors." Sammy soon had more than a thousand hours in his logbook as a pilot.

Like many who started out to become pilots and didn't, future B-29 radio operator Carl Barthold did plenty of moving around after going into uniform in February 1943. "I felt the Draft Board's footsteps getting closer to me so I enlisted in the AAF and was called up around Washington's birthday. I took basic training near home at Jefferson Barracks in South St. Louis County."

Barthold was among the tens of thousands who started out to become a pilot and didn't. He signed up for the aviation cadet program and was shipped to St. Paul, Minnesota, where he learned to fly a light plane, a single-engine Aeronca C-3. "My instructor was a huge and inept man, so the aircraft was always out of balance. I got checked out for ten hours but did not solo. However, I made a really smooth landing on a grass strip near U.S. Highway 61, so I thought to myself, 'Oh, I'm going to be a great pilot.'" Not long after being introduced to handling the controls of an airplane, Barthold was told he couldn't become a pilot because of his eyesight. "We had tests. I had trouble lining up the two little sticks, which was a test of your depth perception. They decided I was going to be a washout and sent me to Fresno, California, to become a radio operator." Barthold did not know it yet, but they had also decided because of his eyesight to assign him to the only bomber where the radio operator was not a gunner. Barthold had not yet heard of this new bomber. He would learn about it on a train ride.

He would discover that the new bomber had killed a lot of good men in the Eddie Allen tragedy. The crash led to extensive modifications of the B-29. Engineers hunted down and remedied sources of possible fuel leaks. They relocated fuel filler necks and installed a fire-stop bulkhead. These and other changes were introduced retroactively to the first and third planes in the series and subsequently to all production models. Thus began a long series of changes to a basic design that still had too many flaws.

From the earliest days of B-29 development, the top brass in Washington argued over how best to manage the Superfortress and the bombing campaign that would ultimately be mounted against the Japanese home islands. From the beginning, there was discussion about commanding the Superfortress effort from the northern Virginia suburbs of Washington, where, in early 1943, the AAF's top general, Hap Arnold, moved into the newly constructed Pentagon building. Arnold was promoted to four-star rank on March 19, 1943, and would eventually receive another promotion.

Bud McDonald

The growing air-training establishment in the United States was churning out new pilots at an extraordinary rate—so fast, in fact, that over the coming eighteen months it would stop because it was generating too many of them.

As an eager Bud McDonald discovered, flight training usually began in a biplane trainer at a contract flying school. During World

War II, sixty-four contract schools conducted primary training for the AAF, with a maximum of fifty-six schools operating at any one time. During the war, the schools introduced 250,000 student pilots to the cockpit and sent them on to advanced training. As a member of Flying Class 43-C (the number signifying the year of graduation), McDonald went from primary to basic training in the BT-13 Valiant and progressed to advanced training in the AT-6 Texan at Blytheville near the Mississippi River in Arkansas. McDonald had been interested in airplanes since childhood, and he looked like a pilot in a recruiting poster—many who knew him, especially officers' wives, remarked on how handsome he was. McDonald apparently did not disclose to instructors or fellow students that his father had already revealed to him the existence of the B-29.

It was not uncommon for a new pilot to pin on silver wings and second lieutenant's bars and get married all on the same day. At Blytheville, McDonald did exactly that on March 25, 1943. Gloria DeWolf was the lucky maiden who won the hand of the handsome pilot; later, she would reside in California when Bud and his crew began bombing the Empire.

Blytheville was a big place, with all manner or wooden and metal barracks, including some that resembled chicken coops, and with aircraft taking off and landing constantly. There is no way to know whether Bud McDonald ever had occasion to meet a local musician and bandleader who appeared regularly at the base, or whether the movie star–like McDonald ever saw the musician's four-year-old son, the future actor George Hamilton.

Groves and Wolfe

The world's largest structure, the Pentagon boasted a bizarre, five-sided shape so that any office could lie within walking distance of any other. When it opened for business, the Pentagon also boasted twice the number of bathrooms it needed, a gesture to racial segregation in Virginia that did not exist across the river in Washington, D.C. Little fanfare accompanied the opening of the Pentagon, but there was general agreement that the new building was an engineering marvel. No one was quite sure, however, what had happened to its builder, the U. S. Army's arrogant, short-fused

Lt. Gen. Leslie Groves, who had now moved on. No one quite seemed to know where Groves had gone. A rumor circulated that he was heading a secret project to develop a time machine. Imagine, people speculated, if you could travel backward in time to some important date and change everything, perhaps by smothering Adolf Hitler in his crib? Someone said Groves was experimenting with time travel in Manhattan, which was wrong except for a key word.

Arnold, the AAF chief, directed Brig. Gen. Kenneth B. Wolfe to take over all aspects of the B-29 program, reporting personally to Arnold. Wolfe would soon become the first Superfortress combat commander. As chief of the B-29 Special Project Staff, Wolfe had charge of the initial flight and service testing of the B-29 AAF. Wolfe soon applied his talents to organizing fixes for the B-29, especially fixes to its powerful but troubled engines.

On June 21, 1943, Wolfe became the first commander of the nascent 58th Bombardment Wing at Smoky Hill Army Airfield in flat, dry expanses near Salina, Kansas. The wing would eventually be made up of four bombardment groups but began with no aircraft and for many weeks had fewer than a dozen. Wolfe made an early flight in a B-29 and experienced its R-3350 engine overheating, something the engines were constantly doing. Other problems arose with defective pressure seals around the cockpit windows and sighting blisters, which needed precise fitting to avoid leakage. Formation of the wing was premature. The first production B-29 was completed at the new Boeing plant in Wichita in July. By the end of the following month, only fourteen Superfortresses had rolled off the assembly lines.

Given that the program was moving so slowly, how do we explain the bizarre incident that happened to Carl Barthold, who was not a pilot after all but not yet a radio operator, either?

The Army told Barthold it had two schools for airborne radio operators, one in St. Louis and one in Santa Ana, California. "My home is in St. Louis," Barthold told them. "You're going to Santa Ana," they told him.

In mid-1943, Barthold was on the train to California chatting with a young officer, a lieutenant, who was en route to a different assignment. The officer told Barthold about a new plane called the

B-29. The new bomber was still very secret, the lieutenant said, but Americans would be learning more about it. The lieutenant told Carl that his father was working on the new bomber. "That was the first I ever heard of a machine called the B-29," Barthold said.

They were outside a small town in Kansas when the train made an unscheduled stop, with a station nowhere nearby. Parked at the crossing gate was an olive drab Army sedan with a one-star emblem on the windshield, indicating the passenger was a brigadier general.

Several men were in the car. The lieutenant later told Barthold that one of them was his father.

"The boy got off the train, climbed into the car, and spent twenty minutes talking with his dad. He returned to the train. A whistle blew. The train started up. The lieutenant did not say a word about the train stopping, or how and why it happened. He clamped up about the B-29 and never said another word about it. And after that train journey, I never saw the lieutenant again," Barthold said.

Could the lieutenant have been Bud McDonald? It seems unlikely. McDonald's father had inside knowledge but no reason to be in Kansas. Today, we have only Barthold's memory as a source for this account of how someone in the B-29 program halted a passenger train in order to visit with his son.

Sammy and Aldora

Sammy and Aldora Bakshas, with their infant son, Jerry, spent the early years of U.S. involvement in World War II traveling constantly, being separated too often, and staying in lodging that was anything but ideal. In at least one location, Jerry's bed was a laundry basket in a closet.

Sammy's first move during the war was to Salinas, California. From there he was transferred to Alexandria, Louisiana. His group traveled by train. Aldora loaded all their worldly belongings and little Jerry into their brand new Buick and drove to Louisiana. She had never before driven more than 140 miles by herself. Jerry was two years old. While staying in a motel in Houston, Texas, Jerry poured Aldora's perfume down the sink and drew pictures on her luggage with lipstick, but he was such a good-natured little boy she couldn't get angry with him. Aldora remembers Alexandria being a three-month stint, during which Bakshas instructed student pilots. "He had already been on duty at Alexandria Army Airfield when I arrived with Jerry and the car. I was supposed to have a hotel room, but there was no space available. For a time, I was put up in a nice, old-fashioned house. It turned out we didn't see each other as much as we wanted because Sammy was often away overnight on a B-17 training flight."

Sammy was stationed at many bases, including Mississippi, Idaho, and Florida, but never in one place for very long. Finally, Sammy was sent to Great Falls, Montana, to be a permanent part of the B-17 standardization school. After a short while, they sent him back to Texas. While there, two wives and families were invited to fly in a B-17. Aldora rode in the nose over Texas.

Sammy Bakshas must have been eager to get to the war zone, where younger and less experienced pilots were flying in combat. The record does not show how he felt about spending so much time stateside, training pilots. On some date in 1943, Sammy started talking to his superiors about getting an assignment to the new bomber then being developed—and being plagued with technical glitches on the plains of Kansas. Aldora, who had taken constant moving for granted, knew that Sammy wanted this assignment more than anything. When he told her the details, including likely long separations and an eventual journey to the war zone, she nodded and smiled.

"It's what you do," she told him.

Groves

When he dropped suddenly out of sight, few people knew what had happened to Brig. Gen. Leslie R. Groves Jr., who'd played a key role in constructing the Pentagon building.

Groves was only one of several key figures who'd led the thousands of civilian and military workers building the Pentagon under the leadership of Brig. Gen. Brehon B. Somervell. He believed the building was larger than it needed to be. Like the B-29 bomber being wrung out on the plains of the American West, the Pentagon was the newest, the biggest, and maybe just a little too superlative. And just like the B-29, the Pentagon was plagued with early teething troubles.

Noting that such a large building wouldn't be needed by the

military after the war and that it might be turned over to the National Archives, Groves departed the scene before the first workers began to occupy offices in the five-sized puzzle palace. Groves believed himself in need of a rest. While overseeing the building of the Pentagon, Groves relentlessly overcame one hurdle after another, coping with strikes, supply shortages, conflicting priorities, and engineers who were not up to the task. Groves worked six days a week in his office in Washington, D.C. During the week he would determine which project was in the greatest need of personal attention and pay it a visit on Sunday. Groves said he was hoping to get to a war theater, where his life would be more peaceful.

He did not get the rest he thought he needed. Instead, he became the head of the Manhattan Engineer District. The Army devised the yawn-inducing name to conceal the true purpose of Groves's program. No longer a familiar sight in Washington, Groves was off in the high desert of New Mexico building a new town (and a secret laboratory) with a cadre of civilian scientists. The location was an obscure backwater named Los Alamos. A resident called it a "one-horse town." At the time most Americans never heard of Los Alamos, or of the Manhattan Project, or of the wellspring of other scientific installations that sprang up around the country from Hanford, Washington, to Oak Ridge, Tennessee. Groves, top scientist J. Robert Oppenheimer, and others on the Manhattan Project were not permitted to tell outsiders what their purpose was or what they were laboring to create.

Groves was "the biggest S.O.B. I have ever worked for," wrote Kenneth D. Nichols. "He is most demanding. He is most critical. He is always a driver, never a praiser. He is abrasive and sarcastic. He disregards all normal organizational channels." But, added Nichols, "if I had to do my part of the atomic bomb project over again and had the privilege of picking my boss I would pick General Groves."

One of the few people who knew about Groves, Oppenheimer, Los Alamos, and the Manhattan Project was the commanding general of the AAF, Arnold. Another who would belatedly receive a top-secret briefing about the project was Brigadier General LeMay, who was soon to pin on a second star. Arnold had no control over Groves and Oppenheimer, but he had plenty of direct authority over the troubled program to produce aircraft that would carry what they were making.

Production and Problems

In 1943, Boeing began delivering Superfortresses to the 58th Bombardment Wing commanded by Wolfe, which had been established in anticipation of the new bomber. B-29 production was the most diverse aircraft manufacturing project undertaken in the United States during World War II, with literally thousands of subcontractors supplying components or assembles to the four main production plants: Boeing at Renton, Washington, and Wichita, Kansas; Bell at Atlanta, Georgia (in a location known today as Marietta); and Martin at Omaha, Nebraska.

Eventually, production of B-29s totaled 3,970 airplanes. The figure includes 1,644 from Boeing's Wichita plant, 668 built by Bell, and 536 by Martin. The Renton plant produced 1,122 examples of the B-29A variant with slightly increased span and changes in fuel capacity and armament.

The B-29 Superfortress was coming off factory assembly lines but not as rapidly as AAF boss Arnold wanted. As of January 1944, ninety-seven B-29s had been built, but only sixteen of these were certified for unrestricted flight operations. The other aircraft required some fifty modifications each to be combat ready. Eventually, the productive capacity of Boeing and of other contractors ramped up, and production began to increase exponentially. What didn't improve was a long roster of technical problems with the R-3350 engines.

The R-3350 leaked oil. It caught fire. It seized. Not for nothing was the B-29 the only large aircraft on which the flight engineer was usually an officer trained as a pilot. The engineer was in effect a third pilot; the B-29 needed that many at the controls.

While the big brass and ordinary men in uniform were struggling to make their new bomber work, some of the thousand kids were only beginning the journey that would take them to Guam, Saipan, and Tinian. Having completed boot camp in Greensboro, North Carolina, Bill Carter—the yo-yo whiz from Atlanta, soon to be called "Reb" and eventually to join Dean Fling's crew on *God's Will*—was in the college training detachment at Duquesne University in Pittsburgh preparing to go into flight training and to become an officer and a pilot. He did not know yet that he would never become either. Within a few weeks, he and his buddies would be told that the AAF had too many pilots and not enough gunners. Carter would find himself in gunnery school at Tyndall Field, Florida.

On February 14, 1944, at Duquesne, Carter was focused on using a fountain pen and cursive handwriting to draft a letter to his girlfriend, Phyllis Ewing—daughter of a prominent jewelry distributor—whom he'd met at a swimming pool one Sunday afternoon in Atlanta. Carter was smitten in a big way. He was patiently putting off becoming formally engaged and was a little fearful about the relationship remaining intact while they were separated. He called her his devil and he began his letters, "My dearest, dearest darling Devil . . ." On that day, he wrote, "Your pictures came today and they are wonderful. I am sitting at one of the desks with your pictures spread out in front of me. I have the two large ones and eleven little ones. I write a line then look back at your pictures. Darling I don't see how I could ever get such a beautiful, adorable, darling, sweet girl as you." Later in the letter, perhaps feeling a little anxiety, he wrote: "Don't worry about me quitting loving you because I never will." Carter, seemingly unable to see anything in his mind but Phyllis, wrote to her that they would be able to see each other when he began pilot training at Maxwell Field, Alabama.

Carter was right that he would never quit loving her. He was wrong that he would be going to Maxwell for pilot training.

Concerns about the B-29

On February 20, 1944, Col. Walter Lucas was ordered to take his crew plus two extra crew chiefs from Kansas to Bolling Field along the Anacostia River in Washington, D.C. When Lucas landed, Arnold greeted him and told him that the purpose of his trip was to show the B-29 to President Franklin D. Roosevelt.

The following day in the late afternoon, the president came to Bolling. His chauffeur brought his limousine to a halt in front of the smoothly rounded nose of the big bomber. The president did not get out of his car but scrutinized the bomber closely. His daughter, Anna, and her two children, Eleanor and Curtis, accompanied him. They did get out of the limousine and inspected the aircraft. Lucas said that Roosevelt flashed his famous smile at the crewmembers as he departed.

Wolfe, who'd been the military figure in charge of B-29 development and subsequently the first commander of the 58th Wing, was tapped for command of XX Bomber Command, charged with bringing the 58th and 73rd wings up to combat status. Wolfe was good-natured, hard working, and highly regarded, but his experience lay in research and development; he had no upper-echelon command or operational experience and was viewed by many as poorly equipped for his responsibilities. Plans to form the 73rd Wing in India did not materialize (it later began life on Saipan), and the 58th became the only wing to serve on the Asian mainland.

At their new offices in the Pentagon, Arnold's air staff officers were planning to stand up three B-29-equipped bomber commands to surround Japan—XX in India and China, XXI in the Mariana Islands being wrested from Japanese hands, an XXII in the Philippines. The plan almost immediately collided with AAF boss Arnold's most formidable adversary—not Hitler, not Hirohito, but the U.S. Navy.

Army chief of staff Gen. George C. Marshall, Arnold, and others did not want their new superbomber coming under the command of a Pacific theater boss who wore a Navy uniform. Admiral Ernest J. King, who was both chief of naval operations and commander in chief of the U.S. Fleet, saw the final battle against Japan as a naval battle and wanted the B-29 force to be placed under the command of Pacific naval boss Adm. Chester Nimitz. In the internecine warfare that took place in the Washington bureaucracy, King lost, which meant that Nimitz lost too. So too did southwest Pacific commander Gen. Douglas MacArthur, China commander Gen. Claire Chennault, and Southeast Asia Supreme Allied Commander Lord Louis Mountbatten, all of whom wanted to be in charge of the B-29s. The decision went against all of them and also killed the plan for a XXII Bomber Command in the Philippines.

The B-29 force in the Pacific wouldn't come under local commanders at all. Instead it would go to war with direct command from Washington. It was a unique arrangement. Centralized control of the Superfortresses from Washington marked the recognition of the B-29 as a strategic weapon that transcended theaters and services. The arrangement made Arnold, who was ailing and had other responsibilities, the commander of the B-29 force from behind his desk in Washington. It bestowed on a relatively low-ranking commander in the field—eventually, LeMay—far more authority than his rank called for.

The XX and XXI Bomber Commands would become components of the Twentieth Air Force, commanded from Washington by Arnold. Two of the key figures in fielding the B-29 force, Kenneth Wolfe and Brig. Gen. Haywood "Possum" Hansell, would be virtually unknown to the public by V-J Day, while almost everyone would recognize the name of Hansell's replacement—LeMay.

If Arnold had been in better health (he'd had his second coronary by early 1944), or if things had been more tranquil at home (his wife Bea left him in the final months of the war), he might have taken time to enjoy spring in Washington. Along the Tidal Basin, cherry blossoms bloomed. They were a gift from Japan, decades earlier. The annual cherry blossom festival was on hold. Similarly, in Japan the country's most popular sport, baseball, was suspended for the duration.

Arnold was paying no attention to the flowers Japan had given America, or the pastime America had given Japan. On April 4, 1944, the AAF commander inked an agreement that created the Twentieth Air Force. It was the first time a numbered air force would be commanded from Washington. It was the first time a numbered air force was created to use a single aircraft, the cantankerous and completely unproven B-29 Superfortress. Arnold's AAF did not yet know whether the B-29 could fight effectively, or whether any B-29 would ever get anywhere near Japan, but for the moment at least, the AAF—in the quest for dominance in the Pacific—had managed to vanquish the Navy. The two services waged jurisdictional battles with such vigor, the generals and admirals so impassioned in vying for favor, that they were sometimes accused of forgetting the real enemy.

The Battle of Kansas
Arnold was profoundly impressed by his visit to the Army airfield in Salina, Kansas, where he found the 58th wing in disarray. Flaws in the B-29 design had been fixed, but the R-3350 engine that powered the B-29 wasn't fixed yet, while B-29-related logistical

logjams abounded. Arnold wanted to send off 150 of the new bombers to bases in India. Instead, he found himself spouting orders and launching a major readiness effort that came to be known as "the Battle of Kansas." With Arnold cracking the whip, AAF officers struggled to find logistics shortcuts and to have most of the bombers ready to deploy within a month.

First Lieutenant Nathan Serenko felt some of Arnold's fury over delays. Today, we might say he felt Arnold's pain. Serenko remembered the situation this way:

> The B-29 was not quite ready for prime time when it left the Boeing assembly line. Boeing knew it, and the AAF knew it. That's what happens when you order a couple thousand aircraft before the first prototype has even flown, never mind that they were building the most sophisticated aircraft ever designed up to that time.
>
> Hap Arnold knew the early aircraft rolling off the assembly lines were not ready for combat, and so several modification centers were set up to repair the glitches, such as over-heating engines, frozen guns, bad window seals, flap and rudder problems, and all kinds of electronic problems. There was a major problem with vibration in "cannon plugs," a type of electrical connector with multiple pins inside. We had to remove and re-solder 586,000 contacts, which required 40,000 man hours! If you've ever had to take apart and repair a solder-type cannon plug, you know what a chore that was.
>
> Another problem was that Boeing's sub-contractors had not yet geared up to wartime production pace, so parts that Boeing needed for modifications were not arriving in time to install them on the production line. Therefore, when received, they were sent on to the modification centers to be installed there. The major mod center was in Kansas, where "The Battle of Kansas" took place.

Of all the problems that seemed to keep the B-29 from getting underway toward the war, none was more vexing than the Curtiss-Wright R-3350, the 18-cylinder, two-row, radial "corncob" engine that was the highest displacement engine in the world. A wholly new design from a company that suffered severe management flaws, the R-3350 worked fine when tested in low-altitude, low-load competitions. Even the earliest version was rated at two thousand horsepower at a time when half of that figure was considered respectable. When the first versions appeared, the Wright Aeronautical division ignored design features suggested by the company's best powerplant engineer, German-born Rudolph Daub, and created an air-cooled engine plagued with reduction gear, cooling, and exhaust problems. In retrospect, the company seems to have done almost everything wrong. As Stephan Wilkinson wrote, "Congress—at the end of its patience with Wright—ordered General Arnold to convene a high-level committee to assess the company's problems. The board included William Brennan (a future Supreme Court justice), William O'Dwyer (future mayor of New York) and James McDonnell (founder of McDonnell Aircraft). They found appalling managerial ineptitude and an utterly casual approach to the R-3350 project."

This was the superbomber that was to bring the Reich to its knees, subdue the Empire, and win the war. It was the largest, heaviest, most complex bombardment aircraft ever built, and it was pulled through the sky by powerplants built by a challenged workforce. Wrote Wilkinson: "New Jersey-based Wright Aeronautical decided to build its new R-3350 factory not far from New York City rather than, say, in Kansas where there was a pool of aviation craftspeople with an old-school work ethic. They paid stingy wages—a starting wage of $9.40 an hour in 2011 dollars—and had to compete with New York shipyards in a region that had a high cost of living."

Or, as author William Wolf put it, Wright used "the dregs of the workforce to manufacture the most complex piece of mass-produced machinery built at the time."

Sammy Bakshas, who would fly a B-29 into battle, had mixed reactions when he first saw one. To Aldora, he wrote: "I think a lot of the fellows are going to have difficulty operating this airplane and I don't see any guarantee that it can succeed."

CHAPTER 5

Way Up

Mission to Tokyo
March 9, 1945. 6:05 p.m.–10:00 p.m.

AMONG THOSE NOT TAKING OFF for the long nocturnal journey to Tokyo was Bud McDonald, newly arrived on Guam. In days ahead, he would become airplane commander of a B-29 with the name *City of Philadelphia* painted on the nose but called *The Merry Mac's* by crewmembers. Today, 1st Lt. William Underwood was taking off from Guam at the controls of that plane.

McDonald was the Michigan boy who resembled actor Errol Flynn, or even actor-singer Bert Parks, and who had first heard about the B-29 from his father in Detroit, who was working on remote-control guns. On this evening, as men and machines departed the ground for the long journey to the Empire, Bud McDonald had not yet completed the familiarization flying that had to be logged before he could take off on his first mission.

Before a new crew could go on a mission, they had to take some noncombat training missions. They had periodic ground school. Even after they started combat missions, they still flew periodic training missions. When repairs had been made, such as an engine change, they had to take the plane up for some "slow-timing." If a plane did not have an assigned crew but a plane needed slow-timing, then any available crew would take turns. Other activities when time permitted included reading, writing letters, poker, basketball, baseball, movies, and planting vegetable gardens and grass around their Quonsets or tents. Occasionally they would go to the beach to swim.

There were hundreds like McDonald, men who were caught up in every aspect of B-29 operations but who were not taking off on this evening. It is easy to imagine McDonald sitting on a hillock near runway's end, perhaps with a blade of grass between his front teeth, watching the giant Superfortresses lift aloft without him. In fact, we do not know exactly what McDonald was doing that evening, but we know that his opportunity to make a contribution to the war effort lay not very far in the future.

Tucker's Crew

On Tinian, once inside *Lady Annabelle*, airplane commander Percy Usher Tucker ("Don't call me Percy!") and pilot John T. Kearney settled into their comfortable, armchair-style seats and laid out their maps and charts. By now the configuration of the flight deck of the B-29 was familiar to them; Tucker had remarked earlier in his career how odd it felt to be sitting ninety inches (seven and a half feet) back from the tip of the Superfortress's nose. It was the bombardier, farmer, and all-American boy, Flight Officer Joseph Krogman, in front of Tucker who was truly at the very front of the aircraft and enjoyed a spectacular panoramic view of the world.

By now though, Tucker was accustomed to piloting the plane from this far back.

He and Kearney checked to confirm that the windows around and in front of them were clean. They would be flying a four-engined aircraft under stressful conditions and didn't want any problem that could be solved before takeoff. The two pilots began a lengthy process of preparing to start engines and taxi out.

Lady Annabelle's bombardier climbed up through the nose wheel well, passed between the two pilots already in their seats, and got settled in "the best seat in the house," as Krogman once called it: the bombardier's perch in the forward center of the flight deck. Krogman, earnest and serious, an unkempt mustache on his face, dropped into the centerline seat at the front of the aircraft and adjusted his seatbelt and harness. Before and during engine run-up, each crewmember of a B-29 Superfortress had his own procedure for getting ready. Once in flight, this "was not a place for anyone susceptible to vertigo," another crewmember recalls Krogman saying.

"He was close to the last one entering the plane (this was just our usual routine for our crew)," said engineer Laddie Wale of bombardier Krogman. "After he crawled inside the aircraft, he went to his position in the nose of the plane and checked all of my instruments to see if they were operated okay. He then became an observer watching for other planes and watching the flag and light guys who were giving us signals. If anything that he saw was not correct or if he thought something was possibly wrong, he would pass it on to the airplane commander."

Krogman confirmed that switches on his panel were in the off position, scrutinized his fuse panel for active and spare fuses, synchronized his clock with that of those of Tucker and navigator Edwin J. Koniusky, and jotted down the outside air temperature in his log. Krogman inspected and readied his Norden M-9B bombsight and the remote control sight for the upper and lower forward .50-caliber Browning M2 machine guns. Krogman's gunsight could swing out from almost straight down (-80 degrees) to almost straight up (80 degrees) with a horizontal field sweep of 185 degrees to the left, 140 degrees to the right. Krogman would have the choice of operating the guns or releasing the upper forward turret to the top gunner and the lower forward turret to one of the side gunners.

Once they settled in the plane, Krogman uttered the same word several times. "Sonfoabitch," Krogman said on the interphone. "Sonaofabitch. Sonofabitch."

"Who's he talking about?" said Kearney.

"LeMay," said Tucker.

The tail gunner on the *Lady Annabelle*, Staff Sgt. Joseph Majeski, removed heavy belts of .50-caliber cartridges from their wooden shipment crates and lined them up on the ground before climbing aboard. With help from a ground crewmember, Majeski made certain each round was clean and properly aligned to feed into his guns. "I never heard of having a jam, but we wanted to be sure," Majeski said.

Majeski placed the belts inside his ammunition box and climbed the B-29's rear entrance ladder into the aircraft. He moved toward the tail, the space around him narrowing as he went back. He passed and reached the single metal ammunition can located alongside the left-side interior wall of the fuselage just forward of the tail compartment. Just in front of the compartment, he bumped his right shoulder on the ammunition can—he always did—and passed over the bump on the floor caused by the bomber's tailskid. Majeski was sweating inside the bomber, layering the belts into the rectangular containers.

Majeski fed the end of each belt into the tracks of rollers that led under the pressurized tail compartment and into the separate turret where two .50-caliber Browning M2 machine guns were mounted. He crawled through a round door into the tail gunner's compartment and rose to his feet. The compartment was six feet high and four feet square. Behind him was a seat that could be slid down a rack and unfolded. His one-man life raft pack formed the cushion of the seat.

Looking back from the aircraft—a view he enjoyed, especially on takeoff—Majeski had windows on each side and a slab of bulletproof Plexiglas in front of him (meaning, at the rear of the B-29). After checking that his high-altitude bail-out oxygen bottle, flak suit, flak vest, and life raft were all in place, Majeski climbed down from the Superfortress and made his way to the tail. There, he mounted a ladder and used a screwdriver to remove the covers on his turret, exposing the two .50-caliber guns. He opened their lids and slid the belts of ammunition along their tracks. He fitted the first round into each gun and closed the lids. Now the guns were loaded "hot," and Majeski actuated the weapon with his screwdriver, slamming the first round into the firing chamber. Loaded and ready to shoot, Majeski carefully polished the windows of his compartment until returning to the interior of *Lady Annabelle*.

Although farthest back among the men in the in the ninety-nine-foot fuselage, tail gunner Joe Majeski had the job of taking the first step toward getting the giant bomber into the air. While pilots Tucker and Kearney worked through their "prestart" checklist, Majeski threw on his headset, ready to use the plane's interphone, which was battery-powered. Flight engineer Laddie Wale's voice boomed in his earphones. "Tail, from engineer."

"Tail," Majeski responded.

"Go ahead and start the putt-putt please, Joe."

"Putt-putt. Yes, sir."

Located on the left side of the rear fuselage a short distance forward of Majeski's position, the auxiliary power unit—never called anything but the putt-putt—was a small gasoline engine enclosed in a black cylinder with a handle and knobs. It operated the generator that would power up the Superfortress until the number three engine was started. Now, in a half-crawling, half-lying position, the sweat-covered Majeski pulled the cord, similar to a cord on an outboard motor, and fired up the putt-putt just as he would a lawn mower. The device made a sound that lived up to its name. It would be Majeski's job to shut down the small gasoline engine when it was no longer needed once *Lady Annabelle* was in the air and to start it again before landing.

In the Cockpit

While airplane commander Tucker and pilot Kearney were going over their checklist, each of the eleven men aboard *Lady Annabelle* focused on preparations. Majeski's voice told all: "Putt-putt on line." Tucker exchanged glances with flight engineer Wale. Both peered outside to be certain members of the ground crew were ready with fire extinguishers in front of the number three engine. Tucker held up a finger of one hand, inscribed a circle, and said, "Start three."

On a four-engined Superfortress, the R-3350 engines were identified by engine numbers one through four, beginning with the left outboard engine and ending with the right outboard. The engine-start process began with number three, in board opposite the pilot's side, on the right side of the bomber. "We always started engines in this order—three, four, two, one," said Wale. "That's because the generator was in the number three engine nacelle. Once the engine was started, the generator took over powering the plane from the putt-putt."

The engine numbers were also written on the corresponding thrust levers in the cockpit's center console, sitting between Tucker and Kearney on *Lady Annabelle*. The actual starting process, like so much of controlling the massive B-29, was engineer Wale's responsibility: he turned the boost pumps on, set the throttle and mixture control for the number one engine, and hit the starter switch while intermittently pumping the primer. Tucker was in charge, but he could only watch as the sixteen-and-a-half-foot propeller began to rotate. Beyond the turning propeller, Tucker could see the first hint of sunset arriving at Tinian. A breeze came through the single open glass pane on either side of the pilots; Tucker could hear the sound of other engines beginning to reverberate up and down the line. *It was 6:10 p.m. Chamorro Standard Time, March 9, 1945.*

The Fling Crew

Lifting into the air at Tinian that Friday evening was *God's Will* of the 9th Bombardment Group, piloted by Dean Fling. Left blister gunner Reb Carter wrote in his journal that the target was a "residential-industrial section" of Tokyo. *God's Will* was due to be the seventh plane from its group over the target, right after the group's pathfinders. Neither airplane commander Fling, nor pilot Pete Peterson, nor Carter had any way to know that theirs would inadvertently become the first B-29 from their group to reach the Japanese coast, yet, because of monumental confusion, one of the last to drop its bombs.

Carter wrote that they were carrying "twenty-four 500-pound clusters of magnesium bombs," referring to E-46 bombs. "Different planes are carrying different loads. Some are carrying as many as thirty-three." As *God's Will* leaped off its brakes, plunged down the runway, and gathered lift, Carter apparently felt none of the terror some crewmembers experienced on takeoff. He always seemed to find a level of comfort even during the toughest moments of a flight. He glanced at his Seeland Quadramatic Bumper Gents wristwatch and made a note. *It was 6:21 p.m. Chamorro Standard Time, March 9, 1945.*

Not far behind was Tucker's *Lady Annabelle*. Still in her parking slot with all four engines turning and belching, *Lady Annabelle* strained against her brakes. The ground crew chief took a position on the flat pavement in front of the nose, where Tucker and he were eyeball to eyeball. The crew chief stretched out his arms and swiveled his thumbs to point downward, giving Tucker the signal—the wheel chocks had been removed and the B-29 was ready to taxi. "Bomb bay doors closed," Tucker said on the interphone. "Flaps to twenty-five degrees."

The ground crew chief gave Tucker a salute. Tucker returned it. He eased off the brakes and the fifty-ton bomber came lumbering out of its parking slot. Guided by hand signals from the ground crew chief, Tucker turned on to the taxi strip behind the silvery tails of other B-29s making their way to runway's end to take off.

Said Wale: "The signalers with flags and lights guided the pilots to the proper runway. At the end of the runway, we prepared to take off, paying careful attention to the B-29s in front of us and behind us. The airplane commander [Tucker] revved up the engines to the necessary RPMs and we started the trip toward the runway."

All their lives, the thousand kids who flew B-29s against the Japanese home islands would remember the roar of engines as a strike force began taking off—in this case in early evening, for a journey that would take them over Tokyo in the early morning hours. Tinian and Saipan were so close the roar of engines could be heard from one island to the other, and when both were mounting a major effort, both islands were engulfed in noise. Guam produced its own noise but, because it was slightly farther from Japan, did so about twenty minutes earlier. On this evening, 334 Superfortresses were lifting into the sky from the three islands. While Tucker's crew prepared to take off, the men from Guam—Sammy Bakshas and the *Tall in the Saddle* crew among them—were already leveling off at cruising altitude.

Every man on Guam, Saipan, and Tinian had witnessed what happened when a B-29 didn't gain the right combination of power and lift, failed to get into the sky, and dropped into the ground or the ocean with horrific results. The men setting forth to attack Tokyo on this Friday evening, March 9, 1945, rarely felt fear once they got started. Most were like Carter on the Fling crew, collected and stable and ready. One member of Tucker's crew became so frightened whenever the crew wasn't flying that he would have vomiting fits, yet on the day of a mission, he was cool and calm.

On the day of a mission, once committed, B-29 crewmembers somehow shoved their fear of flying close to other bombers in the darkness, of Japanese fighters, and of antiaircraft fire to the side.

But everyone was afraid of takeoff.

Except for the pilots and the engineer, everyone else aboard a B-29 was a passenger during takeoff. None had any control over what would happen to the giant superbomber as it began hurtling down the crushed-coral runway. All would breathe easier when they got into the air.

When the B-29 Superfortress turned at runway's end and Tucker was signaled into takeoff position, he looked out and saw the Tinian-based chaplains who were always on the scene to bless each plane and crew just at the start of the takeoff roll. Chaplains appeared similarly at Guam and Saipan. Another crewmember wrote: "The blessing and signing of the cross by the chaplains provides [a] feeling of comfort as we accelerate down the runway." Tucker used his throttles (not his brakes) to line up with the runway.

The takeoff of a B-29 fully loaded with fuel and bombs was supposed to be a straightforward proposition. The airplane commander (Tucker, the left-seat pilot) and the pilot (Kearney in the right seat) stood on the brakes and brought the engines up to full power. Tucker searched for signs of problems, nodded, and signaled for both pilots to pull shut the single open window at their opposite shoulders. Flight engineer Wale agreed that the aircraft was ready to go. Feet came off the brakes and the Superfortress began to roll.

Another B-29 crewmember described the spectacle thusly:

> You knew every eye on that flight line was watching, from every hardstand position, from every maintenance engine dock, from the tower—every viewpoint, all watching, holding their collective breath as much as the crew within the rolling ship! And the next ship in line was already cranking up to full power before yours broke ground. But now you were past the point of thumps and bumps on the gear, starting to float a little on the struts, and the airplane commander held it down, forward on the yoke a little, gaining more speed, air speed, precious air speed for a margin of safety if an engine should fail.

Tucker and Kearney walked the throttles forward slowly until they had rudder control at about sixty-five miles per hour. They then moved the throttles forward to the full open position. In this way, they maintained directional control first with throttles, then with rudder. Their pilots' handbook warned of the obvious: "Don't use the brakes to hold the airplane straight on the runway except in emergencies, since this increases the takeoff distance and wears out the brakes."

Kearney made a continuous power check as the throttles advanced during the initial takeoff roll. The pilots' goal was to reach full power—forty-nine inches of manifold pressure and twenty-nine revolutions per minute—during the roll down the first third of the runway. At 90 miles per hour, Tucker began to relieve pressure on the nose wheel by easing the control column back. The airplane began to fly itself off the ground at about 115 miles per hour. The men felt lift building beneath them. Once he felt the ground depart, Tucker called, "Brake the wheels. Gear up."

"Sonofabitch," said Krogman.

They all felt varying amounts of apprehension, but none of the officers in the forward fuselage knew that an enlisted man in the rear was visibly trembling. The prospect of traveling into the night against flak and fighters to assault the Empire at low level was simply too much for him. Right body gunner Cpl. John R. Dodd was clutching a rosary and shaking. "I can't do this," he said aloud. "I can't do this. I can't do this."

"Sonaofabitch," said Krogman.

"Interphone discipline," said Tucker. It meant "Shut up!" and everyone did. From now on, with Tinian falling behind them, they would talk on the interphone only to perform crew duties.

With the onset of night approaching off her left wingtip, *Lady Annabelle* was on her way to the Empire. *It was 6:30 p.m. Chamorro Standard Time, March 9, 1945.*

Uncomfortable Crews

When they began their takeoff roll and there was no way to go back and change any part of what happened next, many B-29 crewmembers held in their minds the thought that their humorless, cigar-chopping commanding general was sending them to die.

There was no way an American warplane with eleven men aboard could survive arriving in the Empire in darkness at altitudes between 5,000 and 9,500 feet. No one had been there before. If you were going up against men with guns, would you fly low in order to give them a shorter distance to shoot?

It wouldn't comfort any of them, but LeMay wasn't sure they were wrong in their fatalism. He spent the early evening hours watching B-29s take off from Guam in the fading daylight. He told his confidante, Lt. Col. St. Clair McKelway, "If I am sending these men to die, they will string me up for it." LeMay later said to another aide, Lt. Col. Robert S. McNamara: "I was under pressure from some people who didn't want a change in the way we were doing things. I felt I had to ignore them and take a chance."

Some called LeMay's decision a gamble. If so, it was a very big one.

With pathfinders roaring into the air first, it took two hours and forty-five minutes for 334 B-29 Superfortresses to take off, one to three minutes apart, from six runways on Guam, Tinian, and Saipan. The noise of so many R-3350 engines traveled across the islands and over the sea; no one in the region could escape it. No one had ever sent this many bombers aloft in so short a span of time. Some planes were tucking in their gear and climbing out while others were still turning engines. The choreography may not have been perfect, but the beginning of the mission to Tokyo was going as smoothly as anyone could expect. For the most part, the largest force of bombers ever assembled in the Pacific got off to a good start.

The noise, we can be certain, carried to handfuls of Japanese holdouts in caves on Saipan, Tinian, and Guam, as well as to Japanese troops on a couple of small islands in the Marianas that had been bypassed and to at least one small vessel in the western Pacific that was listening in to LeMay's communications. "Did the Japanese know we were coming?" said Joe Majeski, a tail gunner on the Tucker crew. "Nobody ever told us for sure, but it's hard to imagine they didn't. We figured they knew when. We figured they knew where."

After the war, some crewmembers said that propaganda broadcaster Tokyo Rose described the markings on B-29 bombers and even the names of airplane commanders and crewmembers. Documentation of this has proven elusive, but the Japanese knew plenty. By the time the first B-29s were tucking in their wheels and climbing aloft into the early evening, Japan's defense network knew the Americans were coming and knew they were coming to Tokyo. It is unlikely, however, that the Japanese knew they were coming at low altitude.

One of the first pathfinders to lift skyward was radio operator Carl Barthold's airplane. Once he could reassure himself that he had survived takeoff, always a tense time, Barthold was gifted with plenty of time to do what military men have done since war was invented—hurry up and wait. He was doing just that at the radio operator's station, which was a kind of minioffice surrounded by gadgetry, wires, codebooks, and papers. "I think I spent about half an hour breathing a sigh of relief that our airplane was climbing instead of crashing," Barthold said. "All of us were uncomfortable about what lay ahead and at least one member of my crew was pretty close to being terrified, but at least we were in the air and all four engines were churning."

Barthold sat facing the outer skin of the fuselage with the back of the flight engineer's panel to his left and the bomb bay bulkhead to his right. He had enough room not to feel claustrophobic, but only one small aperture gave a glimpse of the sky and sea outside, growing darker as night descended. Much of Barthold's world consisted of the wires and dials of his four-channel, very high-frequency SCR-522 command radio set, but while he wore earphones and had a microphone handy, Barthold wasn't using the radio. He was listening to the interphone (on the other side of the world, the British would have called it the intercom), but true to form the B-29 crew was observing interphone discipline. "Looks like about six and a half hours to the Empire," said the flight engineer, who was hidden from Barthold by his instruments. "Hurry up and wait," another crewmember said. "Cut it out," said the voice of airplane commander James M. Campbell, not unkindly. "Let's have some interphone discipline, gentlemen."

"Goddamn LeMay's going to get us killed," somebody said, and then the interphone fell silent.

Barthold settled back in his seat. He'd trained to receive and decode sixteen random, five-letter Morse code groups per minute, but for now he felt, as he recalled later, like little more than a potted plant. The slim, small Barthold listened to the drone of the Wright engines, told himself again that everything was going to be all right, and reminded himself that some people thought General LeMay was going to get them all killed. "It wasn't the hardest part of the mission," Barthold said, "but it was hard, not having enough to do." The pathfinder B-29 continued on its way northwest. They'd been in the air three hours now, and behind them the entire strike force had taken off from Guam, Tinian, and Saipan. For Barthold, it was "hurry up and wait" time, except that every half-hour he would listen to the mission frequency to make certain that if there were a recall order, he wouldn't miss it. He began making the checks, heard no recall, and became certain they would be going all the way tonight. *It was 8:30 p.m. Chamorro Standard Time, March 9, 1945.*

The entire mission to Tokyo was now in the air. Of the 334 aircraft that took off from three islands, 279 were going to make it all the way to their intended objective while the remainder aborted and dropped out for technical reasons. This was an extraordinary showing and a testament to the ground crews, some of which had labored as much as thirty-six hours to get a single Superfortress ready to fly. In America's entire war inventory, no other aircraft was harder to maintain or keep airworthy.

At least one observer would later write of a "loose formation" of B-29s approaching Japan from the Marianas Islands. There was no formation. Each aircraft was on its own, its airplane commander entrusted with the souls on board, its navigator and his special skills never more important than now. The pathfinders were way out in front, with most of the bomb groups from Guam coming next, having taken off early enough to overtake the Superfortresses from Tinian and Saipan. Tommy Power's 314th Wing from Guam (the 19th and 20th Bombardment Groups but not the 39th and 330th, which were still en route to the war zone) was assigned to approach Japan flying between 5,000 and 5,500 feet. Brigadier General Emmett "Rosy" O'Donnell's 73rd Wing from Saipan (the 497th, 498th, 499th, and 500th Bombardment Groups) was ordered to fly toward the target at between 3,000 and 3,500 feet. Brigadier General John H. Davies's 313th Wing on Tinian (the 6th, 9th, 504th, and 505th Bombardment Groups) was under orders to make the long journey to the Empire at 4,000 to 5,000 feet, although 9th group commander Col. Henry C. Huglin would later write that his guys "flew at around 2,000 feet and then climbed to bombing altitude when approaching the mainland." All would climb to arrive over the target a couple of thousand feet higher— but not high enough to feel safe. The separation of bomb wings by height above a dark and cruel sea was the only hope of preventing air-to-air collision, since bombers from the three different islands had no other easy way to avoid each other.

Anyone looking down at this mass flight of B-29s from high above using night-vision goggles—which hadn't been invented yet—would have suspected that Curt LeMay's entire XXI Bomber Command had fallen into chaos and disarray. Anyone familiar with precision daylight bombing formations in Europe—stepped, spaced, boxed aerial assemblages of bombers proceeding together in unison—would have believed that LeMay's entire B-29 force had lost all sense of discipline, and possibly common sense. Perhaps the men at the controls of these planes were completely mad.

They were—but mad as in angry, not mad as in crazy. Tucker was not eager to encourage the cussing fest by his bombardier Joseph Krogman, but on one occasion, as many airplane commanders did, "Tuck" spoke on the interphone suggesting that LeMay had taken leave of his senses.

In fact, the battle order, the same document that identified the target as "the urban area of Meetinghouse," had taken the nature of this mass-gaggle flight into account. If a B-29 airplane commander took off at the prescribed interval, climbed to the assigned height, and cruised toward the target at the assigned altitude, the risk of collision would arise only if someone up ahead suffered a mechanical problem and reacted to it by screwing up. An airplane commander with a mechanical issue was supposed to get down to wave-cap level in order to be out of the way of the onrushing B-29s behind him. Sammy Bakshas in *Tall in the Saddle*, Tucker in *Lady Annabelle*, Dean Fling in *God's Will*, and every other airplane commander in the sky tonight fully understood that there was not supposed to be any chance of a collision, but it's doubtful they really believed it. They struggled to remain alert while many in the B-29 crews struggled to cope with the mixture of tension and boredom that were part and parcel of flying to the target.

CHAPTER 6

Soldiering

The B-29 Superfortress against Japan, April 5, 1944–June 15, 1944

THE FIRST FLIGHT OF B-29s left Kansas for India just a week before the establishment of the Twentieth Air Force. Many of the bombers were attired in the olive-drab paint scheme the AAF had now decided to retire. One or two would retain these colors until war's end. Most, however, were silvery and shiny. The B-29 did not yet work well and its engine problems had not yet been solved, but to some it was the best-*looking* airplane ever built, especially in natural metal finish. It became fashionable to say that the B-29 looked as if Raymond Loewy, the industrial designer who created the Greyhound bus, the Coca-Cola bottle, and the Lucky Strike package, was responsible for the bomber's sleek lines and rounded surfaces.

The Superfortresses made the journey eastward, to Maine, Morocco, and Egypt. The destination was Calcutta, India, where airfields for the 58th Wing were being readied.

During the ferry effort, which continued into early May, several B-29s were lost in mishaps and at least a dozen men lost their lives. At the start of April, Col. Leonard F. Harman was at the controls when the first B-29 landed in India. Eight days later, the Joint Chiefs of Staff formally approved Operation Matterhorn, the plan to bomb Japan using B-29s based near Calcutta and staging through airfields near Chengtu. Matterhorn missions were expected to shore up the flagging morale of the Chinese Nationalist forces of Generalissimo Chiang Kai-shek, which many feared might soon collapse because of war weariness. As it turned out, B-29 crewmembers were going to need a little shoring up of their own.

With some difficulty, the 58th Wing prepared to fight, its four groups scattered in the Calcutta region at Chakulia (40th Bombardment Group), Charra (444th), Piardoba (462nd, the "Hellbirds"), and Kharagpur (468th and wing and command headquarters). Charra turned out to be a boiling hellhole with a main runway that ran uphill, and the 444th Bombardment Group soon relocated at Dudhkundi. But all of the bases were boiling hellholes in the hot season and were inhospitable year around. Airplane commander 1st Lt. Winton R. Close, apparently not bucking for the job of tourism director, wrote the following of Dudhkundi:

It was a little, rural village about 40 miles northwest of Calcutta. It was not a very attractive place. In the dry season, it was flat, ugly, dirty, dusty and hot. During the monsoon season it was flat, ugly, dirty and muddy. During part of the dry season it would become so hot in the middle of the day that one could not touch the aluminum skin of the B-29 without getting burned. It was not a nice place at all. The water supply was suspect, so we drank slightly diluted chlorine from Lister bags. There was no ice. There was no beer. The only distilled liquor came from Calcutta. Its brand name was Carew's. We called it Carew's booze for combat crews. It came in three flavors: gin, rum and whiskey. All three tasted exactly the same. The only difference was the coloring used in each: no color for gin, a light tinge of yellow for rum, and a sort of dark tan for whiskey.

Wolfe's Lair

Kenneth B. Wolfe established XX Bomber Command headquarters near the town of Kharagpur, west of Calcutta in an oddly shaped structure called the Old Institute Building, which appeared to have a control tower protruding above its tile roof. His command problems were complicated by the fact that the building, despite its resemblance to an airfield control center, was close to town and not at the recently completed airfield.

Wolfe's men were still having problems with the B-29 and its R-3350 engines. After an aircraft was lost to an engine fire—one of many to come—Wolfe cabled Hap Arnold in Washington and demanded that a better engine cooling system be developed before the B-29s could be combat ready. New B-29s arriving from the United States each carried as cargo an extra R-3350, but even though the B-29 force now had five engines per four-engined bomber, technical problems persisted.

Wolfe was worried. He did not think his men or machines were ready for war. He was uncomfortable about his own position. Having Wolfe in charge prevented local commanders like Gen. Joseph Stilwell and Chennault from diverting the B-29s away from their primary mission—bombing Japan—but it didn't put a halt to turf wars. Everyone in a position of command, it seemed, wanted to weigh in with some idea of how best to use the new Superfortress bomber and its inexperienced crews. Wolfe wanted latitude in making key decisions and didn't get it. He believed he was being micromanaged from Washington.

One of Arnold's idea men, Col. Emmett "Rosy" O'Donnell, proposed that Wolfe's B-29s be stripped of armament and used for night radar-bombing missions. This of course was exactly what Superfortress crews would do on a mission to Tokyo many months into the future. Arnold did not like this idea and Wolfe apparently didn't either.

O'Donnell probably deserved a more receptive hearing. He'd flown B-17 Flying Fortresses and served as a squadron commander during a time of heartbreak amid losing battles against the Japanese in the Philippines and on Java. Promoted to brigadier general for the job, O'Donnell replaced Col. Thomas H. Chapman as commander of the 73rd Wing on March 15, 1944. Originally, the XX Bomber

Command was expected to operate two wings of B-29s from the China-Burma-India Theater. The 73rd Wing never began operations in China, however, because there weren't enough aircraft: not enough B-29s were leaving the United States and not enough were completing the long flight to the other side of the world. For a time, the 58th Wing in India was in the awkward position of having more crews than aircraft. Construction, especially the paving of runways, lagged. "We wanted runways," said Wolfe. "We found a bunch of Indians making mud pies."

The heat at the bases in India was like nothing most of the Americans had ever experienced. One thermometer measured it at 120 degrees Fahrenheit. Historian Steve Birdsall recalled B-29 pilot Jack Ladd talking about making takeoffs in India:

> The cylinder-head temperature gauges were against the stops and we did not know how high the temperatures actually were. The streamlined engine cowling was designed for low drag but was too close for adequate cooling, which the Boeing engineers admitted later on . . . the first planes had excessively long cowl flaps to try to cool the heads but if they were opened far enough to cool effectively they created a severe buffet. . . . The Chandler-Evans carburetors on these first airplanes were very vulnerable to fires, one good backfire and you usually had an engine on fire. Some engines actually burned off the wing and fell to the ground. The engine-fire stories were not overdone and if anything they were underplayed. I had more two- and three-engine time on the B-29 than I had with all four engines running. It got so I'd tell my flight engineer to keep his mouth shut about how hot they were running. I said I didn't want to know.

Because of the heat and the imperfections of the R-3350 and its carburetors, pilots could not follow the usual practice of keeping the engines running while waiting in a long line to take off. A pilot had to start, shut down, and restart the engines while waiting his turn to begin the takeoff roll. It made tempers flare. It made some men sick. Referring to the bombardment group known as the Hellbirds—an apt name for men garrisoned in India—Birdsall wrote: "The 462nd Group worked out a standard procedure to keep the engines as cool as possible on the ground—they were started as rapidly as possible, and the flight engineer was given exclusive use of the throttles. The airplanes were operating at very high gross weights and therefore flying slower, making the available cooling even less effective."

The insufferable heat in India produced other problems. Plexiglas blisters cracked as they expanded and contracted between the ground and high altitude, and large sections blew out. When this happened at heights, the aircraft depressurized and crews had to quickly don oxygen masks. The supply of blisters was inadequate, and old ones had to be repaired. Metal became too hot to touch, and maintenance could be accomplished only during the early morning or at night using floodlights that attracted swarms of insects.

The bases in India were not within operational range of any inviting Japanese target, and the plan to fly B-29 missions out of China quickly proved more of a challenge than anticipated. AAF transports were bringing supplies and fuel to China by flying "the Hump," the Himalaya range, which boasted the tallest mountains in the world (and finicky weather, a foe from which the B-29 never found relief). Superfortress crews would have to bring their own supplies into China.

Bomber crews, having won the "Battle of Kansas" and all primed up to enter the war against the Empire, were in no mood to be cargo carriers. They were not mentally prepared for anything like the Hump. Unfortuntately, they had no choice. The idea was the B-29s would haul extra fuel and bombs over the Hump and store them at forward bases in China until enough supplies and munitions had been assembled to mount an air strike on the Japanese home islands.

The distance between bases in India and forward locations in China was not an issue. Hauling fuel or cargo, a loaded B-29 could readily traverse the twelve hundred miles from Kharagpur to Hsinching in five hours or so, but the true barrier was the Hump itself. From India the B-29s crossed the Brahmaputra River and the Himalayan foothills, then faced the Hump, where seemingly harmless flocks of clouds were broken by the stark, jagged peaks of the world's highest mountains, some of which had never been climbed. Birdsall wrote: "Wild river gorges lay far below, and pillars of clouds sent trickles of moisture across an airplane's windows, which turned to ice in seconds. Over China the terrain was unchanged, more clouds forcing a continuous high altitude [flight path]." There were "waterfalls, a treacherously beautiful landscape," and then "the sheer mountains gave way to hills, many covered by an amazing pattern of terraces, and soon the plane was roaring across the great Chengdu Plain."

Reb Carter

Before they ever reached the war zone, many B-29 men spent time shuffling around the United States and riding on trains. Reb Carter from Atlanta now had the same experience as Carl Barthold from St. Louis: the Army told him he would not become a pilot and reassigned him as an enlisted crewmember. Carter was being sent to Tyndall Field, Florida, for "flexible gunnery training." His orders were explicit that he would be "utilized to meet B-29 gunnery requirements."

The bad news was that he would never pin on pilot wings. The good news was that his train would pass through his hometown. Carter made a long-distance telephone call (not an easy thing to do at the time) and told his dad the time his train would make a stop in Atlanta on the morning of April 16.

On arrival, Carter's family and his girlfriend, Phyllis Ewing, and her family, were at the station to greet them. It is unclear how he pulled it off, but Carter was the only person allowed off the train during the brief stop. He began kissing Phyllis while soldiers leaned out the passenger car windows and began whistling. It was a brief meeting, but Reb and Phyllis were now engaged in everything but name. Carter arrived at Tyndall in the waning hours of April 16 to begin the transition from pilot trainee to gunner trainee.

In the China-Burma-India Theater, the B-29 build-up continued unabated.

Beginning on April 24, 1944, Superfortresses began hauling supplies into China. An aircraft piloted by one-time West Point football hero Brig. Gen. LaVerne G. "Blondie" Saunders, commander of the 58th Wing, was one of the first to land at an airfield in China. Two days later, a Superfortress piloted by Maj.

Charles Hansen became the first to engage Japanese fighters. Hauling supplies over the Hump en route to Hsinching, China, the B-29 tangled with Nakajima Ki-44 Hayate, or "Oscar," fighters. When one of the fighters was observed limping away trailing smoke, tail gunner Sgt. Harold Lanahan was credited with an aerial victory, the first such credit for a Superfortress crewmember. Claims for air-to-air kills were almost always exaggerated, however—Japanese records show no Ki-44 lost that day. Another member of the Hansen crew, Sgt. Walter F. Gilonske, was wounded, becoming the first B-29 crewman in World War II to receive injuries from enemy action.

Flying the Hump was a fearsome prospect for the young men of Superfortress crews. So far, they had never enjoyed good morale in the history of the B-29 Superfortress, and the Hump hadn't changed this. They worried constantly about Japanese fighters, heavy icing conditions, and the grim prospect of being forced to bail out over the high, barren Himalayas. They worried about violent updrafts and downdrafts that could cause a sudden loss of control, snowstorms, and dense cloud formations. They worried about making a navigation error and flying straight into a twenty-thousand-foot peak. They'd overcome adversity back home in order to bring their mostly unproven new bomber to a war zone, and they wanted to bomb Japan. They were frustrated that hauling supplies over the Hump didn't seem to be accomplishing much. They worried about dying without ever getting into genuine combat. Flying the Hump was deemed so dangerous that it counted officially as a combat mission.

Mechanics stripped twenty Superfortresses of their armament and transformed them into fuel-carrying tankers for this logistical effort. That in itself was an accomplishment, but pilots and crewmembers in India were often given confusing and contradictory instructions. On early Hump flights, B-29s carried fuel into China only to find that in order to return to India they would need to use more fuel than they'd transported. Using the B-29 to haul fuel was a short-lived failure and the job was soon turned over to an aircraft called the C-109, a tanker version of the B-24 Liberator bomber. Eventually, B-29s stopped ferrying other supplies, too.

By the end of May 1944, Superfortresses had completed 245 supply flights into China, assisted by AAF transports. The supply effort persisted into June and July, the Superfortresses bolstered by cargo-hauling C-46 Commandos and C-109s.

B-29 into Battle

Also at the end of May 1944, the Superfortress bombers and crews arrayed near Calcutta were finally ready for a taste of battle. Staff Sgt. Roger Sandstedt, a central fire control gunner, remembers frustration and urgency as crews practiced loading the bombers. Sandstedt recalls a flight engineer saying that the trouble-prone R-3350 engine was "still making as much trouble for us as it ever did." An attempt to bomb any target, but especially any attempt to bomb the Japanese home islands, would be premature, Sandstedt believed.

Sandstedt and his buddies would attack Japan by taking off from India, staging at one of four sites in the Chengtu area of China—Kwanghan, Kuinglai, Hsinching, and Pengshan—and flying onward to the Empire. It was a badly flawed idea, and the principal flaw was obvious: Operation Matterhorn relied on all supplies of fuel, bombs, and spares needed to support the forward bases in China being flown in from India over the Hump. The Japanese controlled the sea approaches to the Chinese bases, so they could be supplied only by air.

Laddie Wale, later to fly a mission to Tokyo with the Tucker crew, was still in the United States while Matterhorn was forming in India and China, but he had a rare opportunity to talk to a sergeant who came home from the war zone. "He described a lot of good men working in harsh, primitive conditions trying to do their very best as they prepared for war," said Wale. "There was a lot of disease. There was a shortage of parts. There was some feeling that the leaders"—meaning Wolfe—"didn't have a clear picture of what they were doing." Always, no matter how hard everyone tried to make things work, there were tales of the R-3350 engine running amok. "I knew we could make the R-3350 perform the way we wanted," said Wale. "A lot of guys thought we never would."

LeMay, too, wondered whether the B-29 Superfortress would ever get to war. The India- and China-based Matterhorn scheme seemed, as LeMay viewed it, to present too many formidable challenges.

"The scheme of operations they dreamed up was like something out of 'The Wizard of Oz,'" wrote LeMay. "No one could have made it work. It was founded on an utterly absurd logistic basis. Nevertheless, our entire nation howled like a pack of wolves for an attack on the Japanese homeland. The high command yielded. The instrument wasn't ready. The people weren't ready. Nothing was ready. Folks were given an impossible task to perform."

That impossible task would begin with the first combat mission flown by B-29s.

The Manhattan Project

Activity continued at Los Alamos, New Mexico, and at other sites around the country, where a hard-driving Leslie Groves was overseeing the Manhattan Project and a quietly demanding Robert Oppenheimer was making it happen. Groves had an office on the fifth floor of the New War Department in Washington, but he was more likely to be seen at Los Alamos. The British had joined the effort there, bringing with them Niels Bohr, Klaus Fuchs, and others.

In June 1944, Oppenheimer oversaw progress in the development of two kinds of new bombs: a gun-type weapon using uranium and an implosion device that relied on plutonium. Oppenheimer implemented a sweeping reorganization of the Los Alamos laboratory to focus on the latter. This was dangerous work. In due course, half of the project's chemists and metallurgists had to be removed from work with plutonium when unacceptably high levels of the element appeared in their urine.

Someone in the project was talking to a handful of specially cleared people on George C. Marshall's staff in Washington, making plans to deploy the new weapons they were developing—two very different kinds of atomic bombs, made with different technologies. The staff in Washington identified several Japanese cities as potential targets. The staff was also taking steps toward forming the B-29-equipped 509th Composite Group later in the year and was reviewing the 201 File—the personnel folder—of Paul W. Tibbets, a veteran of the war in Europe who was now a colonel.

One of the cities to which their deliberations would return was named Hiroshima.

Crews from Clemson

Halfway around the world, Clemson University, a land-grant college in a South Carolina town of the same name, produced several of the thousand kids who flew B-29s over Tokyo. One was an earnest, boyish 1st Lt. Wesley O. Chandler from Hickory, North Carolina, itself a city that has produced an extraordinary number of aviation figures.

A 1940 graduate of Clemson, Chandler returned in June 1944 to marry Norma Sammons before flight school and his eventual role as pilot on the Firman E. Wyatt crew of a B-29 called *Cherry the Horizontal Cat*. It is unknown whether Chandler ever met Bake Baker, future radar operator on the crew of *God's Will* or Marshall D. Long, future radar operator on the Leon M. Keene crew of an unnamed B-29, who were both assigned to the college training detachment at Clemson courtesy of the Army Air Forces.

In June 1944, Baker and Long received the news that their college days at Clemson were over. Baker and Long symbolized the one-two punch of American manpower during the war: while it trained some men for battle, the United States had the luxury of parking others in places like Clemson, where many high school graduates earned a semester's worth of college credits. When the first cohort of trained Americans was ready to come home from the war, the second was ready to go in. The Japanese and Germans had no second cohort.

That month, Bake Baker remembers going into Greenville with the squared-away, "sharp as a tack" Long. Their destination was the USO Club. The nonprofit United Services Organization, subject of a government-sponsored movie featuring Army Air Forces Capt. Ronald Reagan, operated more than a thousand facilities around the country. The public image of the USO is of grandiose entertainments with Hollywood stars like Bob Hope, but most USOs were merely places of convenience: "It reminded me of a two-car garage," said Baker. "It was warm. It had lights. The women who were running it were just delightful and took good care of our utilitarian needs. They would sew on a button for us. They had a pressing machine and could press our pants so we'd look good when we went into town. They would wash our summer shirts. If you got spaghetti sauce on your shirt, they could fix it. They gave us advice about restaurants."

Baker would soon be in gunnery school at Tyndall Field, Florida, although not with Reb Carter, who became his crewmate and best friend later. Baker and Long later went to radar school at Langley Field, Virginia, but not together. Baker and Long would subsequently be stationed at McCook Field, Nebraska, and on the island of Tinian, but they would be in separate squadrons and would not see each other. For now, Baker was impressed that Marshall Long never seemed to need any help from the USO ladies to keep his uniform in shape. Long "always looked as if he had stepped out of a recruiting poster," Baker said.

It was quite a contrast to the appearance of ragged, rugged warriors who were beginning America's B-29 war at primitive airfields in India.

Armed in India

The young men who made up the crews of the mighty B-29 Superfortress flew their first combat mission on June 5, 1944. They took off from India to attack the Makasan railroad shops in Bangkok, Thailand, on a round trip of more than two thousand miles. Although the bosses were scrupulous in preventing anyone from saying so, the mission was a debacle.

At 6:28 a.m. local time, a Superfortress piloted by Maj. John B. Keller took off at a gross weight of 131,250 pounds. Midway on the takeoff roll, Keller lifted his nose wheel off the runway and held it in the air for the remainder of the roll, to the extent of striking the tail skid several times. The airplane left the ground after using 7,000 feet of the 7,600 feet of runway and proceeded in an apparently normal manner. The left wing dropped once but was leveled, then dropped again and continued to drop until the airplane struck the ground about two minutes after takeoff. The aircraft performed a spectacular cartwheel, exploded, and caught fire. Shortly afterward, three of its bombs exploded. All aboard were killed with the exception of the pilot (who would be called a copilot on any other aircraft), who was too seriously injured to give a comprehensive account of the accident. From his brief statement, the accident was due entirely to power loss of an undetermined cause in the number two engine. Examination of the badly burned engine revealed no further evidence. The R-3350 had made the leap from killing Americans back home to killing them on the battlefront.

After that first loss of a B-29 on a combat mission, mechanical difficulties prevented three planes from lining up for takeoff and forced one pilot to cut his engine halfway down the runway. Ninety-three bombers of an intended ninety-eight got into the air. Later, five were forced to ditch, fourteen aborted while en route, and forty-two landed at other locations without enough fuel to get home.

All crews reported a great deal of confusion over the target with B-29s making bombing runs on numerous headings. Exactly eighteen bombs fell near the target area. There was no Japanese antiaircraft fire. There were no Japanese fighters. The Japanese needed no flak or fighters on this day.

To add insult to injury, one B-29 refused to sink after ditching in the Bay of Bengal. While all but two of the crew were picked up by rescue boats, the B-29 floated around, behaving much like a boat itself, until it came to a halt near shore, still on the water's surface. In some aviation quarters there exists a legend that the wayward B-29 is still floating on the water today, timeless because it was passed over by time, visible but unnoticed. The actual disposition of the seagoing aircraft is not known.

Most of the world never knew about the mission. Halfway around the globe, American paratroopers were dropping into Normandy hours ahead of the D-Day invasion. The press found a little space for headlines about the men of the 58th Bombardment Wing, but not a lot.

Bomber boss Wolfe had always seen this mission as a practice run for his fledgling bomber crews. Back in Washington, Hap Arnold saw it that way too.

Wolfe was a skilled administrator and a constant gentleman, caught up in a no-win situation where everything was wrong. While it looked like a Superfortress, the B-29 continued to be a troubled aircraft that was prone to accident, especially the pesky engine fires that plagued the R-3350s, and it required more maintenance than the primitive conditions at airfields in India and China could support. The men and machines of the B-29 force had descended upon an India and China that were not ready for them. Not a fan of Wolfe, one American commander in the region said the B-29 cadre in the China-Burma-India Theater was "an interloper with specious claims of independence and a habit of sponging."

That was a terrible way to characterize men who were trying to use a new aircraft in an unfamiliar setting with minimal support. The men of the B-29s deserved better and so did Wolfe. But somebody had to take the blame, and Arnold, impatient with Wolfe's progress, decided that Wolfe would take the hit.

Assault on the Empire

If bravery and good intentions had been enough, the Superfortress crews that flew the very first mission to the Japanese home islands might have produced better results. Their target was an industrial site on Kyushu billed as the "Pittsburgh of Japan." The attack on the Imperial Iron and Steel Works at Yawata on the night of June 15–16, 1944, mounted from bases in China, didn't produce good results. Five B-29s were lost in accidents during the operation and two more fell for other reasons. Fifty-four crewmen and a correspondent were killed. One loss occurred when a Superfortress flew into debris left by another after being hit—and burst into flames. Also lost was a B-29 that encountered mechanical problems but landed relatively intact at a Chinese airfield. The following day, the crew was laboring to make the Superfortress airworthy when Japanese warplanes arrived abruptly and destroyed it on the ground.

It was the first strike on Japan since the Doolittle Raiders more than two years earlier. One crewmember described the fledgling mission in prosaic terms:

> We were the fourth to take off from our base in China and the second to hit the target. There was no formation flying, or anything elaborate like that. We flew single, bombed single and returned home alone too. We were the second to land back in China. Can't say it was uneventful, because about 40 miles from the target, the number two engine began coughing and running rough. I got it smoothed out in time for the final bomb run, but was questionable most of the way home. Also, the bomb bay doors would not close after we dropped the bombs. The electric motor wouldn't work. Our right blister gunner had to use the

emergency hand crank to crank them shut, once we were clear of the target area.

The mission to Yawata used nearly all of the fuel supplies stockpiled in China. Superfortresses would not be returning to the Empire for three weeks.

On the night of July 7–8, 1944, eighteen Superfortresses launched from bases near Chengtu in China to strike the naval base at Sasebo, also on Kyushu. Later, it was learned that their bombs missed the port facility by as much as a dozen miles due to mechanical problems with the radar bombing system. On the return flight, seven Ki-44 Hayate fighters tangled with the bomber formation, with inconclusive results.

Unfortunately, the three-week delay between the first and second missions reflected serious problems that prevented a sustained strategic bombing campaign from China against Japan. Each mission consumed tremendous quantities of fuel and bombs. There never seemed to be enough of either at Chengtu.

So far, it seemed that the massive bombing strategy that had been the keystone of U.S. airpower doctrine was rapidly going nowhere on all four engines. "You could not blame our generals for being deeply discouraged," said Paul Savko, a historian who served as a B-29 gunner in a later era. "They had built this magnificent flying machine. With difficulty and a nudge from Gen. Arnold, they had overcome the initial logistics problems. But they could not yet see any tangible result, except that some of their buddies were dying."

Red Beach One

While B-29 crewmembers were seething with frustration and accomplishing little from their bases in India and China, on June 13, 1944, a naval armada began shelling the kidney-shaped island of Saipan in the Marianas. At 7:00 a.m. on June 15, more than three hundred landing craft put eight thousand Marines ashore on Red Beach One, on the west side of the island. More Marines and the Army's 27th Infantry Division came ashore later. Private First Class Leon Uris, a Marine field radio operator, had previously fought on Guadalcanal and humped ashore at Tarawa with his radio unit and Thompson .45-caliber submachine gun. Afflicted with dengue fever, he missed the early, bloody fighting on Saipan but took notes from fellow Marines caught up in the carnage there.

Uris marveled at the ferocity of the Japanese who were defending against the onslaught. An aspiring writer, Uris felt he had material for a novel. "The blood ran deep under a murderous staccato of careening bomb bursts and geysers of hot metal mixed with spurting sand and flesh," he wrote of Saipan's Red Beach One. He also wrote that no one had briefed the Marines on why they were landing on Saipan, or why it mattered.

CHAPTER 7

The Way In

Mission to Tokyo
March 9, 1945, 10:00 p.m.–11:50 p.m.

THOSE WHO COULD SEE OUT OF THE B-29s—radio operators like Carl Barthold were not among them—had little to see. Col. Arnold Johnson, commander of the 497th Bombardment Group on Saipan and part of Rosy O'Donnell's command, spoke of looking down at the nocturnal Pacific. Decades later, Doris Goodlett, Johnson's daughter, described it: "One thing I can remember my father saying more than once was that the Pacific Ocean looked so black and foreboding as he flew over it on his way to Japan. He always hung a pair of my sister's baby shoes from the cockpit roof to remind himself of why he was flying on those missions. He couldn't ever talk about the missions, because it weighed on his mind that he had to drop firebombs on old men, women, and children, and he would get tearful about it if he tried to talk about it. He just faithfully did his duty to the best of his ability for his country, countrymen, and family. The moments of looking down at the Pacific, which should have brought some comfort to his soul, were instead a harbinger of what lay ahead."

A B-29 gunner recalled: "Occasionally on a night I would look out my blister at the ocean down below and it would look like we were passing over a series of connected super highways with lights. What I was observing were lines formed in the currents of fluorescent sea life. It was eerie, not in a comforting way but in a troubling way."

Often while the bomber was droning toward its target on a long mission, there was simply too little to do and too much time to think. Tonight's mission was not one on which to benefit from long periods of empty time. Just thinking about arriving over the Empire at low altitude was dangerous for anyone's mental condition. And then there were the other things. A Superfortress gunner recalled dwelling on things that could happen. "One of the dangers was in an over-water bailout. Many opened their chute harnesses early so they could get out and not be fouled by their chute in the water . . . so the admonition was 'Do not attempt to judge your height and jump from your harness until your feet are wet.' Over a calm sea it is very difficult to tell if you are at 100 feet or 1,000 feet . . . even in daylight!"

What is not clear in retrospect is how many B-29 crews ran into weather problems on their way to Tokyo. The body of information available about the weather that day paints a confusing picture. Because the bomber men planned to burn down the Japanese capital, their leaders had waited for a night when the air was dry and there was wind in the target area. The wind, of course, would spread the fire. It was indeed dry and windy at the capital, but all manner of weather conditions were roiling up in the region.

Because they were flying at far lower altitude than usual, the bombers were not confronting the jetstream, those furious high-altitude winds that had been all but unknown until this air campaign began. Many, including Barthold and Trip Triplett, never knew there were snowstorms churning in several locations near Tokyo. One pilot said the weather approaching Japan that night was "unremarkable"—unaware of the snowstorms over land—while yet another said, "There was never good weather when you were flying to Japan." The significance of the weather would become important to the crews of three B-29s in particular, who didn't know they had an appointment with a mountain.

One tidbit about the weather comes from Don Weber, the right-seat pilot of a B-29 called *Old Ironsides* of the 500th Bombardment Group, flying from Saipan. "As is usual, we hit plenty of weather on the way," Weber wrote in his journal. "St. Elmo's fire caused one bright explosion, which fairly rocked the ship." This was a reference to an atmospheric static electrical discharge that could sometimes make an entire B-29 glow like a giant neon sign. It was also happening to *God's Will*, prompting left blister gunner Reb Carter to write that his crew was flying through electrical storms and that "sparks were jumping all over our plane."

Weber noted, "Got plenty of instruments flying on the trip. We split the A & P time [meaning the airplane commander and the pilot took turns flying the plane]." Many pilots didn't expect this. Their attention was focused on the fact that Tokyo was dry and windy under a quarter moon, and some of them hadn't paid enough notice to the part of the briefing that warned of storms along their path and all around the Japanese capital.

Closer to the Empire

Aboard his Superfortress from Tinian, radar operator Trip Triplett performed tasks that were partly preparation and partly make-work while the nocturnal waters of the Pacific slid past beneath. The long hours of in-flight cruise and inaction were beginning to wear on Triplett. *It was 9:30 p.m. Chamorro Standard Time, March 9, 1945.*

Triplett lowered the radar dome, not visible to the crew but hanging beneath the fuselage of the B-29. He turned on his set and tuned it for clear reception on his scope. "Up front, beneath the belly of the plane, the radar transmitter-receiver began turning steadily around," Triplett recalled. "Electrical impulses, traveling at the speed of light, were fired outbound. Impulses striking solid shapes, like islands, ships, heavy clouds and the like were reflected back and displayed on the radar scope as bluish-white silhouettes. One of the tricks of becoming a good radar operator was in knowing how to interpret the images on the scope. We were traveling right on the deck tonight so the reception range of the radar would be low."

Triplett's bomber turned on a course heading of 348 degrees. He drew a long line on his map heading upward toward the distant IP, the initial point from which a bomb run would begin. The IP was a place called Futtsu, just south of Tokyo—and, for now, 1,200 miles to the north. As Triplett remembers, "In the darkness over the Pacific, a long line of bombers was strung out for miles. Bombers carrying names like *Thumper*, *Krowes Kids*, *Lucky Lady*, *Coral Queen*, *Miss Su-Su*, and *Omaha, One More Time*. Names that held memories of frolicsome stateside ventures, a beautiful woman, or just a touch of home. How many would make it back to our little speck in the Pacific we called home base?"

Also among the names scattered in the night sky were *Tall in the Saddle* and *Lady Annabelle*. It's easy to imagine Sammy Bakshas in the left front seat of *Tall in the Saddle*, watching instruments, keeping a grip on the control yoke, working with regularly assigned airplane commander Gordon Muster and flight engineer Leland P. Fishback, monitoring any change in the behavior of the four engines and checking in frequently with navigator John Hagadorn. How annoyed was Muster, a mature pilot and the real leader of this crew, at being displaced by the even more mature, more experienced Bakshas? The pair had gotten along famously until today, but Muster apparently felt his squadron commander was overstepping by taking the pilot-in-command role. On the other hand, some who knew this crew believe that talk of tension between Bakshas and Muster was overstated.

Fishback was checking instruments constantly, continuously shifting fuel to adjust the balance of the aircraft and giving spot checks on the interphone. The other crewmembers saw Fishback as serious, unemotional, and functional. He was very much like the job a flight engineer performed—solemn and straightforward. He was also one of the many who had expressed clear but calm misgivings about making a bombing run at low level. He expressed his displeasure quietly before the crew went out to the airplane and then, evidently, he forgot about it and got on with his duties.

Busy as pilots Bakshas and Muster and flight engineer Fishback were, the most important crewmember on the long journey toward the Empire was navigator Hagadorn. If he screwed up, nothing else would matter.

Hagadorn sat on the left side of the aircraft behind the airplane commander. It was his job to keep up with the current position of the plane at all times. He did this through dead reckoning (keeping track of the aircraft's speed and direction and any changes in course) and making observations of landmarks, celestial objects, and radio beacons. When he wanted to make a "fix" with his hand-held sextant, Hagadorn crawled into the tunnel above the bomb bay and, just a couple of feet back toward the tail, looked up into a transparent astrodome. Another navigator called the job "constantly monitoring, monitoring" and said "you were always busy but you weren't too busy to worry about the consequences of a mistake"—the B-29 did not have a great deal of excess fuel if the crew found itself in the wrong place on the map—"or, for that matter, to worry about Japanese fighters and antiaircraft guns." Hagadorn knew he might also be called upon to calculate a new course if there were deviations to the flight plan as well as give travel time estimates. He was one of two crewmembers—the other being the flight engineer—who could not doze off, even for a few minutes, at any time during the mission.

The very long-range nature of most B-29 missions, including this one, placed unprecedented demands on navigators like Hagadorn. In Europe, a bombing mission could last eight hours; in the Pacific a mission typically lasted fifteen. The war in Europe was fought mostly by daylight over land when navigation cues were visible everywhere, with bombers staying in formation and thus helping each other get to the right place. Hagadorn and the men of *Tall in the Saddle* were over a dark sea at night and weren't part of a formation: hundreds of B-29s and thousands of men were speeding toward Tokyo, but each aircraft and each crew was alone.

The Tucker Crew

Aboard *Lady Annabelle*, occupying its own place in the night sky, Percy Usher Tucker's navigator was Edwin J. Koniusky. He looked like a happy kid with a broad smile and a forelock of black hair dangling over his forehead. A perfectionist, they called him, even though he radiated youth and charm. "A perfectionist who had to be satisfied we were in exactly the right place in the sky," flight engineer Laddie Wale said. The stuff around Koniuksy was uncommonly tidy—a drift sight to measure wind drift, the inevitable sextant for celestial sightings, a radio direction finder unit to take bearings on known radio stations—useless tonight—and a slew of outdated and inadequate maps, which were also useless when rising over a dark sea devoid of recognition features.

The truth was, Koniusky was scared. He had watched the gunners prepare their weapons and ammunition, just as those aboard many other B-29s had done, all in violation of the battle order, and he had sat through the intelligence briefing about fighters and flak, and Koniusky was afraid that tonight's mission might be his last. Diligently, and never losing his cheerful look, he worked on his navigation tasks and occasionally said something to Tucker on the interphone. "Tucker is going to get us home," Koniusky was thinking. "Believe it. Tucker is going to get us home." Unlike another crewmember aboard the same aircraft who was beginning to lose it, Koniusky kept his concerns under control as *Lady Annabelle* droned ahead on a northwesterly course. *It was 10:30 p.m. Chamorro Standard Time, March 9, 1945.*

Tucker's crew was fortunate to have a serious and well-regarded airplane commander. But if Tucker was a man of few words, his bombardier Joseph Krogman was a study in contrast. Krogman was always cheerful, even when LeMay's change in tactics was eating up his stomach. A bit of a prankster, he grew up on a farm in Iowa and "cussed like a storm," as another crewmember put it. Krogman used "damn" and "hell" all the time and the f-word regularly, in comparison to Tucker, who once surprised everyone around him once when he uttered "Damn!" when he hit his thumb with a hammer.

Krogman could "talk your ear off," many said of him. Affable, open, vocal with his very strong opinions, Krogman absolutely hated LeMay and regularly used barnyard jargon to describe the general. Today, and on other days to come, Krogman used the words "that sonofabitch" as if they were interchangeable with LeMay's surname. He stopped uttering the term on the interphone, but his feelings didn't change. He hated LeMay in part because, like so many, he was certain LeMay would get them killed today. But he could talk, and cuss, and hate, and still have it under control—unlike the guy in the rear fuselage, who was losing it.

Krogman had the best view in the plane. He could peer out over his bombsight through the rounded nose of the Superfortress and watch the Pacific pass by beneath. Krogman, too, kept his concerns under control.

If Tuck was going to keep *Lady Annabelle* flying properly and heading to the right place, it was going to take a lot of work from flight engineer Laddie Wale, who sat behind the pilots facing rearward and looking at his instruments. The "college professor in uniform" who wasn't really a professor at all, Wale was uncomfortable with the decision to fly tonight's mission at low altitude, uncomfortable with LeMay's order to leave guns and ammunition at home, and even more uncomfortable with the decision made by Tucker—and half the other airplane commanders on Guam, Saipan, and Tinian—to bring the guns and ammunition along anyway. "I didn't like anything about the way we were getting into this," said Wale. At least he had plenty to keep him busy while the nocturnal Pacific waters slid past below.

Wale instructed tail gunner Majeski to turn off the auxiliary power unit now that *Lady Annabelle* was operating on her own power in flight. Majeski returned to his tail gunner's position and did a routine check of his guns. Having been relieved that nothing terrible happened at takeoff—"a B-29 could make a big hole in the ground on takeoff"—Majeski received a call from flight engineer Wale. "Why don't you come up here, Joe?" And later: "I've been fooling with weights and balances, Joe. For the next hour or so, it would help to have your weight a little farther forward."

Majeski wriggled his way forward. He passed right blister gunner John R. Dodd, "a good-looking guy from Boston" who was clutching rosary beads with both hands. "He was really afraid," said Majeski. "He made everybody nervous."

Dodd had never faltered in his duty. This may not have meant a lot because a side blister gunner actually had very little to do except keep watch, acting as an extra pair of eyes for the airplane commander. Still, Dodd had never done anything wrong, not once. But other crewmembers aboard *Lady Annabelle* often saw him trembling. Tonight, no doubt as fearful as everyone about flying at low altitude, Dodd was visibly shaking. Wale later commented that he had enormous respect for someone who could be so apprehensive and still go out to the plane, climb aboard, and fly to the Empire.

Next to takeoff, what frightened Majeski most was the prospect of an engine fire. Majeski, a nonsmoker, had never quite understood why Tucker, a smoker, allowed the men to puff on cigarettes aboard *Lady Annabelle*. He crawled through the tunnel above the bomb bay and kneeled next to Wale, who was shifting fuel from one tank to another—again. "Smoking lamp's off," Wale said over the interphone. And, a few minutes later: "Smoking lamp's on." Majeski knew the R-3350 engines were prone to catching fire—in the course of the war, engine fires killed more B-29 crewmembers than Japanese bullets, and it upset him when crewmembers puffed away. "We had a bond when we were in the air, but we were not that close the rest of the time," Majeski said. "There was a solid line between the officers and the enlisted men. We saw Captain Tucker only when we were on the airplane with him."

When he wasn't using his body to assist one of Wale's endlessly complicated and ever-changing weight-and-balance equations, Majeski had a little freedom during the first part of the mission.

> Between Tinian and Iwo Jima, I would wander about the airplane. Sometimes I would crawl through the long tunnel over the bomb bays and visit with the crew up front—the airplane commander, copilot, bombardier, navigator, radio operator, and the flight engineer. Most of the time I would remain in the Central Fire Control [CFC] compartment with the right and left blister gunners, the CFC gunner, and the radar operator. After passing Iwo Jima I would then go back to the tail compartment because we would now be getting into the range of Japanese fighters. It is interesting to note that many times over a target (a Japanese city) I would point my two powerful .50-caliber machine guns and fire bursts down into the city. In retrospect now when I think back, I had been praying for my life and shortly after I was firing my guns in anger hoping to kill some Japanese. War does create some mixed feelings. However, remember the sneak attack on Pearl Harbor by the Japanese. That—and the wanting to be home enjoying life—is what motivated my hatred towards the Japanese.

With Wale monitoring instruments, Majeski watching for fighters from the tail, Krogman adjusting his bombsight, and the crew increasingly tense and nervous, Capt. Percy Usher Tucker's *Lady Annabelle* continued northwest and began closing the distance between the men aboard the B-29 and the Japanese capital. *It was 11:30 p.m. Chamorro Standard Time, March 9, 1945.*

In the hands of the Japanese, Iwo Jima had been a springboard for lethal, air-to-ground attacks on the B-29 force in the Marianas. When the thousand kids first began arriving at Guam, Saipan, and Tinian—while the earlier B-29 campaign mounted from China, known as Matterhorn, was winding down—those Japanese air-to-ground attacks from Iwo Jima killed several of the kids, blew up some of their aircraft, and exacerbated the feeling of failure that hung darkly over the faltering B-29 effort.

Iwo Jima's ultimate significance was that it could be an emergency landing spot for a B-29 in trouble on the way home from Japan. By the end of the war, the tally would be an extraordinary 2,400 Superfortress emergency landings on the sulphur island.

Tonight, outbound toward the Empire, the thousand kids flying northwest in darkness regarded the island of Iwo Jima—still embattled, not yet secured—as a navigation point. It was also a kind of "last chance" for anyone with mechanical problems, although it offered no facility for a landing at night. The radar aboard a B-29 could pick out a land mass and a qualified operator could readily identify the location. If Iwo Jima showed up on the scope in the right place at the right time, a crew could be assured that they were burning precious fuel flying in the right direction.

The Bertagnoli Crew

Rather than a tightly disciplined aerial formation, the swarm of Superfortresses boring through the night was an unruly gaggle of aircraft operating individually, protected from colliding with each other only by staying at their assigned altitude and navigating properly. But navigating properly was easier said than done.

Navigating, in fact, was the hardest part of the mission. "The navigator was the most important man on that airplane, hands down," said a B-29 gunner.

The lives of two airplane commanders, and their connections to their navigators, were going to be intertwined in the days and weeks ahead. Both airplane commanders were in the 9th Bombardment Group based on Tinian, and both were heading toward Tokyo tonight. Captain George "Bert" Bertagnoli at the controls of *Queen*

Bee and Dean Fling piloting *God's Will* were both having unexpected and unwelcome navigation problems. Neither Bertagnoli nor Fling was going to be over Tokyo at the prescribed time.

Aboard Bertagnoli's *Queen Bee*, the situation was unspeakably frustrating. The crew's regular navigator had been trying since takeoff to use the tools available to him to get the B-29 on the right path, headed for the right place, but he was bumbling it.

Looking over his shoulder was squadron navigator 1st Lt. George Edwin Albritton, who was not a member of the crew. He was flying with a crew that, according to him, had lost confidence in its regularly assigned navigator. Bertagnoli had, in effect, fired the regular navigator, but instead of sending the young man packing, the squadron had sent Albritton to check out the situation. Albritton was performing what crewmembers called a "supervised position." "He was there," said one crewmember, "to see if this young man was doing his job." He wasn't.

"I'm going to have to take over," Albritton finally told the young navigator firmly. Albritton calmly replaced the navigator and began calculating their location. That young man now moved to a bucket seat with no equipment, no job to perform, and a seething resentment over being replaced by an interloper. He had the sympathy of some of his crewmates.

"When we were in the states, he was a wonderful navigator," said a crewmate. "When we were crossing the ocean and flying to Tinian, he was a wonderful navigator. But when they started to shoot at us, he forgot how to do arithmetic. When he took us in the opposite direction from what had been planned, Bertagnoli started to think about getting rid of him. When we were supposed to go to the ocean and he took us to the mountains instead, Bertagnoli said, 'Now I'm going to get rid of him for sure.'"

But Bertagnoli hadn't. Now instead the navigator sat, useless, while Albritton worked to get *Queen Bee* and her crew to the target. "We passed between Iwo Jima and Chichi Jima with radar identification and headed on a west-northwest course after which we were to turn north-northwest on the final leg to Tokyo."

Some time later—he did not remember exactly when—the crew navigator notified Albritton that Albritton had forgotten to note the time of his fix on Iwo Jima. It was an important lapse. "We did not have any idea how far we had gone," Albritton said. It was a humiliating setback for the usually even-headed Albritton because he, after all, was aboard the bomber to replace the man who'd just corrected him.

"'All is not lost,' I said to myself. 'We will fix our position with celestial navigation,' which is measuring the elevation of the stars with a bubble sextant. This we did and after three fixes found that we were some one hundred miles east of course."

The crew navigator then gave the airplane commander a course intended to get *Queen Bee* back on the planned flight path and gave Bertagnoli an estimated time of arrival at Tokyo. One of visitor Albritton's duties later in the mission would be to position himself in the tunnel (the passageway above the bomb bay) looking out the astrodome for other planes during the time in the target area. But first, they had to reach the target area. To Albritton's frustration, the findings by the crew navigator appeared to be wrong. When Albritton did further celestial navigation, he found the B-29 was not on proper course for the target.

"We're lost," said the crew navigator. His tone was unmistakable—*If I had been navigating instead of you, he seemed to be saying, this wouldn't have happened.* Albritton was the outsider, the other navigator seemed to be thinking and would now have to bear the blame for putting the aircraft and its entire crew in trouble.

The tension between *Queen Bee*'s regular navigator and Albritton was thick enough to cut with a knife. Had they not been strapped inside a cramped steel cocoon moving through the night at almost three hundred miles per hour, they might have come to blows. Albritton had to admit that the words no navigator should ever utter were accurate. They were lost. It was the damndest thing to happen in the middle of the biggest B-29 mission in the war, and it was no one's fault, really, but yes indeed, they were lost. *It was 11:10 p.m. Chamorro Standard Time, March 9, 1945.*

The Bowers Crew
One of LeMay's nightmares was a gaggle of B-29s fanning out in different directions, missing Tokyo, and burning up fuel at a suicidal rate. They would be lost, all of them, B-29s sucked up by the storms

and murk surrounding the clear and cold Japanese capital. By flying off course, heading off toward all points on the compass, they would transform today's bombing mission into an epic failure and end the bombing campaign, to say nothing of LeMay's career. And they would be astray and alone, lost and imperiled, *before* encountering Japanese flak and fighters.

It was happening, and not just aboard Albritton's airplane.

It was happening aboard *Ready Teddy*, a B-29 of the 9th Bombardment Group flying from Tinian. Airplane commander Capt. Alvin Bowers began the mission with a smooth takeoff, leveled off for the cruise, and got off to "a pretty good start," said left blister gunner Sgt. Donald R. Dacier. Those who could see outside the aircraft looked down at the Pacific and felt their tension growing. At times they could see some sort of life form roiling up near the surface of the dark waves. It was luminescent and it streaked the black waters with tiny slender flecks of shiny light.

While airplane commanders tended to be serious and tight-lipped (the model was the taciturn Tucker of *Lady Annabelle*), Bowers was cut from a different mold. His angular face almost always seemed to be on the verge of breaking into a grin, his eyes sparkled, and he was almost always cheerful. Bowers was from Little Rock, was married, and was a very experienced and much-admired pilot who'd gotten plenty of experience handling airplanes before the war. He encouraged the nonpilots in his crew to sit in a pilot's seat and handle the controls from time to time. He took pleasure in explaining principles of aeronautics to those who hadn't attended flight school.

Tonight, Al Bowers was not grinning. "Something's not going right here," he said.

Bowers had an almost magical rapport with pilot 1st Lt. John Swihart, who in postwar years would be a senior official with Boeing. Swihart rarely gave the impression that he didn't know what was going on.

"Where are we?" Swihart said.

It was the Bowers crew's fourth mission, but the first three had been easy daylight flights. The only experience they had flying at night was in training flights back in the United States. Bowers wanted the whole crew on this mission because he wanted as many eyes as possible looking for Japanese night fighters. But all the eyes in the world couldn't discern their exact location over the dark Pacific waters.

From his gunner's position in the rear fuselage, Dacier listened on the interphone while Bowers, the navigator, and the radar operator became flustered. In the best of times, the radar was not a terribly effective aid to navigation, but it was supposed to pick out land masses. Right about now, it was supposed to pick out Iwo Jima, the volcanic sulphur rock where Marines were locked in close-quarters battle and an airfield was just barely in friendly hands, a possible refuge for a B-29 in trouble.

Right now, the radar wasn't picking out anything.

"We were about fifty miles off course," said Dacier. "The navigator was trying to work with the radar operator, but the radar was not functioning properly. The navigator crawled up into the bubble [the astrodome], performed some celestial work, and told Bowers, 'We're heading on course toward Tokyo Bay.'" No one else thought the navigator was right.

Heading northwest toward the Empire (maybe), it took Bowers's crew another hour of trial and error, and of rising levels of frustration evident in their voices on the interphone voices, to realize the obvious. "We don't know where we are," Bowers said finally, not a hint of his usual cheerfulness in his tone. *It was 11:50 p.m. Chamorro Standard Time, March 9, 1945.*

Shrouded in nocturnal darkness, flying low over black waters streaked with tiny licks of illumination, the eleven men aboard the sixty-five-ton *Ready Teddy* were lost.

CHAPTER 8

Striving

The B-29 Superfortress against Japan,
June 16, 1944–December 3, 1944

WHILE A WET-BEHIND-THE-EARS cadre of B-29 airmen struggled to make a mark from bases in India and China, and while other B-29 crewmembers continued training at stateside airfields, the amphibious war in the Pacific surged ahead.

On Saipan, beleaguered Americans faced an unprecedented *gyokusai* attack—a suicidal onslaught—and later witnessed hundreds of Japanese killing themselves by jumping off the sheer cliffs near Marpi Point. The battle killed 2,949 Americans, the costliest toll of any battle in the war thus far. More than ten thousand Americans were wounded, including twenty-year-old Marine Pfc. Lee Marvin from Connecticut, who wanted to become an actor. Despite embarrassing turf issues between Army and Marine leaders during the invasion and subsequent battle, the top brass were able to declare Saipan secure on July 9, 1944. By the next day, Navy construction battalions, the famous Seabees, were underway, transforming Saipan's crude airstrips into B-29 bases. Saipan became home to the 73rd Wing Rosy O'Donnell.

On July 21, 1944, the invasion of Guam began. It was not as heavily fortified as the other Mariana Islands such as Saipan that had been Japanese possessions since the end of World War I, but Guam did have a large Japanese detachment, and resistance was stronger than the western allies expected.

On July 24, 1944, Marines began their assault on yet another island in the Marianas chain, Tinian. It was flat, desolate, and decidedly unimpressive. One of the Marines, Pfc. Victor Parissis, looked at the smoke-strewn island, saw "what I would call a desolate place of sand, slag and rock," and wondered what conceivable benefit, if any, Tinian could offer the war effort. Yet Tinian would soon become the busiest airfield in the world by far, as well as home to the 313th Wing led by Brig. Gen. John H. Davies and eventually to the 509th Composite Group under Col. Paul W. Tibbets.

On the day the Marines invaded Tinian, Reb Carter, soon to be left blister gunner on the Dean Fling crew of *God's Will*, paused during his new training assignment at Lincoln, Nebraska, to write to his sweetheart Phyllis Ewing. He had just listened to a lecture from "guys that have been in combat." "Honey," he wrote, "I love you so, so, so, so, very, very, very, very much and I know I always will. We will be so happy when we are married and can be together always." His was a generation that could wait to fulfill its dreams, and Carter was willing to wait as long as necessary.

Days later, still at Lincoln waiting to go to McCook, Nebraska, to see a B-29 for the first time and to join a B-29 crew, Carter wrote: "The way I feel, knowing you want to marry me now and love me so much, I could lick the whole Jap Army so don't worry about me. I do want to come back so very, very much and know I will." It was a beautiful thought, but it did not prevent Ewing from worrying about Carter. After all, as she told family members in Atlanta, he was "getting ready to do something dangerous."

China-Burma-India Theater
So far, B-29 crews were still fighting from India and China. Their supplies refreshed and their experience growing, they attacked the Showa steelworks in Manchuria on July 29, 1944, and Nagasaki on the night of August 10–11. On the latter night, Superfortresses also staged from Ceylon to attack an oil refinery at Palembang, Sumatra.

On the Nagasaki mission, Tech. Sgt. Harold C. Edwards was credited with shooting down a Japanese fighter with his bomber's tail-mounted 20mm cannon, the first tail gunner to rack up a kill. B-29s rolled out of the factory with two .50-caliber machine guns and one 20mm cannon in the tail, but crews often discarded the latter weapon, which had a different range and trajectory than the "fifties."

A participant in the July mission made an emergency landing at Vladivostok and became the first of three Superfortresses to be interned by Soviet authorities. Captain Howard Jarrell, the pilot, expected that the Russians would greet him and his crew with open arms. After all, the United States and the Soviet Union were allies in the struggle against Hitler's Germany, and there was talk, premature as it turned out, of the Soviets entering the fight against Japan. In fact, Jarrell and other Superfortress crewmen who landed on Soviet soil—like some of the Doolittle B-25 Raiders who preceded them—were treated as anything but brothers in a common cause. The men were interned, received more as enemies than as friends.

Jarrell and his crew were greeted with no caviar, no vodka, and no trip back to American lines. The Soviets were not even cheerful, Jarrell said later, but they were overjoyed with the gift Jarrell had brought them. Feasting his gaze over the sheer beauty of the Superfortress, one Russian general called it *dar Bozhii* (a gift from God). Moscow strongman Josef Stalin had an air force heavily populated with small tactical planes but no strategic bombers. He realized how vulnerable this made him. Stalin made copying the B-29 a top priority for his military. Eventually, the Soviets received two more B-29s, and Stalin ordered vaunted engineer and designer Andrei Tupolev to reverse-design the B-29. The Soviets moved one of the bombers to Moscow for flight-testing. In a newly established office in the Soviet capital, Tupolev himself did a lot of hard work and a great deal of running around and giving an impression of near panic. As Tupolev knew from his personal experience of being in and out of prison for the past seven years, if you crossed Stalin, you could end up in the slammer—or dead.

Stalin belatedly developed an appreciation for strategic bombing and made at least three requests for B-29s under Lend-Lease. Americans had no wish to export four-engined bombers to Russia, not even the B-17 Flying Fortress or B-24 Liberator. Stalin placed his chief of secret police, Laventriy Beria, who was also in charge of the development of the Soviet atomic bomb, in charge of the B-29 program.

Tupolev interpreted his directive strictly—a wise decision where Stalin was concerned—and the engineers followed the rule so rigorously that even obvious individual flaws of the individual B-29s were included in the copying process. Said one Russian, "When Stalin orders you to copy, you copy." Amid the haste of its own manufacture, for example, the crew tunnel connecting the two pressurized crew areas in Jarrell's B-29 had been only partially painted. The Soviets duplicated this incomplete paint job flawlessly on their version of the Soviet bomber. Also duplicated were some small holes in the wing that were apparently mistakes or locations where equipment had been moved around.

The Tu-4 project produced absurdities. Soviet experts debated American penis size as they contemplated the B-29's large-diameter relief tube. Among the absurdities, according to legend, was the word "Boeing" embossed on the rudder pedals of the Tupolev bomber. Tupolev is reported to have asked Beria if the U.S. Army Air Forces insignia was to be reproduced on the wings of the Tu-4. Afraid to alter his master's edict, Beria put the question to Stalin in a joke. The dictator's laughter told him to put the Soviet Union's red stars, instead of the U. S. emblem, on the aircraft. Like the B-29 itself, the Tu-4 became a player in the postwar tensions between Moscow and Washington.

Yawata Again

Other than giving the Russians an airplane they were unable to develop on their own, Operation Matterhorn was not producing the results American planners wanted.

A decision was made to mount a second attack on the Yawata steelworks. "Blondie" Saunders, commander of the 58th Wing, decided make it a daytime strike. Those who took part called it Yawata Day to distinguish it from their experience back in June, which they dubbed Yawata Night.

On August 20, 1944, ninety-eight Superfortress crews, having moved forward from India, were in position in China for their second go at the steel-producing complex. Their efforts were marred

by crashes on takeoff, delays, and some navigation problems, but most of the B-29s dropped on Yawata, despite steady antiaircraft fire, and achieved reasonable accuracy.

In Hollywood blockbusters, when a plane ploughs into the ground, it erupts in a red-orange storm of pyrotechnics. On this Yawata mission, one bomber careened to the side of the runway an instant after its wheels left the ground, crashed at a nose-first downward angle, and lay in brush and dirt—so far as anyone could see from the outside, completely undamaged. An observer heard its impact with the ground as "a dry, clumping sound, very soft, lasting for only an instant." Every man aboard the Superfortress died.

Approaching Yawata, antiaircraft fire claimed at least two Superfortresses. With flak still swirling about, a solitary Kawasaki Ki-45 Type 2, also known as a "Nick" fighter, made a head-on assault on a B-29. The Nick banked abruptly, its wings vertical to the ground, and sliced through the leading edge of the Superfortress's wing. Fuel tanks on both aircraft ignited. A crew in another B-29 witnessed a stop-motion image of two aircraft stuck together in midair, but only for an instant. Then, in a flash of pyrotechnic brilliance, red-orange flames swallowed up both the Superfortress and the Nick.

Debris and flaming metal flew everywhere. A fragment slammed into the tail section of another Superfortress, and it, too, went down. American intelligence analysts concluded that the Nick fighter was on a suicide mission and rammed the B-29 intentionally. Japanese records dispute this. Japan had not yet fielded the kamikaze forces (named for a "divine wind" that had saved the nation at an earlier juncture by toppling a foe's naval fleet), but ramming—not necessarily with the intention of suicide—would soon be a tactic of some Japanese fighter pilots.

During Yawata Day, Japanese aircraft attempted several times to drop bombs on the B-29s from above. A Mitsubishi G4M, or "Betty" bomber, dropped a bomb that detonated atop the Superfortress piloted by Col. Richard H. Carmichael, commander of the 462nd Bombardment Group, the "Hellbirds." Carmichael had survived the attack on Pearl Harbor and an earlier tour as a group commander in the Pacific. With his aircraft on fire, Carmichael did some difficult flying that enabled most of the crew, including himself, to parachute from the bomber. They became prisoners of war.

During Yawata Day, B-29 gunners claimed seventeen Japanese aircraft—a claim that appears to have been wildly exaggerated. A B-29 damaged in the battle diverted to the Soviet Union, but Stalin and Tupolev didn't get this one. Instead, the crew bailed out over Soviet territory and was summarily interned.

Palembang Mission

Operation Matterhorn was moving in fits and starts. On the night of August 9–10, 1944, fifty-six B-29s from Kharagpur, India, staged in Ceylon in order to fly to the Japanese oil fields and refineries at Palembang, Sumatra. Documents from the time cite this as the longest military mission ever flown, listed as a round trip of 3,855 air miles to Palembang and 4,030 miles for the handful of Superfortresses that traveled farther to drop mines in the Moesi River. That same night a different batch of B-29s traveled in the other direction and bombed Nagasaki, the port city on the westernmost Japanese main island of Kyushu. These flights were excellent training tools for Superfortress crewmembers, but their execution showed a lack of operational control and inadequate combat techniques, drifting from target to target without a central plan. The bombing was largely ineffective.

Kenneth B. Wolfe was the only combat commander who ever arrived in the war zone with solid experience in the still-evolving B-29. It was not good enough. Even before Palembang, Arnold had decided to replace Wolfe with Saunders as temporary commander until Major General Curtis E. LeMay could arrive from Europe to take over.

The Fling Crew

Many B-29 crewmembers were arriving at their final training centers in the United States and would go to Guam, Saipan, and Tinian without ever setting foot in India or China. These men came together, formed crews, and pressed ahead with preparations, planning, and training. When men from all over the country came together to create the team that would be responsible for a single B-29, a combination of factors decided how fate would treat them later. Many of the crew assignments were made at random by officials in Training Command, but at times an airplane commander was given a list of names and files and allowed to choose his pilot, bombardier, flight engineer, navigator, radio operator, radar operator, and gunners. On August 21, 1944, at McCook Field, Nebraska, airplane commander Dean Fling was doing just that. Fling had been assigned an aircraft, soon to be named *God's Will* (in the mind of pilot Harold "Pete" Peterson, the name already belonged to the plane, although it was not yet agreed upon or painted on the nose). Fling was handed a list of potential crewmembers. He liked the looks of several of these men.

Peterson, the right-seat pilot and the most fervent among the crew, had been a varsity athlete in two sports and two schools—football at California Polytechnic Institute and baseball at the University of California–Davis. In flight training, Peterson's flight instructor was a Hollywood actor whose career on the silver screen was interrupted by war: Robert Cummings had learned to fly from his godfather Orville Wright and instructed hundreds of pilots during the war.

In addition to Peterson, Fling acquired bombardier Don "Red" Dwyer, navigator Phillip H. Pettit, flight engineer Lawrence Eginton, radio operator Thomas Sulentic, radar operator Bake Baker, central fire control gunner Noah A. "Pappy" Wyatt, left blister gunner Reb Carter, right blister gunner John Emershaw, and tail gunner Norman "Shorty" Fortin. Baker, of course, had been at Clemson before going to radar training. Baker and Carter almost immediately became best friends.

The crew met for the first time in a large briefing room at McCook. A handful of B-29 crews never recovered from this initial convocation. These were the crews that never found a way to fit together; they would remain dysfunctional to the end of the war, and regrettably there were too many such crews.

Not part of the Fling crew was Marshall D. Long, who had served with Baker at Clemson and was now in the same bomb group but a different squadron. Also not part of the Fling crew was Samuel N. Slater, the navigator who had almost made it on the Doolittle Raid. Fling may have had a crack at Slater when he chose Pettit, or maybe not. But Slater had now graduated from the

B-25 Mitchell to the B-29 Superfortress, and he would eventually see Japan.

At McCook, the Fling crew bonded and thrived. Baker wrote that the crew was "in good spirits and quite well trained." He never had a chance to observe Carter's prowess with a yo-yo—Reb left that behind in Atlanta—but Baker wrote that Carter was "friendly as a cocker spaniel" and "did not have an enemy in the world."

Baker noticed that Carter was confident and thorough, whether handling his machine guns or cleaning their barracks living area or pulling the much-disliked kitchen police, or KP, duty that helped keep the troops fed. Later, Baker and Carter would be reminded repeatedly that military life consisted of "hurry up and wait" and would develop interests in everything from gardening to photography. At McCook, however, free time was at a premium, and crewmates could socialize with the lovestruck Carter only when he was not writing letters to Phyllis Ewing. Carter also wrote to his mother and in one letter said: "We are now on a seven day a week schedule and it is rough. Part of our ground crew has moved out so we have to work on the line during our free time. The last two days I had to get up at three a.m., and will have to get up at three Sunday and Monday. They are going to let us sleep late tomorrow. We only have to get up two hours before the sun (five a.m.)." The Fling crew completed a grueling training flight to Cuba and back, and there was a heightened awareness among them that they would soon be taking their B-29 to the western Pacific. They were heading for the real thing.

In the War Zone

LeMay, now one of the America's most accomplished bomber generals, took command of XX Bomber Command in India on August 29, 1944. LeMay nominally reported to the ailing Arnold, who was both Army air boss and Twentieth Air Force commander in Washington. No one was peering over LeMay's shoulder, however, and he was quick to seize as much autonomy as he could.

If it was hard to feel warmth toward him, his men at least respected LeMay. He had risen through the ranks on merit and not because of personal contacts. Arnold summarily relieved Wolfe, with Saunders filling in temporarily, not so much because of Arnold's attitude toward Wolfe but because from a distance, Arnold was certain LeMay was the leader he wanted.

LeMay was rarely seen without a pipe or cigar, but while he always carried a Ronson lighter, he chewed on his cigars more than he smoked them. Often portrayed as a one-dimensional, gruff, and unforgiving brute, LeMay was in fact a complex and brilliant figure who had to work harder than most to succeed. Arnold chose him, but the two did not know each other well. Because he never talked about it, some did not know that LeMay had earned a Distinguished Service Cross, the second-highest award for valor, for a mission to Regensburg before leaving Europe to journey to India. Now, LeMay had inherited the troubled Operation Matterhorn and knew he was expected to improve the performance of the B-29 airplanes and crews.

Another view of LeMay came from Army Maj. James Gould Cozzens, better known as a novelist and later to publish *By Love Possessed*. Wrote Cozzens:

> He had a dead cigar in his mouth when he came in [to a meeting] and he never moved it for three quarters of an hour, though talking around it well enough when occasion arose. The superficial first impression was that he was dumb or gross; but he has one of those faces that grow on you—real intelligence and even a kind of sweetness—as though he would not do anything mean, or even think anything mean, though he is well known to be a hard man, and you can see that too—becoming more apparent the longer you look at him. Around the motionless cigar he spoke sensibly.

LeMay revamped tactics and shifted from nocturnal flying to daylight precision attacks, a step he would reverse for the great Tokyo firebomb mission. He instituted twelve-plane formations aimed at concentrating defensive firepower. He went along on a September 8, 1944, mission by 108 bombers from Chinese bases to the Showa steelworks in Japanese-occupied Manchuria.

The pace of Superfortress operations flatlined for a time, with crews distracted by weather and maintenance issues. Twentieth Bomber Command mounted only one additional mission in September, a revisit to the Showa works.

In October 1944, China-based Superfortresses struck Formosa and supported U. S. troops landing in the Philippines. On October 25, XX Bomber Command attacked the Omura aircraft factory on the Japanese main island of Kyushu. As happened all too often amid the pressures of launching a mission, a B-29 of the 468th Bombardment Group crashed on takeoff, killing all aboard.

Japanese fighters met the fifty-plus B-29s that arrived over Omura. Some of the fighters dropped air-to-air bombs and one fired air-to-air rockets. Gunners aboard the B-29s received credit for seven fighters shot down, but fighters swarmed over another B-29 and riddled it with gunfire. The Superfortress limped back to China, where the crew had to bail out. All but one survived.

The Superfortress armada was growing rapidly, but bombing missions against Japan were still occurring only infrequently. In August, September, and October 1944, the total number of missions had been two or three. In November 1944, there were five, including an ostensible milk run to Rangoon. Sadly, a mission to Singapore in November claimed the life of Col. Ted S. Faulkner, commander of the 468th Bombardment Group, and all of his crew, plus war correspondent John J. Andrew who was aboard. They were flying a B-29 named *Lethal Lady*.

The loss of *Lethal Lady* in the Bay of Bengal was puzzling, not least because Faulkner was one of the most experienced pilots in the B-29 force. An official report described an eyewitness account of the B-29 exploding in midair. Another B-29 crew reported seeing red and green flares, and yet another reported seeing a yellow life raft with either a man standing erect or a mast. No one aboard the Faulkner aircraft was ever recovered.

In manner of speaking, Faulkner had been the first American in World War II. He'd been assigned to take a B-24 Liberator to the Pacific to photograph Japanese installations in the Caroline Islands. On his way he stopped at Hickam Field in Hawaii and there his B-24 became the first American aircraft to be destroyed during the Pearl Harbor attack. Faulkner and his crew were unscathed then, but not this time.

So far, no B-29 had gotten near Tokyo.

The term F-13A applied to the photo-reconnaissance version of the Superfortress, although troops referred to it in conversation simply as a B-29. F-13As joined XX Bomber Command in November 1944 as part of the 1st Photo Reconnaissance Squadron, which operated initially from Kharagpur in India and then Hsinching in China. Early flights by the F-13A were aimed at supporting the now-ubiquitous high-altitude, precision bombing missions such as the one conducted on December 7, 1944, when LeMay launched 108 B-29s against the Manchuria aircraft factory located in the city then known by its Japanese name, Mukden, which the Chinese called Shenyang.

The saga of difficult and undramatic B-29 sorties by XX Bomber Command continued through the end of 1944 with missions to Hankow (December 18), Omura (December 21), and Shanghai (December 22). In the new year, the India- and China-based Superfortress fleet was slated to cease operations against targets on the Japanese mainland, which were far more readily accessible to XXI Bomber Command in the Marianas, then preparing to fight from Guam, Saipan, and Tinian.

Marianas Mission

By the end of October 1944, XXI Bomber Command boss Possum Hansell and 73rd Wing commander Emmett "Rosy" O'Donnell were setting up shop on Saipan. After a lengthy and indirect journey from Washington, Hansell arrived aboard the B-29 named *Joltin' Josie, the Pacific Pioneer*, piloted by Maj. Jack J. Catton.

There was considerable hoopla when the men dropped to the ground from *Josie* (named for Catton's wife). Hansell looked out at the crowd and said, "When we've done some more fighting we'll do some more talking." When he realized these were the same words Lt. Gen. Ira Eaker had uttered upon forming the Eighth Air Force in Europe, Hansell sent a cable to Eaker's headquarters to apologize. Although Hansell had not told his wife where he was going, someone had told Tokyo Rose, who broadcast a "Welcome, Possum Hansell" on Tokyo Radio.

From the start Hansell was assailed by problems that some had predicted, some had glossed over, and a few never saw coming. These included the now-familiar teething problems with the B-29 and its engines, tardy delivery of aircraft, aircrews untrained in high-altitude formation flying, primitive airfield conditions, lack of an air service command for logistical support, no repair depots, and a total absence of target intelligence thanks in part to the fact that no real photo-reconnaissance effort had yet been mounted with any success. To Hansell, high-altitude precision bombing was a religion, and he ran into stubborn internal resistance to daylight operations within the 73rd Wing. O'Donnell is thought to be among those who lobbied Arnold for Hansell's removal.

O'Donnell's wing boasted the 497th, 498th, 499th, and 500th Bomb Groups. The wing's first mission (October 28, 1944) was a fourteen-plane shakedown mission against the island of Truk, followed by five more missions flown primarily for training against soft targets not located on the Japanese home islands.

At first, Hansell and O'Donnell were in the awkward situation of having more generals than bombers on Saipan. The number of Superfortresses went up when two F-13As arrived (on October 30, 1944) on the long ferry flight from Smoky Hill, Kansas. The crews were exhausted, but that did not prevent Capt. Ralph D. Steakley from launching at 5:50 a.m. the following morning. Everyone understood the importance of preparedness for bombing missions to Tokyo, and Steakley's first full day in the Pacific turned out to be the only one in World War II when the weather over the Japanese homeland was flawless. "The air was so smooth it was like flying on glass," said an observer who watched Steakley's takeoff from Saipan.

The F-13A became the first American warplane over Tokyo since the Doolittle Raid of twenty-eight months earlier. In the brightest, clearest weather any American crew ever saw over Japan—ideal for snapping pictures from the air—Steakley arrived over Tokyo at 32,000 feet without observing any opposition. He began flying around as if he owned the place. Many Japanese looked up into the shiny sky and beheld his Superfortress with more curiosity than fear, having never seen one before. Steakley's F-13A criss-crossed Tokyo as if its crew were thumbing their noses at the emperor's defenses. Exactly why the Japanese fighter force did not take early advantage of the beautiful flying weather remains unknown. Steakley's crew, all of them over enemy soil for the first time, shot seven thousand still-photo frames of the city that was the heart of the Empire.

It was later learned that some Japanese antiaircraft batteries fired on the aircraft, but Steakley never knew it. With fuel running low and film running out, Steakley banked in a long wide circle above the Imperial Palace and turned for a flight path that would take him home to Saipan. Only then did his F-13A crew come under scrutiny from a Nakajima Ki-44 Shoki, or "Tojo" fighter, apparently piloted by Maj. Noburu Okuda, commander of the Japanese Army's 47th Air Regiment. Steakley's tail gunner put the Ki-44 in his crosshairs, but the Japanese pilot decided not to engage, perhaps because he lacked the speed to catch up with the departing Superfortress.

After fully fourteen hours aloft, a weary Steakley touched his Superfortress down at Saipan carrying a wealth of valuable photos. That day or possibly the next, he and his crew named their aircraft *Tokyo Rose* after the radio personality who broadcasted propaganda from the enemy capital. The crew received awards for the mission. Reconnaissance flights by F-13As would continue until war's end (an F-13A was lost over Nagoya on November 21, 1944). Steakley's pictorial "take" was such a treasure trove that intelligence analysts perused the negatives and photographs for many months.

Mission to Tokyo

By early November 1944, about sixty Superfortresses in the colors of the 497th and 498th BGs were ready for action on Saipan. Hansell and O'Donnell launched a mission on November 3 aimed at the Japanese-held island of Iwo Jima. It was expected to be an easy milk run and good for training. But the 73rd Wing lost its first bomber when a B-29 suffered an engine fire and other mechanical woes. Some of the crew parachuted and some ditched with the bomber, but only two were rescued. The incident was the genesis of lore among crewmembers that ditching a bomber in the Pacific almost always guaranteed death.

Thanks in part to Steakley's clear-weather photography, XXI Bomber Command plotted a mission to the Nakajima aircraft engine factory near Tokyo, known as the Musashino plant. After weather delays, the mission was mounted on November 24, 1944. Code-named "San Antonio 1," this was the first bombing mission to the Japanese capital since the Doolittle Raid, and it would be carried out by daylight, but the bombers would return after dark;

conditions at Saipan were still so primitive that they would have only smudge pots alongside the runway to light their path.

The lead B-29 was *Dauntless Dotty*, piloted by O'Donnell. The airplane commander was Maj. Robert K. Morgan, who had flown the B-17 Flying Fortress *Memphis Belle* in Europe. *Dotty* led a strike force of 111 bombers, of which 94 actually reached Tokyo. Here, crews encountered the phenomenon Americans were only beginning to learn about: furious jetstream winds roaring to speeds of up to 140 miles per hour. It would take them a long time to appreciate the effects the jetstream would have on their lives.

The winds scattered the strike force. Twenty-First Bomber Command boss Hansell insisted on tight formation, which had worked well in Europe but was not working here: more than half of O'Donnell's B-29s dropped their bombs on secondary targets. While this was going on, over a hundred Japanese fighters and moderate flak met the attackers. Gunners aboard the Superfortresses claimed seven fighters shot down.

A Kawasaki Ki-61 Hien, or "Tony" fighter, collided with a B-29 and tore off the bomber's starboard stabilizer. A second B-29 sustained hits and began trailing smoke. Both Superfortresses went down in the water, although all twelve crewmen aboard the second bomber were rescued. This would be the command's only positive experience with a ditching for weeks to come.

A tropical storm swept Saipan before the B-29s could make their after-dark return, prompting considerable apprehension in Hansell's headquarters. Wrote St. Clair McKelway, "This night, this unforgettable night, Possum and Rosy stood in the rain for twenty-five minutes in a silence that ached and groaned with agony, screamed with apprehension, and made no sound." The weather broke just in time to avert disaster, as Hansell watched the air traffic control sergeant bring each plane in "without a hint of panic."

Overall, the mission was viewed not merely as a success but as a triumph for Hansell, who could legitimately claim to be America's most important proponent and practitioner of high-altitude precision daylight bombing.

In direct retaliation for the November 24 mission to Tokyo, the Japanese air unit on Iwo Jima sent a pair of Mitsubishi G4M Betty bombers to attack Saipan accompanied by Zero fighters that strafed

Isley Field and killed at least one airman. A Zero hit by ground fire crashed into a throng of B-29 crewmembers, wounding several. One Superfortress crewmember observed that having the Japanese just 725 miles away at Iwo Jima was "a damned nuisance." In fact, the distance was a monumental challenge to the Japanese, who had to stretch their aircraft capabilities to the limit to make the trek. Iwo Jima was clearly a thorn in Hansell's side.

The B-29 force struck back with a December 3, 1944, mission to the Mitsubishi aircraft factory at Nagoya. The products of that factory, Zero fighters, engaged a B-29 called *Rosalia Rocket*, piloted by Col. Richard T. King, commander of the 500th Bombardment Group, and airplane commander Maj. Robert F. Goldsworthy. Also aboard the brass-heavy *Rosalia Rocket* was Col. Byron E. Brugge of the 73rd Wing staff.

The attack began quickly, but the downing of *Rosalia Rocket* did not happen with any haste. Goldsworthy later wrote that

> [Zeros] were everywhere, mostly making head-on attacks. The gunners on my plane were all busy and to good effect. I saw one Jap plane explode from direct hits. Another went down trailing smoke. Others appeared to suffer varying degrees of damage. But we were taking a terrific beating. Three of our engines were shot out and the communication system, too. All control cables with the exception of one aileron were inoperative. One wing was burning and the front compartment was in flames.

With fire loose in the fuselage and the B-29 disintegrating, Goldsworthy tried to save bombardier 1st Lt. Walter J. "Pat" Patykula by dragging him to an escape hatch and pushing him out into the airstream. "I saw Pat's chute open, turn brown, and burst into flame. A fine boy, a grand friend, and one of the best bombardiers in the Air Force," Goldsworthy said.

Rosalia Rocket and her crew struggled for thirty minutes trying to get to safety. Twelve crewmen were aboard. Three died when the aircraft finally succumbed to the fighter attacks and battle damage. Three others were severely wounded and died the next day. Three including Brugge died subsequently while captives of the Japanese. The remaining three, including King and Goldsworthy, became prisoners and survived the war. In one of so many horror stories in a horrible war, the Kempei Tai, Japan's security service, interrogated Brugge—one of the highest-ranking B-29 men to be captured—for fully three months before he died as a result of beatings. Back on Guam, Saipan, and Tinian, no one knew about Brugge's private hell, but every one of the thousand kids knew what was possible. All were struggling to make the B-29 more effective and none ever lacked for good reason or firm resolve.

CHAPTER 9

Squabbling

*The B-29 Superfortress in the Campaign against
Japan, December 4–December 31, 1944*

POSSUM HANSELL, IN COMMAND OF XXI Bomber
Command (meaning all B-29 Superfortresses in the Marianas),
was feeling the pain. Back in Washington, AAF boss Hap Arnold
had reminded Hansell that a B-29 set back the American taxpayer
$605,000, or enough to purchase three B-17 Flying Fortresses.
The B-29 had to be viewed differently from other warplanes that
routinely fell from the sky in the heat of battle, Arnold cautioned.
"We must consider the B-29 more in terms of a naval vessel, and
we do not lose naval vessels in threes and fours without a very
thorough analysis of the causes," Arnold wrote. Hansell was not, in
fact, losing a huge number of planes—just nine on the first three big
missions over Japan—but he was also not being effective. Hansell
was not, in truth, a poor leader, but he was at the beginning of a
kind of warfare that no one had undertaken before; it was all new,
and Hansell was by nature impatient. He was frustrated with his
aircraft, his engines, his equipment, and his men. He wondered if

Arnold was hinting that his own—Hansell's—future was at risk unless something improved.

Aware of Arnold's impatience, Arnold's deputy Lt. Gen. Barney Giles, who was doubtful that Hansell could accomplish the task given him—setting up an air campaign in a brief period using a prematurely operational and trouble-prone aircraft—obtained a commitment from Arnold that he would not relieve Hansell in only a few months "because he is going to be involved in deals out there, getting stuff started, opening bases, and getting the bombs, the ammunition, the crews all trained."

Hansell had come to the Marianas from duty as Arnold's chief of staff and had helped frame the early American argument, contrary to the policy of the British, against bombing cities in favor of precision attacks. However Hansell's tenure was threatened from the start because his replacement on the air staff, Maj. Gen. Lauris "Larry" Norstad, was by now no longer a supporter of daylight precision bombing, instead advocating massive destruction of Japanese cities by firebombing, a tactic that had been promoted within the Pentagon for more than a year.

It didn't matter that Norstad and Hansell and their wives had been extremely close before the war and had played cards and socialized frequently. Norstad believed in the incendiary and Hansell used it only reluctantly in small numbers, repeatedly and forcefully telling anyone who would listen that he considered firebombing repugnant and militarily unneccesssary. To Hansell, using fire as a weapon meant targeting civilians, an abhorrent departure from striking military and industrial facilities.

Hansell's busy, serious work ethic also placed him in conflict with others. Lieutenant General Millard Harmon, the senior AAF officer in the Pacific region under Adm. Chester Nimitz, made repeated efforts to insert himself into the chain of command, even though the B-29 force did not belong to Nimitz. In fact, it was Hansell, in his former job as chief of staff to Arnold, who had recommended the arrangement actually adopted, with the Twentieth Air Force directly under Arnold in Washington. In an extraordinary coup, Hansell had even sold the idea to chief of naval operations Adm. Ernest J. King, despite King's vocal distaste for strategic bombing and for the now-ending Operation Matterhorn in particular.

Hansell would never have similar success with Nimitz, with whom he met in Hawaii while en route to the Marianas. Nimitz despised a command arrangement that required him to provide logistics but gave him no say over operations. Nimitz warned Hansell that the naval commander in the forward area, Vice Adm. John Hoover, "breaks my admirals and throws them overboard without the slightest compunction. God knows what he will do to you." Hansell later wrote:

> Under General Harmon was another senior Army Air Forces officer, Maj. Gen. Willis H. Hale, who commanded our land-based air forces in the Forward Area. Whereas my relationship with General Harmon had been tolerably agreeable, if somewhat formal, that with Willis Hale deteriorated after a confrontation on Saipan. When the second air base built for the 73rd Wing of the Twenty-First Bomber Command on Saipan proved technically unsuitable for B-29 operations, I based the entire wing at Isley Field, Saipan. I agreed to turn the other base over to General Hale's units since it was suitable for operations by other types of aircraft. When I arrived on Saipan with the first B-29, I found a half-completed base and over a hundred of General Hale's airplanes on Isley Field. Several times I requested Hale to clear the field for my impending operations. He agreed to do so but failed to move his planes. Finally, in desperation, I forced a showdown; the situation had become intolerable and threatened to prevent our first strike. [Nimitz's staff] offered to clear up the matter with a direct order to General Hale. But I thought it would be better if two air officers settled their problem between them. Hale moved his aircraft, then went straight back to Washington to complain to General Arnold about my arrogant attitude. General Arnold backed me up, but I suspect the incident did me no good.

Nor did Hansell have good relations with 73rd Wing commander Rosy O'Donnell, who could be insubordinate at times and who never hesitated to repeat his view that B-29s should be bombing Japan at night. O'Donnell was a very popular commander and a brave leader and would have helped Hansell if they had seen eye to eye. When O'Donnell found it necessary in early December 1944 to hold a meeting of all his key officers, he invited Hansell to sit in. O'Donnell then stood before an assembly of pilots, navigators, bombardiers, and staff officers and, true to his nickname, described a rosy picture of the way the bombing campaign was going. O'Donnell, who had once proposed stripping B-29s of armament and attacking Japan during the nocturnal hours, now gave an optimistic assessment of the way fully armed Superfortresses were carrying out their bombings in daylight. O'Donnell said nothing about the ongoing mechanical problems with the B-29 and its R-3350 engines. He praised his men and told them the situation would improve as more aircraft and crews arrived, and more experience was gained.

Hansell lost it. He simply could not believe that Rosy was delivering a rah-rah speech. As reported by Barrett Tillman and in an official history, Hansell stood before the group and unloaded.

"I am in sharp disagreement because in my opinion you people haven't earned your pay over here," Hansell said. "Unless you do better, this operation is doomed to failure."

Hansell was tired of saying there was still much to learn. He wanted things to improve now. He openly contradicted his wing commander and made it plain to everyone in the room that he was displeased with just about everything, including O'Donnell.

Martin Caidin described Hansell's reporting about his problems, all of which were now increasingly familiar but none of which was amenable to any easy solution. Wrote Caidin:

[Hansell] had been driving his crews relentlessly. The excessive aborts and appalling losses at sea stemmed not from any faults of weakness in the men, Hansell stressed, but from inadequate maintenance and depot facilities. There were other factors to consider—factors that extended the life of the Japanese targets and gave Japan a lease on combat and industrial strength they never realized was being afforded them. The fierce resistance on Saipan had delayed the entire B-29 campaign. But worst of all was the absolutely wretched and unexpected weather that crippled many strikes. So entangled was the logistical system and the manpower shortage that the planned buildup in the strength of the raids could not be achieved. The installations on Saipan, to say nothing of those expected on Tinian and Guam, were far behind original construction schedules.

At the start of December, Hansell's command began launching small-scale weather-strike missions. One of these was to precede each major bombing mission, usually by twenty-four hours so experts would have time to analyze the intelligence but would finish the job before the weather changed. On these missions, B-29 crews were tasked as their first priority to gather information on cloud cover, temperatures, and barometric information, but they were also sent to drop bombs, typically incendiaries. On one such mission, Robert Morgan of *Dauntless Dotty* and *Memphis Belle* fame looked down and saw Tokyo lit up all over—"just like flying over New York," he said. For the rest of the war, Tokyo's streetlights would be on at odd times and off at others.

Building upon the bedrock of intelligence gathered earlier by the F-13A named *Tokyo Rose*, these bomber crews brought home a wealth of knowledge. But throughout December, the weather foiled several attempts to fly weather-strike missions.

Bombing Iwo

On December 7, 1944, the third anniversary of the Pearl Harbor attack, Japanese warplanes from Iwo Jima did a repeat of an earlier raid by strafing and bombing Isley Field on Saipan. Although antiaircraft gunners laid claim to six Japanese aircraft destroyed, the attack destroyed three B-29s and damaged many more. On December 8, Superfortresses went in the opposite direction and bombed Iwo Jima, the "nuisance" island that was causing so many problems for Hansell and his men, hoping to neutralize the Japanese air threat in the region.

On December 13, 1944, Hansell launched his most ambitious attack on the Japanese home islands yet, sending ninety-one Superfortresses against the Mitsubishi aircraft factory at Nagoya. In official circles, this was viewed as support for the Mindoro invasion in the Philippines scheduled for two days later, even if the B-29s were heading in the opposite direction. There had been some discussion of a more direct use of B-29s to support the invasion, but every time such an idea came up, every air general from Arnold on down opposed any attempt to transform the B-29 into a tactical weapon.

The Nagoya strike was another high-altitude, daylight, precision-bombing mission. By now, the air staff in Washington was talking about Hansell's lack of success with daylight precision bombing and debating wholesale destruction of Japanese cities with firebombs, a weapon that had held support in planning circles for more than two years.

Hansell's Superfortresses bored through mushy weather and into hurricane-force headwinds. Most of the B-29s carried conventional, 500-pound bombs, but some were hauling incendiary cluster bombs. Hansell had ordered the incendiaries loaded aboard the bombers only after objecting in a cable to Norstad and receiving a reply, written by Norstad in Arnold's name, overruling him. The United States had been developing firebombs since the earliest days of the war, well aware that Japan was a nation of buildings made of wood and paper. Incendiaries were deemed useful against a facility like the one in Nagoya, where fuels and chemicals were stored in an industrial setting.

On this trip to Nagoya, four B-29s were damaged badly enough that they needed to ditch. The 500th Bombardment Group suffered its first casualty on this mission even before reaching Japan. While still about a hundred miles from the coast and climbing toward a bombing altitude of 28,500 feet, the left blister in a Superfortress named *Mustn't Touch* blew out, taking the left blister gunner, Sgt. August Renner, and his gunsight with it. His loss became something of a legend among B-29 gunners, who knew that a simple harness would have prevented Renner from flying like a cork out of a bottle into the void. One of those gunners was Sgt. James Krantz on Saipan, who resolved that what happened to Renner wouldn't happen to him.

Renner tumbled as he fell. His parachute was seen to open about two thousand feet below the formation, but he was never found. Back on the plane, the explosive depressurization caused a four-foot metal ladder stowed in the forward part of the tunnel to shoot toward the rear. Fortunately for the central fire control gunner, Sgt. Bill Agee, the ladder caught on some padding around the rear end of the tunnel; otherwise it would have struck him at about knee level. A bitterly cold wind whistled through the gunner's compartment, nearly freezing Agee and right blister gunner Robert Schurmann. A less determined pilot might have aborted, but Capt. Robert McClanahan decided to complete the mission—and so the crew did, shivering all the way. Schurmann later discovered that the water in his canteen had frozen solid.

Lost on the Nagoya mission was a bomber called *Tokyo Local*. After turning away from the target, she dropped out of formation with one engine windmilling and another belching smoke. *Tokyo Local* made it across a wide swath of Japanese soil and ditched at sea, but Capt. Charles Grise and his crew were never seen again. As a result, the perils associated with a ditching gained new strength in men's minds.

The Arnold Crew

That first Nagoya mission was a horror for radio operator Staff Sgt. Barthold of the 497th Bombardment Group's 870th Bombardment Squadron, who remembers being in the soup most of the way to the target but eventually breaking into clear sky. His B-29 Superfortress, *Texas Doll*, ran into headwinds blowing at 130 miles per hour while the aircraft was showing an indicated air speed of 200 miles per hour. "From the initial point to the target, it took eleven minutes for the bomber to travel thirteen miles," said Barthold. It may have seemed for a time that the B-29 would never get there but would, instead, be forced by the winds to stand virtually stationary in the air. Everything seemed to take forever. It was perhaps appropriate that where the pilot's name was stenciled on the side of the fuselage beneath his window, the inscription read "PILOT: CAPT. (FOREVER) J. C. ARNOLD," a reference to Carter Arnold, who did not expect ever to be promoted—although, eventually, he was. Barthold had not yet shifted to another crew led by Capt. James M. Campbell.

Barthold was the compact Missouri-born radioman who lived in a Quonset hut labeled The Exclusive Elite. On the interphone, Barthold heard a gunner saying, "Hey, they're taking off down there." The B-29 was moving so slowly relative to the ground that Japanese fighters easily reached the bomber's 31,000-foot altitude, surrounded it, and opened fire. Some of the Japanese pilots attacked from a few degrees to the right front of the B-29. Some were good enough to perform a difficult frontal attack from a few degrees above the centerline of the B-29 as it rushed toward them. They were in the position the Americans called twelve o'clock high.

A 20mm shell from a Japanese fighter exploded in the nose of the Superfortress, where bombardier 2nd Lt. James D. "Dave" Holloman sat. Barthold felt the impact when that single shell exploded against the Superfortress's rounded nose and sprayed the bombardier, pilot, and copilot with glass and metal fragments. The aircraft decompressed. Abruptly, it was colder than Barthold had ever been aboard an airplane, as the air rushed out of the fuselage through the open nose. A voice boomed in Barthold's earphones, apparently pilot Arnold: "Radio, we need you!"

"I got myself in gear," Barthold said. "I grabbed a first aid kit and a walk-around oxygen bottle. I grabbed his collar and moved him to where I could try to help."

The bombardier lay on the floorboards. He was motionless between and behind the two pilots and directly in the path of the frigid windblast from the shattered nose. Barthold was the crewmember trained as a medic and issued first aid equipment and "some very long, sharp needles for injections." Now, the bombardier appeared to be unconscious and Barthold saw no blood. Barthold attached the bombardier's oxygen mask, gave him plasma via an intravenous feed, and worked on him for ten minutes, struggling on the floorboards of the B-29 with the wind blasting into his face while the pilots fought to control the bomber.

Feeling around, looking, touching, Barthold discovered that Holloman had an almost imperceptible nick on his neck. While *Texas Doll* struggled home to Saipan, her pilots battling windblast from the nose, it became obvious that Holloman had died the moment Barthold reached him. In a diary he kept on an Army-issue tablet marked with the warning "Do not write anything of military activities," Barthold that evening wrote:

We were flying #3 ship of a 3 plane formation and had 14 Tojos and Nicks attack us from out of the sun at 11 o'clock. A 20-mm got Dave Holloman, the bombardier, and he died with 15 seconds as the jugular vein was severed. The plane was shot up. The nose was a mess. Simon, the tail gunner was wounded. The rudder was badly damaged. So was the right elevator and left aileron. The bomb bays, too, had some holes along with the horizontal stabilizers. We had only the magnetic compass to get back home on. We made Saipan, thank heaven. I took sleeping powder for the first time in my life. Simon is okay but *Texas Doll* is in the plane hospital for some time.

Many dozens of crewmembers on Saipan participated in a memorial service for Holloman. Among them was a newly arrived airplane commander, 1st Lt. Edward W. Cutler, who would take over *Texas Doll* with a new crew. Cutler was a third-generation alumnus of West Point (of the class of June 1943, the only year in its history in which the U.S. Military Academy graduated two classes). Cutler wrote, "The entire nose of the *Texas Doll* had to be replaced and the original crew was broken up and never flew the *Doll* again."

Early in their acquaintance, Barthold said to Cutler, "Your grandfather went to West Point. Your father went to West Point. You went to West Point. I'm a civilian. I was a civilian before the war. I'm a civilian now. I'll be a civilian after the war." Barthold, of course, was exactly that—a specimen of a citizen army fielded by a nation that went to war only reluctantly and only with the force and commitment of its entire population. Not until a new century would the United States rely instead on a professional armed force.

"You know what?" Cutler replied. "We'll get along."

Breaking up a crew after a member was killed on board was apparently a standard practice. Barthold was surprised that he was able to keep his aplomb in the aftermath of this horrific, close-up loss of a crewmate. Barthold wanted payback, and in his mind Tokyo would be the place for that. He was assigned to a new crew and continued his war.

The Tucker Crew

Not every B-29 crewmember destined to participate in the great Tokyo firebomb mission had yet reached the Marianas. While Hansell was grappling with command, his crews were struggling, and the air staff was squabbling. Norstad, despite being an old friend of Hansell's, was becoming increasingly animated in his arguments with supporters of the B-29 commander, especially Arnold's immediate deputy, Giles. Many of the men who would fly the great Tokyo firebomb mission were still getting ready stateside.

On December 14, 1944, flight engineer-pilot Laddie Wale and others in the crew led by Percy Usher Tucker were at Borinquen Field, Puerto Rico, following a long-distance training flight from their home base in Grand Island, Nebraska. As was routine on a long-distance round trip, their B-29 was equipped with an extra fuel tank in its bomb bay. Similar in appearance to the oval-shaped, long and thin oil tank in a home heating system, the 610- to 640-gallon tank was supposed to be attached by shackles to racks designed for 500-pound bombs. A Superfortress could carry two of these tanks in each bay for a total of four, although only one was in place on this day.

Tucker was at the controls taking the Superfortress home to Nebraska during the nocturnal hours when the Superfortress entered turbulence and began shaking. This, too, was routine. Not routine, however was the sharp clanging sound in Wale's ears when the tank broke loose from one of its shackles, remained affixed to the other, and slammed against the closed bomb bay doors.

Had the tank fallen loose completely, its weight would have taken it through the bomb bay doors. As Wale remembered, "The bomb doors don't have enough tension to stay closed if the auxiliary tank fell on them. A man's weight could open them. But this was a partial breakaway and the tank was only partly loose in our rear bay."

"We don't have enough fuel now to get back to Grand Island," Tucker told the crew. Among those aboard the B-29 that day, memories differ as to whether Tucker declared an in-flight emergency. Before engineer Wale could chip in and say exactly the same thing, Tucker told the crew that the nearest airport that could possibly handle a B-29 was located in Nashville, Tennessee. It was at that time a rather small commercial airport. The site of the present-day Nashville International Airport was then known as Berry Field in honor of Col. Harry S. Berry, state administrator of the Works Projects Administration. Tucker probably knew that the airport was now a military base, taken over by 4th Ferrying Command. The length of its longest runway was six thousand feet. It was not deemed absolutely impossible to halt a B-29 in that space, but it was a challenge, to say the least.

Staff Sgt. Joe Majeski, the tail gunner on the Tucker crew, recalled what happened next. "Captain Tucker had a very slow and deliberate way of speaking. He used very few words. I switched the frequency on the interphone and listened to him calling the tower. He gave the usual identification and requested an emergency landing. A female voice asked, 'What type of aircraft are you flying?' Tucker replied that our aircraft was a B-29.

"A screaming female voice said, 'If you're a B-29, you can't land here!' Tucker in his usual slow and deliberate calm way said, 'Lady we are coming in anyway.'"

Tucker, Wale, Majeski, and others worried that the jolt upon hitting the runway and the weight of the bomb bay tank might force the bomb bay doors open. Bombardier Joe Krogman, the grin-and-cuss all-American type from Remsen, Iowa, was, of course, farthest to the front of the fuselage, so he uttered something about the nose of the aircraft being smashed.

This did not happen. Upon reaching the airport, the B-29 settled smoothly at runway's end, bounced once, used almost every inch of pavement, and came to a halt.

"This happened about 3:00 a.m.," said Majeski. "Later that morning hundreds of people thronged the airport to get a look at a B-29. We were treated like celebrities." Using George Wale's Argus camera, Wale and Majeski took turns standing on the forty-three-foot horizontal stabilizer of the big bomber, each capturing a portrait of the other peering with mock aloofness out into the distance. Years later, Wale would remember incorrectly that the photos were taken before departing Puerto Rico, but he would never forget how the men needed to unwind in Nashville. "The truth is," Wale said, "the situation we'd experienced with the tank frightened us more after it was over, and we were all a little nervous."

With Tucker and Wale overseeing the effort, the crew reinstalled the troublesome fuel tank. Word was spread around the airport that the great new bomber seen in Nashville for the first time would soon be taking off. Said Majeski,

> Finally after some makeshift repairs and refueling we were ready to take off. Lining both sides of that short (for a B-29) runway were fire apparatus of all types. There were hundreds of people all around the airport. It was quite a spectacle.

We taxied off of the runway onto the grass near the airport fence. With the brakes on hold, the engines were revved up so that the plane was shaking. Finally, with the brakes released, we started the takeoff roll.

A grove of trees was located at the end of the runway and we cleared them (or so we thought). Everyone up forward held their breath because of the trees looming directly ahead. I was in the tail during takeoff and I think I could have reached down and taken hold of a branch.

When the B-29 finally arrived at Grand Island, Tucker was told to circle because of plows clearing snow from the runways. After landing, the men looked at the landing gear of the B-29 and were amazed to find tree branches sticking out. As Majeski noted, "A few feet lower and we might have been history."

Arnold and Hansell

It is unclear whether and to what extent Hansell was briefed on the stateside activities of Groves, Oppenheimer, and the others in the Manhattan Project. At some point Arnold sent Hansell a message forbidding him from flying on combat missions; knowledge of the Manhattan Project may have been the reason, but the record is uncertain and some historians say Hansell never knew. In any event, Hansell and the burgeoning population of Americans on Saipan, Tinian, and Guam had plenty to think about without contemplating the cool, parched salt flats near Wendover, Utah.

There, on December 17, 1944—a date some may have recognized as the forty-first anniversary of Orville Wright's first powered flight—Paul Tibbets formed the 509th Composite Group. Tibbets had been told verbally "organize and command a combat group to develop the means of delivering an atomic weapon by airplane against targets in Germany and Japan." In addition to a flying squadron of B-29 Superfortresses specially built in Omaha by the Glenn L. Martin Company and known as Silverplate airplanes, Tibbets's outfit had a flying squadron of C-54 Skymaster four-engined transports to make it as nearly self-sustaining as possible, so it was given a "composite" rather than "bombardment" appellation.

Tibbets was a pilot and a commander, not a scientist. "I will go only so far as to say that I knew what an atom was," he later told St. Clair McKelway. Tibbets began operations at Wendover accompanied on his assignment by his wife Lucy Wingate, to whom he was forced to lie, saying that all of the nuclear physicists running around were "sanitary engineers"—but he was already thinking of a way to honor his mother, Enola Gay Haggard.

Christmas Bombing

The heavy bombers went to Nagoya again on December 18, 1944, encountered heavy cloud cover, and bombed by radar. This time Japanese fighters engaged the attack force, which consisted of sixty-three Superfortresses out of eighty-nine launched. The Japanese shot down one B-29 over the target. Two more ditched and one crashed on arrival at Saipan. The crew of the crashed aircraft walked away from the mishap.

A December 22, 1944, return trip to Nagoya was a tough mission for the increasingly frustrated Hansell and his men. They were beginning to use firebombs now, but they were scattering them too widely when dropping from high altitude. The December 22 mission spread incendiary bombs by radar through solid cloud undercast. The target—once again, the Mitsubishi aircraft factory—experienced some disruption in its daily activity but suffered little real damage.

On December 24, 1944, Hansell sent Superfortresses to bomb Iwo Jima for the second time in the month. The B-29s hammered the airfields on Iwo that might otherwise launch raids against the B-29 force. This was a monumental distraction that Hansell disliked but found necessary. Throughout the history of the B-29 effort, every general in charge had tried to preserve the B-29 as a kind of silver bullet—a long-range asset to be used directly against the Japanese home islands and not to improve a tactical situation, support naval forces, or support an amphibious invasion.

The Japanese retaliated on Christmas Day with strikes on Saipan from Iwo Jima by two dozen Japanese aircraft. It was the last time Iwo-based warplanes struck the B-29 force successfully.

As 1944 ended, O'Donnell's 73rd Wing on Saipan was becoming a seasoned outfit and learning plenty of lessons, with the powerful impact of the jetstream winds over Japan always at the top of the list. The B-29s returned to Tokyo on December 27 for their final mission of the year. Only thirty-nine of the seventy-two bombers dispatched actually reached the primary target. The B-29 crews encountered moderate antiaircraft fire and persistent attacks by Japanese Tony fighters.

One of the fighters made a head-on attack on a B-29 named *Uncle Tom's Cabin* while the bomber was just a minute from bomb release at the vanguard of a formation of nine Superfortresses. With short bursts of gunfire, the Tony blew off part of the central fire control gunner's blister. Then, the Tony's wing ripped open the side of the bomber from nose to wing, creating a huge cavity that emitted smoke and flames.

Uncle Tom's Cabin remained in formation briefly with pieces of equipment pouring out of the hole on its side. The bomber then began to fall from the formation, hounded by additional Tony fighters including one that rammed the bomber on its starboard side. Yet even after a third Tony rammed this B-29, the bomber was still airborne. Several minutes elapsed before *Uncle Tom's Cabin* plunged straight down and hit the ground, leaving a rising plume of smoke in its wake. There were no parachutes.

Another bomber on that final 1944 mission had to ditch while attempting to return to Saipan. Again, the crew was lost, and again the news rippled through the ranks.

Later in December, Hansell lost it again, so to speak. He issued a statement that said, among other things, "We have not put all our bombs exactly where we wanted to put them, and therefore we are not by any means satisfied with what we have done so far. We are still in our early, experimental stages." His three principal targets in December had been hit hard but "not destroyed by a damn sight," Hansell said. By this time, the eloquent St. Clair McKelway was Hansell's public affairs officer, and McKelway should have known better, but the statement was pure Hansell, who never liked to sugarcoat anything and was merely uttering the truth. Hansell's statement directly contradicted a press release from Curt LeMay, which had proclaimed, "the experimental phase of B-29 operations is over."

On December 31, Hansell moved his headquarters from Saipan to Guam and took receipt of a cable from Arnold praising him. "You have brought to a great many Japanese the realization of what this war holds for them," Arnold wrote. What the cable didn't say was that Arnold—more seriously ill than ever, always short-tempered, and unhappy over the blunt honesty of Hansell's reports from the field—was now furious at Hansell over his latest statement. In response, Arnold began a series of steps that would send Larry Norstad on a journey to the Pacific.

CHAPTER 10

To the Target

Mission to Tokyo
March 9, 1945, 11:50 p.m.–March 10, 1945, 2:00 a.m.

HOURS PASSED. THE DARK SEA rushed beneath the B-29s. Tokyo drew nearer. On Guam, many on Curt LeMay's staff caught up on their sleep with the general's permission. LeMay usually had no difficulty sleeping, but tonight he was wired up. He would not know until the main force began to bomb Tokyo two hours after midnight whether his shift in tactics was a brilliant stroke or a death warrant. LeMay always looked grim because of a condition called Bell's palsy, which paralyzed facial muscles near his mouth and made it almost impossible for him to smile. Tonight his bluntness, his ability to intimidate physically and intellectually, and his grimness seemed to have been washed away. LeMay's face was both blank and expectant, like a small boy anticipating a long-sought gift.

The general in command of thousands of bomber crewmembers was alone in his Quonset headquarters but for St. Clair McKelway, the public relations officer who had become a confidante and who'd been told to wait to hear the "bombs away" message expected in early morning. LeMay and McKelway exchanged small talk. Neither was good at it. Both felt the tension as they awaited news from Tommy Power, at the cutting edge of the attack force.

While they waited, the Quonset flooded with electric light all around them in the night, LeMay mentioned his wife and child back in Cleveland. This was out of character. McKelway later wrote that LeMay had no life, "beyond games of medicine ball to keep fat off a body that tends toward fat, games of poker to relax as best he can a mind that actually never stops thinking about how to do the job better the next day, and a little reading, mostly fairly serious, to improve a mind he considers inadequate."

With midnight approaching and the first pathfinders due over the Japanese capital within a half hour, a curious kind of loneliness bonded McKelway and LeMay. They seemed, finally, to run out of small talk in the brightly lit room covered with charts, maps, graphs, and mission-control boards. For a split-second, McKelway sensed it was as if there was no difference in rank between them. "We won't get a bombs-away for another half hour," LeMay said, looking at his watch. "Would you like a Coca-Cola? I can sneak in my quarters without waking up the other guys and get two Coca-Colas and we can drink them in my car. That'll kill most of the half hour."

They drove the hundred yards to LeMay's tent in his staff car and he sneaked in and got the sodas. "We sat in the dark, facing the jungle that surrounds the headquarters and grows thickest between the edge of our clearing and the sea," McKelway wrote—two men, no rank between them now, pulling on the six-ounce Coca-Colas and knowing that within a very short time the thousand kids would be arriving over the Empire. *It was 11:50 p.m. Chamorro Standard Time, March 9, 1945.*

The Bertagnoli Crew

For navigator George Edwin Albritton of the 9th Bombardment Group, flying with the George "Bert" Bertagnoli crew, nothing seemed to be going right. As far as Bertagnoli knew, everybody else was in the same situation as himself and the men aboard *Queen Bee*. Bertagnoli imagined hundreds of Superfortresses flying individually rather than in formation and scattered, now, all over the map. The weather was not remarkable over the intended target tonight—it was clear and windy, just as LeMay had wanted—but on the flanks of the approach route, threatening weather fronts loomed everywhere. Even in darkness with a quarter moon and the ocean surface playing tricks on the eye, the storm clouds were thick and angry—just like the unspoken tension between Albritton and the regularly assigned navigator on Bertagnoli's B-29. Albritton explained the situation:

> About the time we should have reached the coast of Japan and begun picking it up on radar, we were in a terrible storm and the radar would not function due to the storm clouds.
>
> We flew on for some time in the storm and tried flying as wingman on another B-29 in the storm. He banked away and left us so we kept on a northwest course for quite some time. About 30 minutes after our estimated time of arrival had elapsed, the clouds cleared enough so that we could see Polaris, which is the North Star. You can measure the elevation of it and with the small correction obtain your latitude which is the distance north of the equator. After this calculation, I notified the airplane commander that we were 60 miles north of Tokyo, and that we had to be northeast for if we were northwest, we would have flown into Mt. Fuji which is northwest of Tokyo and about 13,000 feet high about 20 minutes ago. We were at 5,500 feet.

Airplane commander Bertagnoli ordered the crew to strap on oxygen masks. He increased power and began a climb that would take him to 14,000 feet. He headed southeast. "We began shooting and plotting more celestial fixes," said Albritton. "After three such fixes, we determined that we were about 175 miles southeast of Tokyo."

The dilemma: Would their fuel supply permit the Bertagnoli crew to belatedly change course for Tokyo and drop their bombs? Or would proceeding to the target jeopardize the crew and airplane and force them to ditch in the ocean short of their Tinian base? "We had been in the air a long time during the high fuel consumption phase of the mission," said Albritton. "The airplane commander asked me what I thought we should do. Everyone had been deeply concerned about this mission and that we would be sitting ducks for the antiaircraft guns going in at [low altitude]. If we didn't make it to the target, would our decision be questioned? Would we lose a valuable B-29 and maybe crewmembers if we ran out of fuel and had to ditch in the ocean?"

For the first time that night, *Queen Bee* was no longer lost. The crew would be able to return to base if they got on course for Tinian now. The flight engineer told Albritton there was not enough fuel to continue to Tokyo and then make it back to Tinian. Albritton got on the interphone to Bertagnoli: "If we jettison the bombs and return to base, we can always come back on other missions."

Another of LeMay's fears was that too many of the B-29s, prone to engine fires and jammed fuel lines and radar malfunctions, would be forced to abandon their journey toward the target. Even if you traveled 90 percent of the way to the target, once you turned around for home it was an abort; it didn't count as a mission for the crew and it didn't place any bombs on their objective. If enough B-29s aborted, the Japanese wouldn't need flak or fighters.

The Bertagnoli crew did exactly that. Discretion, not valor, became the virtue of the moment as *Queen Bee* made a wide turn in the nocturnal sky and pointed its nose away from Japan and toward the Marianas. Bertagnoli, Albritton, and the others were aborting and heading home. *It was 11:55 p.m. Chamorro Standard Time, Friday March 9, 1945.*

The Fling Crew

On Guam, LeMay and McKelway awaited news, first at their hideaway in the general's Jeep and later in the command's corrugated tin operations building. Bud McDonald, the B-29 pilot who was newly arrived on Guam and hadn't yet flown a combat mission, walked around a bit after watching the bombers take off, watched night descend over his island, and headed for his Quonset. While the bombers were still trying to find their way to Japan, McDonald had no reason to be awake. Days away from his own baptism of fire, McDonald crawled into his cot while B-29s bored toward Japan.

The Dean Fling crew was out there in the night, hugging the dark Pacific, the Japanese home islands approaching. Fling in the left front seat was listening to his navigator and engineer on the interphone and glancing back and forth at Harold L. "Pete"

Peterson in the right seat. Fling was from Windsor, Illinois, and was apparently not as devout as Peterson. In the night, no one could see the garish emblem painted on the nose of the bomber: a giant bluish purple shield enclosing a Christian cross bisected by a wide-bladed sword.

On their first mission, one of those wasteful expeditions to Truk where crews traversed vast distances and achieved little, the B-29 lost an engine and had to turn back and descend to wave-cap altitude. Describing the Truk experience, left blister gunner Reb Carter used very sparse prose to describe what he considered a life-or-death crisis: "Our ship turned back due to the loss of the no. 1 engine. We were only 150 feet above the water and came very close to ditching. To stay in the air, we threw out the ammunition and dropped the bombs and were ready to throw out other equipment."

When the bombload was jettisoned, a bomb jammed on its shackles in the bay at the instant of release. The ground crew had installed the bomb in an incorrect position. Three bombs above it didn't jam, came loose as they were supposed to, and struck it with a resounding clank.

"The navigator felt it when the first bomb from above hit the stuck bomb," wrote Carter. "There was nothing he could do since the switches had been thrown and he was too scared to say a word anyway. He said that in those long seconds he almost died of a heat attack."

The stuck bomb didn't explode; the impact shook it loose. All of the bombs departed the bay and fell. If the bombs had detonated, they would have splattered bits and pieces of the aircraft for miles and killed everyone on board. "I don't know what will happen to the guys that loaded the bomb incorrectly," wrote Carter, "but I think they will be dealt with severely."

Peterson's voice was the one on the interphone. "Those bombs didn't go off," said the devout Peterson. "It's God's will."

That day, aborting its travel to Truk, the crew had a new name for its new aircraft: *God's Will.*

Even if Carter didn't know it and Peterson wouldn't admit it, bombardier 1st Lt. Don "Red" Dwyer, a New Jersey boy with a touch of the prankster and a more subdued kind of devoutness, knew that God had been given a little help. Each bomb fuse was attached to a tiny propeller that was wired to the shackle. Releasing a bomb broke the wire. When a bomb encountered the airstream, the propeller would turn. After the bomb had fallen two hundred feet, the propeller unscrewed itself from the bomb and the fuse became live. Dwyer knew the stuck bomb wouldn't detonate inside the bay even if you banged on it with a sledgehammer.

What Dwyer didn't know was that the very devout Peterson had been planning the name for the Superfortress for months, going back to the crew's stateside training. Now on the night of the great Tokyo firebomb mission, *God's Will* was boring over the ocean and both midnight and the coast of Japan were drawing close.

Dwyer used his bombsight to give the navigator drift readings. He took off his headset and chatted with pilots Fling and Peterson. One thing about the B-29: it wasn't unduly noisy on the flight deck. "We talked a lot of shoptalk," said Dwyer, but the men were tense, no doubt about it.

Reb Carter acted as a scanner early in the flight, keeping his eyes on the number one and number two engines ready to utter a warning if a mechanical problem revealed itself. On this mission, Carter had no guns to prep and no ammunition to load. Some crews had left their gunners at home, but not Fling's. Some crews had brought both gunners and guns, but not Fling's. Carter was unarmed and had few tasks to perform while his best friend, Bake Baker, the radar operator, was unable to find Iwo Jima on his six-inch scope.

Navigator 1st Lt. Phillip Pettit had a radar screen identical to Baker's that wasn't working either, since the crystal in the radar transmitter that powered both screens was malfunctioning. For practical purposes, that meant the radar screen went blank. In reality, the only thing Baker or Pettit could see was the illuminated lubber line as it swept around the scope like a second hand sweeping around the dial of a clock. Nothing else was visible.

Pettit struggled to make everything right, but Baker felt helpless. Pettit was the navigator who'd been assigned to this crew when Samuel N. Slater, who'd almost made the Doolittle Raid, was tapped for another Superfortress crew in the same squadron. Pettit was more junior and less mature but was universally respected among the crew. Always a little rummaged, he was the poster child for an old piece of Air Corps doggerel:

> *You can always tell a gunner by his greasy hands and vacant stare*
> *You can always tell a bombardier by his manners debonair*
> *You can always tell a navigator by his pencils, books, and such*
> *You can always tell a pilot—but you cannot tell him much.*

"We had something to fall back on," said Baker. "We had an excellent navigator in Pettit. In addition to our navigator, both pilots and the bombardier had some navigation training. But I was not in any position to help. I didn't have an air speed indicator. I didn't have anything on my scope. I was completely blind."

The situation aboard *God's Will*, commanded by Fling tonight but destined to become Bertagnoli's plane in the weeks ahead, was strikingly similar to the situation aboard *Queen Bee*, Bertagnoli's plane on tonight's Tokyo mission. But while Bertagnoli was said to be flustered and fussing, Fling was stable and calm. Fling was not the silent type (not like the restrained Tucker of *Lady Annabelle*), but he was not one to express displeasure in any setting except a private one.

"Fling taught college physical education before he came into the Army Air Corps, so he had a good way with people," said Baker. Even if a heavy bomber carrying eleven men was going to get lost on its way to the Empire, "Fling would never demonstrate that he was dissatisfied with any one of us in front of anyone else. If we did anything wrong, that was considered a private matter and when no one else was around he would handle it.

"Besides," said Baker, "it was no one's fault, really, that the radar was malfunctioning."

On some missions gunners like Carter, with an okay from Fling, could take a nap while *God's Will* was churning northwestward. With the radar inoperative and everybody keyed up trying to navigate, tonight was not the night for sleeping. Fling, Peterson, Dwyer, Baker, Carter, and the rest of the crew were all in a state of high readiness when Fling announced, as they all knew already, that the hour of midnight had arrived.

"We were the first ship to reach the coast of Japan," wrote Carter, "but we were lost because the radar went out and we were flying in electrical storms." A dark mass of land to their left gave way to a yellowish glow of the kind that could come only from electric lights.

"That's a city," Carter said over the interphone. "All lit up."

"I think that's Tokyo," said Dwyer from his ringside seat in the nose. "I wonder why they have lights on in the city with us coming to visit them."

"No," said Pettit. "It's Yokohama."

As if considering, Pettit added, "Surely, Tokyo, the seat of government and the number one military target in all of the Empire isn't going to be all lit up like a Christmas tree."

He was wrong. Incredibly, even as the first pathfinder B-29s were on their final approach, and as a new day began—before the bombs, before the burn—streetlights in Tokyo were lit.

"I see what you mean," said Fling, "We'll continue north. We'll find our IP at Choshi Point."

He was wrong too.

It was 00:05 a.m. Chamorro Standard Time, Saturday, March 10, 1945.

Tokyo Alight

So did streetlights really have Tokyo lit up before American bombers arrived to shower the sky with rivulets of fire and take the city into the bowels of hell? Some B-29 crewmembers interviewed for this book said the city was aglow when they arrived, with no sign of a blackout in effect. Others insisted it was not. Japanese records and Japanese survivors indicated later that standard air-raid precautions were taken, but Japan's on-the-ground performance rarely matched expectations. Through a variety of means—agents in the Marianas, picket ships at sea, radio intercepts—the Japanese knew that a maximum-effort mission had been launched against them just before sunset. They probably knew that Tokyo was the target. They probably knew the first pathfinder B-29s would be overhead shortly after midnight, with waves of planes to follow. They could not have anticipated that the B-29s would be approaching at low altitude.

Some B-29 crewmembers listened to Japanese radio stations while they flew toward the Empire. In defiance of official Japanese policy (which had banned baseball for the duration, confiscated American literature, and forbidden the study of English except for military purposes), broadcasters were playing American music. A crew led by Capt. Thomas Hanley of the 497th Bombardment Group entered the final hours of the approach to Tokyo listening to a song whose title they would remember later with strange irony: "Smoke Gets in Your Eyes."

There was a quarter moon that night. Perhaps to the surprise of their crewmembers, most B-29s were on course. Many were making a key turn at Choshi Point, east of Tokyo, the IP, or initial point where they would turn west to begin their planned run-in. Crewmembers squeezed into their flak vests, heavy and cumbersome garments with steel plates that could absorb shrapnel. Some donned helmets that interfered with earphones but promised head protection. None saw any night fighters stalking them. Antiaircraft gunfire would be a formidable adversary, but the fighters were somehow missing.

The defense of Tokyo was a paradox. Americans were warned about, and on occasion reported seeing, barrage balloons— gas-filled aerial bags that were used to string vertical cables in the path of approaching airplanes—yet the Japanese had never had any. Japan had night fighters and very capable night fighter pilots, yet most Americans never saw one. At night, Japan's network of antiaircraft guns and searchlights could be terrifying, and sphincters tightened whenever a searchlight beam locked onto a bomber, yet there appeared to be little coordination between the guns and the lights.

An intelligence summary called the Tokyo region a "jigsaw puzzle" of antiaircraft installations totaling five hundred guns, "as many guns as ever protected the German capital of Berlin." Bomber crewmembers feared these guns, yet they were never as effective as their German counterparts, which inflicted far higher casualties. American intelligence experts created various diagrams, some entitled "flak clocks," showing a trapezoid with concentric rings. Each ring was made up of flak gun batteries, the modern-day equivalent of a moat surrounding a castle.

Radio operator Carl Barthold remembers being briefed that the Japanese antiaircraft guns were effective from the ground up to 5,500 feet, but that a "gap" existed going up to about 10,000 feet where coverage resumed. The need for coverage above

10,000 feet was obvious because the Americans had wasted many months flying at great heights. "We were told that we were going in through a 'window' where they wouldn't have the capability to shoot us."

That was not quite true. Sammy Bakshas of *Tall in the Saddle* would learn that it wasn't. Yet the Americans were approaching a city where leaders had gone through all the motions. Every manner of lip service had been paid to defending the urban area and its population, but few practical measures actually had any impact.

Japanese cities had been equipped with air-raid sirens, blackout facilities, and underground shelters for almost twenty years, yet people at home and on the street often ignored them. In Tokyo, shelter construction, especially in the area near the bay, was complicated because they could not be dug more than a few feet without encountering ground water. Many people simply stayed where they were when the bombers approached. Perhaps inured by the apparent inability of the Americans to hit anything with their bombs, urban residents dismissed the appearance of the *bi ni ju ku*, the B-29, as a "mail run."

The previous day, a strong wind had been rattling the panes in doors and windows all over the city, the same wind the Americans hoped would spread the fire they were bringing; most people had gone about their day routinely. For the past few nights, single B-29s had appeared over the city, not dropping any bombs but flying very low and setting off the searchlights and antiaircraft fire. This was reconnaissance and it made many in the capital uneasy, yet routine activities continued and, after dark, the lights may have stayed on.

Or they may not have. Yukiko "Yuki" Hiragama, an eight-year-old schoolgirl who happened to be outdoors that night, remembers nothing about streetlights. "Before the bombers came it was a night of darkness and shadows," said Hiragama. "The sirens made their powerful sounds in the evening and then night came and there were no B-29s. The sirens were silent and the lights were off when the B-29s arrived." While Hiragama remained awake, most in Tokyo went to sleep after the sirens halted, many of them hungry because food supplies were short.

The bombers came.

The first B-29s overhead were pathfinders, sent to burn a fiery X across the target area of the city to mark it for the main attack force.

Ready or Not . . .
Also awaiting the arrival of the B-29s was Japan's fragmented air-defense network and Tokyo's nearly dysfunctional civil-defense system.

Army and Navy airfields were scattered all over the Japanese main island of Honshu, but the specific job of defending Tokyo from air attack was assigned to the Japanese army's 10th Flying Division with 210 fighters, 12 observation aircraft, and a claimed operational strength of about 90 percent. The division's plan was to attempt to screen Tokyo as much as possible by setting up barrier patrols dozens of miles outside the city. The division had no real coordination with the Japanese navy air units that defended nearby Yokosuka and Yokohama. The army and navy had separate ground-control intercept centers that had little communication with each other. Both service branches worried about a shortage of skilled pilots and insufficient fuel and spare parts. An attempt to use a substitute for standard aviation fuel called A-Go, a mixture of gasoline and alcohol, proved to be dangerously unreliable and sometimes caused engines to quit in flight.

The army was similarly responsible for antiaircraft gun batteries in and around Tokyo. The guns included a copy of the highly successful German "Eighty-Eight," an 88mm cannon as well as 120mm and 150mm guns. There were only two of the latter, with an actual bore diameter of 149.1mm, but they were credited with destroying two B-29s in a single engagement.

Quite remarkably, the total of army warplanes near Tokyo included only twenty-five or twenty-six night fighters. One of the most effective night fighters was the Nakajima J1N1-S Gekko ("Moonlight"), known to the western allies as an Irving, a two-man, twin-engined fighter that had traditional forward-firing guns plus an upward-firing cannon mounted atop the fuselage and pointing up at a thirty-degree angle. A handful of Gekko pilots scored as many as six to eight aerial victories each against B-29s, but Irvings relied on an air-to-air searchlight instead of radar and performed poorly when fully loaded.

Not as advanced but more numerous was the Kawasaki Ki-45 Toryu ("Dragon Killer"), called a Nick by the allies, another twin-engined, two-man fighter that also lacked radar. The Gekko was operated by the Japanese navy and the Toryu by the army, and that was a problem: even this late in the war, the two service branches had never learned to coordinate their efforts. The navy and army that were fighting for the survival of the Empire often seemed to be preoccupied with fighting each other.

Some of the better-known single-engine fighters, including the navy's Mitsubishi A6M5 Zero (called Zeke by the Allies), and the army's Nakajima Ki-84 Hayate ("Gale"), alias Frank, were used in small numbers during night operations. So, too, was the Kawasaki Ki-61 Hien ("Swallow") or Tony, which had an unsettling resemblance to the American P-51 Mustang but nowhere near the performance. The Hien was the only mass-produced Japanese fighter of the war to use a liquid-cooled inline V-engine. The Hayate was one of the best-performing propeller-driven fighters of the war but was hampered by poor production standards, a high-maintenance engine, and landing gear that tended to buckle. Gekko, Toryu, Zero Hayate, and Hien fighters—to the Americans who bothered to learn them, the Allies' names were Irving, Nick, Zeke, Frank, and Tony—were in the air just after midnight into the early minutes of Saturday, March 10, 1945, but they were receiving little direction from ground controllers and their flights were not coordinated with searchlight and antiaircraft batteries. Hien fighters prowling the Japanese coast were within a few miles of where Dean Fling was flying due north and unknowingly bypassing Tokyo instead of approaching it. The Japanese fighter pilots had no guidance from ground radar stations and never came within eyesight of *God's Will.*

One of the world's great capitals now had fighters patrolling its suburbs, bombers approaching from the Marianas, and relatively little proper readiness for what was coming. The battle for Tokyo was about to begin, and both sides were having problems. *It was 00:15 a.m. Chamorro Standard Time, March 10, 1945.*

The Simeral Crew

Capt. George A. "Tony" Simeral was airplane commander of *Snatch Blatch*, also called *City of Los Angeles.* This was the bomber carrying mission commander Tommy Power and functioning as one of the first half-dozen pathfinders. On this sinister night, it was appropriate that the B-29 drew one of its names from a black witch in Francois Rabelais's writings. As for Tony Simeral, he was one of the most experienced combat pilots in LeMay's command. He'd flown thirty combat missions in the Mediterranean as a B-24 Liberator commander. When they later assigned him stateside to instruct in Liberators, Simeral often and loudly complained about being bored. He had another gripe too: training bomber crews, he believed, was more dangerous than being in combat. He volunteered for B-29 combat duty and found himself in the 29th Bombardment Group.

With Simeral and Power together on the flight deck—in an interview, Simeral said he retained the airplane commander's left-seat position with the senior Power leaning over his shoulder—*Snatch Blatch* and other pathfinders locked in on the section of the city that had been chosen for tonight's treatment. The M47 bombs began to fall. *It was 00:25 a.m. Chamorro Standard Time, March 10, 1945.*

For three hours to come, the roar of R-3350 engines would shake the clear, windy air over the Japanese capital. Simeral's radio operator Staff Sgt. Henry "Red" Erwin would later remember someone on the crew comparing Tokyo ablaze to the ninth, or lowest, level of suffering in the fiery depths of Dante's Inferno.

Simeral circled. He and Power observed a light and color show created by incendiaries, fires, searchlights, and flak. Power climbed down into the nose of the Superfortress, unfolded a map, and began sketching the bombing results he was observing with the naked eye. Radio operator Erwin, using an extension line to his interphone set, climbed up into the navigator's astrodome and looked out in awe as Simeral continued to orbit, oblivious to Japanese defenses. Erwin recalled later that the night was clear and crisp before the smoke began building up. That was true over Tokyo, yet in the region around the capital, snowstorms churned.

Six weeks from now, under circumstances involving a very different kind of fire, Red Erwin would become the most famous enlisted crewmember of the entire B-29 force.

The Keene Crew

The Japanese knew the B-29s were coming. Some night fighters launched into the sky above and around Tokyo. Antiaircraft gunners and searchlight crews were ready. But the low-level approach and the unusually large number of bombers confused the troops manning the gun and searchlight installations. As the fire spread, antiaircraft fire waned. Flames were overrunning the gun positions. Searchlights sought out the B-29s, but once the fire caught, the searchlights were not needed: the sky was bright with flame. Some Japanese fighters came up and about forty closed in for attacks while a searchlight beam held one of the B-29s.

After the pathfinders left their mark on the city, one of the first bombers over Tokyo was a B-29 that hadn't yet been given a name and didn't have a busty blonde or a garish cartoon painted on its nose. Captain Leon M. Keene was airplane commander. The Superfortress belonged to the 99th Bombardment Squadron, 9th Bombardment Group flying from Tinian. The Superfortress came from the southwest at 4,800 feet and about two hundred miles per hour, its silvery skin reflecting the initial fires below and its bomb bay doors hanging open. *It was 1:30 a.m. Chamorro Standard Time, March 10, 1945.*

Keene was not at the controls. The situation on the flight deck was not happy. A senior officer from squadron headquarters, Maj. John C. Conly, sat in the left-hand airplane commander's left seat that Keene usually occupied. Keene was in the right, where pilot 2nd Lt. Richard D. Gordon was supposed to sit, and Gordon was bent forward in the bucket seat between Conly and Keene. Resentment filled the cockpit, just as the stench of burnt flesh would saturate the cockpits of Superfortress crews to follow.

Conly had been trained in the United States as a B-29 airplane commander but before shipping overseas switched to other duty as a radar specialist. Tonight, he was "acting airplane commander"— the term appears in a document—because squadron and group leadership feared that Keene might face a mutiny from his crew. The crew disliked Keene, universally and intensely. On some airplanes, this happened solely because the airplane commander was doing his job, which demanded leadership, not popularity. On others, it happened because the airplane commander was a strutting martinet. Keene's problem was different: he was competent, but lacking in personal skills. He was a better flyer than a leader.

Tail gunner Sgt. James T. Hash said the crew referred to Keene behind his back as "that shithead." Conly was on board to observe Keene and also to refresh his own piloting skills, which had gotten stale while he was doing radar work. Headquarters was planning to make Conley the new airplane commander, at least temporarily, in order to consign Keene to a ground job.

As the Japanese capital, marked with an X left in fire by the pathfinders, fell beneath, Conly worked with the Keene crew's regular radar man, Marshall D. Long—the same Long who had briefly enjoyed college life at Clemson en route to the war.

Long was six feet tall, muscular, a weightlifter, and a close friend of Bake Baker, the radar operator on the Fling crew in *God's Will*. "He was just a fantastic young man," said Baker. "He was sharp as a tack. Everything about him was top grade." With Conly and Long working together, the Keene crew should have been in the best possible hands. But the tension in the aircraft was palpable.

Conly took the Superfortress over the city. He was planning to make a radar-guided bombing run when the radar malfunctioned. It happened a lot. Conly ordered Keene to take over the controls. Under the circumstances, the changeover, taking place over the target, had to be unpleasant. Conly stood, worked his way back to the radar compartment, and took over from Long. The rest of the crew heard Keene say over the interphone that they would be making a second pass over the burning city below. The thermal blasts that would fling around other B-29s to follow had not yet reached the Keene's crew altitude of 4,800 feet, but making a second bombing run seemed risky. No one in the crew was happy.

With Keene piloting but Conly giving orders, the B-29 passed over Tokyo again and dropped its bombs. By now, other Superfortresses were dropping plenty of bombs as well, and the conflagration in the city was spreading. As Keene turned away from the target, tail gunner Hash got on the interphone to report what he was seeing. "It's burning, burning, burning," said Hash with all the crewmembers listening in. "This mission should be called 'Operation Hot Time in the Old Town Tonight.'" The B-29 was approaching shore, ready to leave the Empire, when the Keene crew heard a loud noise and felt an impact. Hash spoke for all of them: "I think it's small arms." At that instant, with Conly monitoring the situation, both airplane commander Keene and flight engineer 2nd Lt. John R. Jewett *knew* they'd been hit by small arms and that the hits had shredded a fuel tank.

Controlled by men with ugly leadership issues, riddled with bullets, leaking the precious fuel needed to make it home, the Keene aircraft began to descend, departed the Empire, and flew straight into a snowstorm. *It was 1:50 a.m. Chamorro Standard Time, March 10, 1945.*

The Tucker Crew
Into the fiery furnace came Percy Usher Tucker and the crew of *Lady Annabelle.* As they reached Choshi Point, the capital of Japan, now due west and readily visible, was burning furiously. Tucker followed standard procedure and prepared to turn his plane over to his bombardier.

Whatever was going on with Joe Krogman—thoughts of death, thoughts of his best friend in Remsen, Iowa, killed in a stateside training crash—when it came time to squint into the Norden bombsight, there was no one who could do it better. "I'm ready," Krogman told Tucker on the interphone. From his front-seat perch, he looked ahead and could see an inferno on the ground and searchlights and shell bursts in the sky, but Krogman would spend no more time looking straight ahead through the Plexiglas. He would now look down into his crosshairs.

Airplane commander Tucker brought *Lady Annabelle* into a level attitude, set the speed at the IP, and hooked in the autopilot. Tucker was no longer flying the B-29. Krogman's Norden bombsight connected to the autopilot. The bombsight controlled the ailerons, which meant the aircraft could turn if Krogman wanted it to. "Okay," Krogman said. The interphone went silent as the bombardier concentrated.

"You put figures into the bombsight for the speed of the aircraft, the temperature outside, the altitude, and so on," Krogman later explained. "You set the 'trail distance,' which determined the number of feet that the bombs were going to trail behind the aircraft when they struck the ground. The IP isn't your Bible. It's not an exact point.

When you pick up the target, you can change whether the plane moves left or right." Tonight, Krogman did not have an exact aiming point: he was tasked simply to drop his bombs into the city below, preferably at a spot not yet afire but close to the conflagration.

Its R-3350 engines groaning, buffeting from heat blasts, *Lady Annabelle* churned into the middle of the burning city. Krogman lined things up vertically, so the crosshairs wouldn't be left or right of the target. He concentrated on the crosshairs. He concentrated on the attitude of the plane. He was silent, silent, silent . . . and both engineer Wale and tail gunner Majeski later recalled some suspense as the bomber continued straight ahead and the silence continued.

"Bombs away," Krogman said.

Lady Annabelle suddenly bucked upward, gaining a little altitude with the release of its load.

"Got it," said Tucker, retrieving control of the aircraft from the bombardier. "Pierce? Dodd?"

As they'd briefed before takeoff, radio operator John Pierce looked through the window in the hatch at the front portion of the bomb bays to make certain all of the bombs were gone and none had gotten stuck inside the plane. Right blister gunner John Dodd, the shakiest member of this crew, the rosary-clutching Boston kid whom Tucker was going to transfer the next day, performed the same task at the rear portion of the bomb bays. All this happened while *Lady Annabelle* was in a turn, navigator Edward Koniusky helping Tucker to plot the way home.

All of the bombs were gone. The bomb bay doors closed without difficulty. The Tucker crew had done its job.

Beside and behind Tucker, the B-29 main force arrived over Tokyo. Carl Barthold working his radio as part of the John M. Campbell crew and listening in the night for signals; the Bakshas crew in *Tall in the Saddle*; the Tucker crew in *Lady Annabelle*; the Bowers crew in *Ready Teddy* . . . they were arriving, all of them, and as fire began to spread in Tokyo, the sound of aircraft engines overhead, those troublesome R-3350s that could also be terrifyingly loud, grew to become a rolling thunder.

It was 2:00 a.m. Chamorro Standard Time, March 10, 1945.

CHAPTER 11

A City Ignited

Mission to Tokyo
March 10, 1945

"I'LL TELL YOU WHAT WAR IS ABOUT," LeMay said in a meeting with B-29 Superfortress commanders. "You've got to kill people, and when you have killed enough they stop fighting."

"They were the enemy," said B-29 radio operator Cart Barthold when interviewed for this book sixty-five years later. "They were Japs. The only good Jap was a dead Jap. In World War II my mother, who had never been outside the house, went to work at a small-arms plant in St. Louis. They made .30- and .50-caliber ammunition. If they could have bombed the ammunition plant, or my mother's house, or the elementary school nearby, the Japanese would have done it without hesitation. If the war was serious enough for my mother to leave the house for the first time in her life, it was serious enough for us to kill the enemy."

"He was never into killing," said a family member of Joe Krogman, the bombardier aboard *Lady Annabelle*. "There was nothing personal to him about killing Japanese with his bombs. I think he shared that with many of his fellow fliers. He once said that a bombing mission was a bombing mission to him, only that and nothing more. The target was reached, the bombs dropped, end of story. He never really allowed himself to think of people dying as a result of one of those bombs. To him it was not killing."

Reb Carter, the Georgia-boy left blister gunner on the Dean Fling crew, left no clue in his journal or in any surviving letters to his girlfriend or his parents of how he felt about Japanese suffering on the ground. Journals, diaries, and memoirs from many other B-29 crewmembers are similarly silent about what was taking place on the ground.

Most of the thousand kids in B-29s had only a very general idea of the horror they were inflicting during the great Tokyo firebomb mission. Most gave little thought to the question of whether their bombs were falling on innocent civilians or on a legitimate military target, although their bosses insisted it was the latter. Most B-29 pilots and crewmembers felt they were doing the job assigned to them, and they hoped they were helping to move the war toward its conclusion. They were not philosophers. They spent little time pondering the deep inner meaning of it all.

Civilian vs. Military

The debate over civilian versus military targets is a postwar phenomenon and is being conducted mostly in Western Europe, where atrocities were fewer and animosities were less intense. Europe was the scene of the Holocaust, but although the Nazis operated camps for the sole purpose of exterminating human beings, their campaign of mass murder was separate from the war being fought between the Axis and the Allies. When fighting the war itself, the Germans followed the existing Geneva Convention and the law of war when operating prisoner of war camps, at least until the final months, when everything began to break down.

Throughout most of the war, while the British relentlessly bombed cities at night, Americans carried out high-altitude, precision daylight aerial attacks on military and industrial targets. B-17 Flying Fortress and B-24 Liberator crews flying out of England and Italy may have killed civilians, but they did not set out to do so. That changed on February 3, 1945, when Eighth Air Force commander Lt. Gen. James H. "Jimmy" Doolittle was ordered to send 1,003 B-17s to bomb Berlin and to use a location near the city center as the aiming point. Doolittle objected strenuously, arguing that Americans did not conduct indiscriminate bombings of urban populations. His bosses overruled him and Doolittle fumed, but he orchestrated the mission to Berlin, carried it out as ordered, and never mentioned the debate in his autobiography.

No such debate took place in the Pacific.

Americans knew little or nothing about any Nazi atrocities, whether they took place while waging the war or while slaughtering innocents at murder camps like Auschwitz. But Americans knew plenty about Pearl Harbor and the rape of Nanking. Moreover, there was a racial component to the way the enemy in the Pacific was perceived. Rightly or wrongly, it is all but impossible to find any B-29 pilot or crewmember who felt moral misgivings about bringing fire to cities made of wood and paper, or about, on March 10, 1945, igniting the hottest fires ever to burn on Earth. Had there been misgivings on any significant scale, LeMay's brave men would not have been able to perform. Instead, they performed with courage and brilliance.

LeMay's B-29s dropped nearly half a million M69 incendiary bomblets on the Japanese capital in the dark early morning hours of March 10, razing sixteen square miles of the city, transforming darkness into an eerie artificial light and immersing tens of thousands of human beings in raw heat against which there was no defense. As Joseph Coleman of the Associated Press described it, "The M69s released 100-foot streams of fire upon detonating and sent flames rampaging through densely packed wooden homes. Superheated air created a wind that sucked victims into the flames and fed the twisting infernos. Asphalt boiled in the 1,800-degree heat. With much of the fighting-age male population at the war front, women, children and the elderly struggled in vain to battle the flames or flee."

Overlooked in the quote is the fact that nearly every Japanese family home was a cog in the Japanese war machine. Many weapons and tools employed by Japanese forces were the products of a home-based cottage industry. Other homes were the dwellings of workers who supplied the manpower for Japan's war industry. Moreover, the Tokyo district called Shitamachi, at the center of the X laid down by the pathfinders, was packed with light industries, called "shadow factories," that produced prefabricated war materials destined for Japanese aircraft factories.

So there was a military justification for bringing fire to the heart of the Empire. But it was a convenient justification, to say the least. Most of those burned alive were indeed women, children, and the elderly.

Lieutenant Colonel Robert S. McNamara, an officer on LeMay's staff, quoted LeMay as saying, "If we'd lost the war we'd all have been prosecuted as war criminals." "And I think he's right," added McNamara. "He, and I'd say I, were behaving as war criminals. LeMay recognized that what he was doing would be thought immoral if his side lost. But what makes it immoral if you lose and not immoral if you win?"

Prepared and Unprepared

Despite a lot of lip service, a few public pronouncements, and some rehearsals, the real crime in Tokyo on morning of March 10 was that the authorities were unready. Civil defense, emergency response, and fire-fighting personnel were shamefully—yes, criminally— unprepared to handle an all-out assault from above.

Steve Birdsall wrote, "The residents, accustomed to B-29 raids, had become almost nonchalant about them, dubbing them the 'mail run.'" Lacking insights from their leaders, everyday people were accustomed to Superfortress missions where bombloads were scattered widely with minimal damage to people and property. They were constantly being reassured in radio broadcasts and newspaper headlines. The war was not going so badly, they were being told. Yes, the western allies were closer to Japan now, but that made the western allies easier to defeat.

Although neighborhood associations served to mobilize the population in a citywide civil-defense effort, in practice this effort varied greatly from one urban area to another. Nagoya, the city where much of Japan's aircraft production was centered, boasted neighborhood associations with good leadership and up-to-date information. Tokyo did not. In both cities and many others, neighborhood associations were charged with learning and disseminating knowledge of how to treat the injured, fight fires, and neutralize incendiary bombs. In fact, there was no defense ordinary people could take against a confetti of exploding M69s. Ideas such as smothering a bomb with a blanket were a waste; that idea would have worked on earlier incendiary bombs but not on the bombs being used now. In Tokyo, the authorities sought to equip each household with a grappling hook, a shovel, a sand bucket, and a water barrel. Some items were in short supply or rationed, but most homes had a barrel of water, which was useless against firebombs.

Wrote Birdsall, "Air raid shelter construction, particularly in the lower area of Tokyo, was complicated because [shelters] could not be more than a few feet deep without encountering ground water. Most dwellings had some kind of shelter, but usually about like a foxhole, and useless in a raging fire storm. People suffocated as they lay there or were roasted alive."

Most people never reached a shelter at all because there were shamefully few of them. Home affairs Minister Genki Abe later said, "The reason we had no definite policy of air raid shelter protection . . . is that we did not unduly wish to alarm our citizens concerning the necessity for underground shelters, as we feared it would interfere with normal routine life and have some effect on war production." He added that after seeing what B-29s could bring to their city, most residents considered civilian defense "a futile effort."

Although the situation was better in other Japanese cities, the Tokyo fire department was a joke. Barrett Tillman quoted an expert as saying that the Tokyo fire department was driven "by ritual more than science." One of the great capitals of the world, filling an area of twenty-three square miles and with a wartime population of five and a half million, was midway through a process under which the Ministry of Home Affairs was overseeing a transition from a volunteer to a professional firefighting corps. In recent months, the strength of the Tokyo fire department had increased from 2,000 to 8,100 firefighters. In contrast, the fire department of New York, which no longer faced any likelihood of being bombed from the air, was made up of almost 10,000 firemen at the time.

A study just after the war, edited by firefighting expert Horatio Bond, concluded that

> In 1943, the Tokyo department had 280 pieces of fire apparatus, in early 1945 it had 1,117 pieces. Tokyo received most of the new fire apparatus built during the war. It purchased 559 new 450-GPM pumpers, which by the way, were the largest pumps in the entire country, except a few early 1920 American-LaFrance 750-GPM rigs. The cities increased the size of their departments by borrowing pumpers from nearby volunteer fire departments in rural communities. Unfortunately for the rural districts there were very few pumps to return after the war. Much of the apparatus acquired from rural communities were hand-drawn 120-GPM gasoline-driven pumps.

In Tokyo, a shortage of mechanics and spare parts, coupled with incidental damage from earlier, high-altitude raids, idled more than half of the fire department's small inventory of vehicles. Only one of Tokyo's large, ladder-carrying fire units was in operation, a German-built, eighty-five-foot extension.

A fire company's typical inventory included a four-pound axe, two twelve-foot ladders, two pike poles, two four-foot crowbars, an eighteen-foot length of one-inch rope, two smoke masks, three spare nozzles, forty sections of two-and-a-half-inch single-jacketed linen hose, and two hose carts. One of the most densely packed urban centers in the world, Tokyo had just three aerial ladders.

Although the use of incendiary bombs by the Americans was neither a surprise nor a new idea, Japanese firefighters were still being trained to work in an environment where they would surround the fire rather than having the fire engulf them. Many were very young and about 40 percent were rated only as auxiliary firemen. Their primary method of fighting a blaze consisted of spraying water on it, a method that was useless against incendiaries. Fire apparatus, appliances, and special tools common to fire departments of American cities were conspicuous by their absence in Japan. Special mobile rigs and companies, such as salvage, light, CO_2, foam, rescue, demolition, airfield crash rigs, and even water tanks with booster pumps were never a part of their fire departments. Japanese firemen did not use the common portable fire extinguisher of the CO_2, carbon tetrachloride, foam, and water-pump can types.

Although the authorities in the capital were doing their best to catch up with reality, expanding civil defense and firefighting capability created its own problems. A postwar assessment concluded, "Men were recruited so rapidly that proper training was not possible. Peacetime fire departments were increased from three to five times their normal size. [In Tokyo] an effort was made to increase personnel to 12,500, but the manpower shortage in Japan made it prohibitive."

As Tillman put it, "Japanese administrative policy only complicated the situation. As in Germany, in major metropolitan areas the police oversaw fire protection, but the Japanese variant lacked the Nazi advantage of competence. Consequently, Allied analysts deemed Japanese efforts unprofessional because local police were incompetent in firefighting. Vastly different work cultures and mind-sets compounded the situation: the police focused on controlling a large population rather than protecting it from external threats of biblical proportions."

Heat and Horror
It began just after 11:00 p.m. Tokyo time, or midnight according to the Chamorro time (Guam time) by which the Americans set their watches. It was exactly twenty-five minutes past midnight when *Snatch Blatch* and the Simeral crew, carrying on-scene commander Tom Power, became one of the first pathfinders overhead. Sirens sounded throughout the city, warning residents who had previously been instructed to stay inside their houses. Inexplicably, it appears that many city lights were still on, despite the certainty of impending attack and the lateness of the hour.

The pathfinders, radio operator Barthold among them, began dropping the self-scattering incendiaries the Japanese called *molotoffano hanakago*, or "Molotov flower baskets," inscribing an X throughout the target zone by igniting the first fires. The Japanese capital then experienced a brief pause before the main force of B-29s came overhead, loud enough to shake the city, and began sprinkling incendiaries by the thousand. The main force of B-29s was four hundred miles long and took two and a half hours to pass over Tokyo, roughly midnight to 2:30 a.m. Tokyo time, or 1:00 a.m. to 3:30 a.m. to the Americans. They unleashed a fire that was more severe than the conflagrations that razed Moscow in 1812, San Francisco in 1901, or even the fire that followed Tokyo's terrible earthquake of 1923. The 1923 disaster registered 8.3 magnitude on the Richter scale, destroyed 60 percent of Tokyo and 80 percent of Yokohama, and killed an estimated 140,000 people. In a harbinger of a different kind of firestorm to come, the 1923 earthquake created a blaze that was carried on high winds and consumed much of the region, including much of its industrial facilities, with long-term economic consequences.

Robert Guillain, a French journalist, was in the middle of the erupting firestorm of March 10, 1945. He was familiar with the earthquake of twenty-two years earlier.

Now, Guillain wrote that the bombers "set to work at once sowing the sky with fire. Bursts of light flashed everywhere in the darkness like Christmas trees lifting their decorations of flame high into the night, then fell back to earth in whistling bouquets of jagged flame. Barely a quarter of an hour after the raid started, the fire, whipped by the wind, began to scythe its way through the density of that wooden city."

Guillain also wrote:

The bright light dispelled the night and B-29s were visible here and there in the sky. For the first time, they flew low or middling high in staggered levels. Their long, glinting wings, sharp as blades, could be seen through the oblique columns of smoke rising from the city, suddenly reflecting the fire from the furnace below, black silhouettes gliding through the fiery sky to reappear farther on, shining golden against the dark roof of heaven or glittering blue, like meteors, in the searchlight beams spraying the vault from horizon to horizon. There was no question in such a raid of huddling blindly underground; you could be roasted alive before you knew what was happening. All the Japanese in the gardens near mine were out of doors or peering up out of their holes, uttering cries of admiration—this was typically Japanese—at this grandiose, almost theatrical spectacle.

Admiration changed to horror as the fire arrived. Once it came, there was no escape. In thirty minutes, the fires were out of control. Even if the Japanese had had more and better firefighting equipment, they would have been hard-pressed to combat the raging firestorms that boiled water in canals and melted the glass of store windows.

The conflagration quickly overwhelmed Tokyo's wooden residential structures. The firestorm replaced oxygen with lethal gases, superheated the atmosphere, and caused hurricane-like winds that blew a wall of fire across the city.

The B-29s that came over appeared to be so close that Katsumoto Saotome, a fourteen-year-old middle school student, could see flames from the burning city reflected, mirrorlike, on their fuselages. "They looked like tropical fish," said Saotome. Some of the people around Saotome were under the impression that the silvery B-29s were chasing individuals who ran through alleyways and along boulevards seeking safety.

Kiyoko Kawasaki, a thirty-six-year-old mother, ran into the street with two buckets on her head for protection, jogging into a sea of fire and seeing burning bodies floating in the Sumida River. "The prostitutes who hung out by the riverbank jumped into a nearby pond," she recalled. "But the pond was boiling so they all died." Kyoko Arai, a middle school student, watched people perish when dancing fireballs set their hair alight.

Among residents of Tokyo who survived the blasts, flames, heat, and suffocating effect of the very air being burned out of existence, two children, both eight years old, were at opposite ends of the firestorm. They did not know each other then and have never met since. Yuki Hiragama had been sent outdoors by her mother, perhaps out of some premonition that being out of the house would be safer (even though the authorities insisted otherwise). Bespectacled, she wore a pale spring dress, shoes, and socks. With the noise of bombers overhead and fires erupting at her back farther into the city, Yuki stood with her back toward home facing the Sumida River, whose black waters now reflected the growing fires in the distance. Yuki had no idea that she was standing at ground zero.

"I was alone," she said. "People were rushing past in all directions, but I saw no one I knew. We had heard the bombers before, but I had never been sent outdoors. I stood very still and was not certain what to do next."

She turned around. The Sumida Ward of Tokyo was ablaze in front of her. People were pouring out of houses and crowds were forming just as a rain of incendiaries fell into their midst. People were suddenly, abruptly, caught up in a storm of light and heat and were incinerated, trampled, and suffocated. Yuki backed toward the river knowing that her own house was now inside the wall of fire erupting before her as the planes droned overhead.

A neighbor who was well known to her, a middle-aged man, ran across her path screaming and flailing. The man was wearing traditional Japanese attire, including long robes, and it was afire. His hair was afire. Another neighbor, also a man she knew, curled himself up into a ball on the ground. It was very hot now. The ground was hot. The air was hot. Screaming voices seemed to be all around her. The scent of burning flesh was in her nostrils.

"It was everything terrible you can imagine," she said many years later in an interview for this book. "The sights, the smells, the sounds—all of it was surreal and impossible. Several people whom I'd known for all of my brief life simply disappeared in the flames. Many of my neighbors, including schoolmates, escaped but were never the same afterward."

Gasping for breath and feeling the heat in the air, Yuki turned away from the conflagration and ran. A pedestrian bridge took her over water to an open field that had not been bombed. Other people, too, were running. Some made the mistake of thinking the river would protect them. Yuki could see, however, that the surface of the river was swirling and frothing: the Sumida River was beginning to boil. Near the bank where Yuki had stood, each B-29 was dropping twenty-four 500-pound E-46 clusters each containing forty-seven M69 incendiary bomblets, with a bomblet hitting the ground every fifty feet. Yuki saw no smoke, only flames and flying sparks.

In later years, an elementary school textbook in Japan would tell of a little girl who gets separated from her family during the firebombing and later finds out that she is an orphan. This did not happen to Yuki: she passed an area where frantic neighbors were stacking charred corpses in a corner of a field. She kept going. She would later be reunited with her parents and a brother, and all would survive not only this night of horror but other bombing raids to come.

Yoko Ono

Twelve-year-old middle school student Yoko Ono saw the inferno from nearby and felt the heat but was more distant from it than the Kawasaki or Hiragama children. Yoko was part of the privileged elite in a society where stature meant everything. She was a stern-looking child whose father, a banker, was being held in an Allied prison camp in Hanoi in Indochina. She'd been trying to break away from the privileged upbringing imposed on her by the accident of being born into an aristocratic family, and to create space for her aspiration to be an artist, but for the moment her unwanted status in the upper class may have saved her life.

As the firebombing progressed, Yoko took shelter with her mother and two tiny siblings in a special bunker reserved for those near the top of the social hierarchy. It was in the Azabu district of Tokyo, within eyesight of the burning carnage but at a safe distance. As the air assault progressed during the early-morning darkness, now almost transformed into artificial daylight, they wondered whether any of the bombers would change course and bring the fire down on them.

As soon as they could get free, Yoko's mother and the three children joined neighbors in a headlong flight away from the burning city, out into open country. But the farmers in the countryside were starving and unenthusiastic about sharing food with a horde of urban refugees.

In the weeks ahead, reduced to foraging from farm to farm, Yoko's family experienced hard times. She would have to beg for food while homeless and pushing her family's belongings in a wheelbarrow. "I did not need to be told about hardship," she said. "I experienced it, along with everyone around me."

Hidesaburo Kusama

About ten miles to the northeast, in an outlying village near a wooded area called Itabashi-mura, Hidesaburo Kusama and his ten-year-old brother wore hard hats, clutched an emergency bag of uncooked rice, and looked up. The growing fire in the city was beginning to reflect off the B-29s passing overhead. Searchlight beams were everywhere in the sky, even though they added little visibility as the fire pushed away the darkness. Kusama believes he had some awareness, even at his very tender age, that he was witness to history. "I wanted to take everything in," he said. For the rest of his life he would remember being totally and completely focused.

Kusama wrote that at the sound of the air-raid alarm, townspeople "except little children and sick persons" got up and prepared to protect themselves. Everyone in Kusama's village, including schoolchildren, was trained to fight with bamboo spears in case they encountered Americans.

Kusama wrote:

[My] elder brother [and I] joined the people gathered on the high ground of the Yatabe Senior High School of Architecture, from where we saw Tokyo burning—the great seat of fire—in the middle of the air raid by 334 B-29s. Not only did we see the burning city, but also searchlights moving like clock hands overlapping one another ominously. The school ground was about 30 miles away from Tokyo, and we couldn't hear the noise of bombs or antiaircraft gun fire, but it was not difficult even for little pupils like [me] to think what was going on there.

Kusama and his brother returned to their home, but then, another alarm sounded. They rushed out of their house again. Now Kusama's gaze locked on a "red-burning aircraft coming slowly down toward us writing a big 'S' in the sky . . ."

Kusama was about to have an indelible meeting with Sammy Bakshas's *Tall in the Saddle*.

Dead City

According to one account, the "all clear" sounded at 2:37 a.m. Tokyo time, or 3:37 a.m. on the clock the Americans used. The firebombing of Tokyo was over. "Stacked up corpses were being hauled away on lorries," wrote Tokyo resident Fusako Sasaki. "Everywhere there was the stench of the dead and of smoke. I saw places on the pavement where people had been roasted to death."

Many months later, after B-29s carried out a "fire blitz," struck other cities, and returned to Tokyo, Staff Sgt. Bob Speer wrote the following in a publication intended for Superfortress crewmembers:

> The great city of Tokyo—third largest in the world—is dead. The heart, guts, core—whatever you want to call everything that makes a modern metropolis a living, functioning organism—is a waste of white ash, endless fields of ashes, blowing in the wind. Not even the shells of walls stand in large areas of the Japanese capital. The streets are desolate, the people are dead or departed, the city lies broken and prostrate and destroyed. The men who accomplished the job study the photographs brought back by their recon pilots . . . and stand speechless and awed. They shake their heads at each other and bend over the photos again, and then shake their heads again, and no one says a word.

The cost to Japan's ability to wage war was enormous. Vast warehouse areas, big manufacturing plants, railroad yards, stocks of raw materials, the whole complex of home factories—all of it was gone, beyond any prospect of salvage. The broadcast studio from which the voice of Tokyo Rose was sent out to taunt B-29 crewmembers—JAOK, the most powerful transmitter in Japan— was heavily damaged, and radio masts a mile away were leveled. The famous Imperial Hotel, designed by American architect Frank Lloyd Wright, was in need of serious repair. The biggest railroad stations in Asia, Ueno, and Tokyo Central were completely wiped out. The Ginza shopping district was damaged and the Asakusa shopping district no longer existed.

The bombing also obliterated the Japanese branches of famous American companies, including the Harley-Davidson motorcycle plant, Ford and Chevrolet facilities, and the Otis Elevator Company. Spared from the horrors of the bombing were the Diet, Japan's legislature, the Imperial Palace, and the Yasukuni Shrine, dedicated to the spirits of Japanese soldiers who died fighting for the emperor.

The world was now seeing the horrors of the costliest decision in human history—the decision raised by American President Franklin D. Roosevelt at the Casablanca Conference to require unconditional surrender from the Axis powers of Germany, Italy, and Japan. The other allies did not favor unconditional surrender;

Britain's Winston Churchill and the Soviet Union's Josef Stalin acquiesced to it only reluctantly, and most senior U.S. officers opposed the policy, with the singular exception of Gen. Dwight D. Eisenhower. But for the demand for unconditional surrender, the war in Europe would surely have ended the previous fall, and the war against Japan would have ended after this first major firebomb raid.

Emperor Hirohito (in the Japanese language, no one would ever utter his name; he would be called simply *tenno haika*, or "the emperor"—had made no public appearance in recent months. The Americans had spared his palace on purpose, recognizing early that they would not help their own war effort by attacking Japan's royalty directly. Hirohito's exact whereabouts on that fiery morning of March 10, 1945, do not appear to have been recorded, but he did not make it a practice to flee the city that was at the center of the Empire. He probably never knew that Hap Arnold's chief of staff Lauris "Larry" Norstad had proposed bombing the Imperial Palace and gotten a rare rebuff from his boss.

Although Americans did not appreciate the fact, he had been reluctant to get into this war, and now some around him believed he was reluctant to continue it. Japanese leaders, including Prime Minister Admiral Kantaro Suzuki, had never expected to conquer the United States, never expected to see their tanks roll into Chicago; they had always assumed the war would end with a negotiated settlement. In all of their planning, including their expectations for the attack on Pearl Harbor, they had expected to seize and hold vast areas of the Asian mainland and Pacific islands, and then sue for a settlement with the United States, one in which they would be able to retain at least some of the new territory they had conquered. All such prospects were gone now. Even the most warlike in the cabinet knew Japan was defeated, but they also believed they had to keep fighting—or had believed it, at least, until tonight—because of the unconditional surrender demand.

The torching of Tokyo and Hirohito's subsequent viewing of the ravaged sections of Tokyo are said to have marked the beginning of the emperor's personal involvement in the peace process, a start toward the final debate in Tokyo about whether, when, and how to surrender.

CHAPTER 12

Thirty Seconds over Tokyo

Mission to Tokyo
March 10, 1945, 2:00 a.m.–3:05 a.m.

O NE OF THE EARLY CASUALTIES in the flickering sky near a burning Tokyo was *Zero Auer*, the B-29 piloted by airplane commander 1st Lt. Robert Auer of the 19th Bombardment Group from Guam. A witness later wrote, "when *Zero Auer* approached the target the flak was heavy and heat from the fires kicked up heavy thermals that made the aircraft bounce around." An Auer family member later wrote of "the brute physical challenge" of controlling the sixty-five-ton Superfortress while it was being batted around like a toy, describing the situation as demanding every ounce of muscle and ability Auer and his right-seat pilot 2nd Lt. Harold D. Currey Jr. could come up with.

The Auer Crew
Although there was not supposed to be a formation that night, *Zero Auer* had fallen into a makeshift formation of seven or eight B-29s that had spotted one another on the way in to Tokyo, banded

together, and entered the target area together. The others were being sought by flak and batted around by thermals too, but the beam of a Japanese searchlight latched onto *Zero Auer* and stayed with it. The beam was powerful enough to blind the men on the Superfortress flight deck. An antiaircraft shell hit the *Zero Auer* dead center, possibly detonating inside the open bomb bay.

Every ounce of muscle and skill in the cockpit went into enabling *Zero Auer* to pass over the Tokyo fires. The aircraft traveled several miles to the north. Then, a witness watched the cigarlike fuselage of *Zero Auer* break into three distinct pieces, with red-orange torrents of fire pouring out of the gaps.

The witness saw an object fly out from the bomber's broken, fire-swept fuselage. That must have been right blister gunner Cpl. Walter Grubb, who fell through the night near a city ablaze and grabbed frantically for the ripcord on his chest pack. Grubb's parachute snapped open and he dangled in the sky, unnaturally still for a moment before he began to drift downward, not into the burning city but very close to it. Grubb was going to come down in the middle of the people he'd been bombing. And it was going to take time because hot bursts of turbulence kept lifting his nylon canopy and delaying his descent.

The others had no such chance. Killed were Auer, Currey, navigator 2nd Lt. William Lemmons Jr., bombardier 2nd Lt. Homer Allington, radar operator 2nd Lt. Robert Booker, flight engineer Tech. Sgt. Pedro Closener, radio operator Cpl. Jack Anderson, central fire control gunner Cpl. George Micott, left blister gunner Cpl. Michael Chalanyca, and tail gunner Cpl. Edward Yuda. The sheer force of the thermal winds and the flak blast carried major chucks of *Zero Auer* still farther to the north to Kawaguchi, an outlying city on the alluvial plain of the Ara River north of Tokyo. *It was 2:05 a.m. Chamorro Standard Time, March 10, 1945.*

The Bakshas Crew
About a third of the way through the three-hour procession of B-29s over Tokyo, Japanese antiaircraft artillery connected with *Tall in the Saddle.*

Tall in the Saddle carried its regularly assigned eleven-man crew led by Capt. Gordon L. Muster plus a twelfth person, Maj. Sam P.

Bakshas—Sammy—who according to the report "was serving as acting command pilot with this crew." The report confirms that Bakshas was sitting in the left seat controlling the aircraft, Muster was in the right seat helping, and the usual copilot, 2nd Lt. Eugene G. Cook, was in a jump seat behind them. Flight engineer Leland P. Fishback was busy at his own instrument console monitoring the progress of the aircraft and its instruments.

Just after "bombs away," an exploding flak shell made a direct hit on *Tall in the Saddle*. According to the missing aircrew report, the B-29 was shot down in a location that is "unknown" and at a time that is "unknown." But from accounts provided by crewmembers in other bombers, it appears the Auer crew and the Bakshas crew were hit within minutes of each other. *It was still 2:10 a.m. Chamorro Standard Time, March 10, 1945.*

Directly over the gathering firestorm, the Bakshas bomber appeared to halt in midair, tilted strangely, and descended to the northwest, fire spurting back from its wing fuel tanks.

The missing-aircrew report was written in haste while search and rescue efforts were still thought to have some prospect of success. There is no reason to believe that Bakshas's status as a squadron commander contributed to its haste.

Tall in the Saddle was apparently the only Superfortress to be shot down directly over the Japanese capital and to fall into the center of the target area. It would have taken between thirty seconds and one minute for a B-29 to traverse the nearly sixteen square miles of densely packed Tokyo that were now white-hot with flames—burning so intensely that ashes streaked the noses of B-29s a mile overhead, while crewmembers could smell burning flesh—and *Tall in the Saddle* appears to have been struck by a direct hit shell squarely at the midpoint of that traverse. It would likely have been an 88mm high-explosive shell, detonating with a kinetic force sufficient to tear the thin aluminum skin of the B-29 to pieces. All the evidence suggests the shell made a direct impact on the forward underside of the aircraft, ahead of the wing.

The Savage Crew

Also high over Tokyo was a Superfortress piloted by George J. Savage, an airplane commander viewed as brash, an upstart, and a seriously tough guy. No one in LeMay's command had more experience handling the control yoke, throttle, and rudder pedals: Savage, now twenty-four and from Collinsville, Illinois, had been a pilot since age sixteen when his father gave him his own airplane, an Aeronca C-3, often called a flying bathtub because it sat so close to the ground. Savage liked to joke that his father had given him this bountiful introduction to aviation to dash his dream of becoming a singer. It was widely said that you needed earplugs when Savage was singing, even in the rickety, wood-frame outdoor shower at Guam. Not yet known, as a signature ingredient of his reputation, was that Savage was going to crack up a record number of B-29s. "George looked to the skies and was forever running into things on the ground," his buddies wrote in a tongue-in-cheek but accurate biography. Savage, like Robert Auer and Sammy Bakshas, belonged to the 19th Bombardment Group.

Over Tokyo hoping to evade antiaircraft fire, Savage later wrote that he was "zigging and zagging like the book said and hoping we wouldn't run into another B-29." Savage saw other B-29s caught in searchlight beams that stuck to them like glue. One of these may have been Auer's.

On the interphone, Savage's bombardier Flight Officer Malcolm G. "Mac" Wooldridge called out that he'd identified a perfect target while squinting into his Norden bombsight. Just ahead of Savage's B-29 "was a lovely island of darkness not yet ablaze and at the front of it was a magnificent building that looked like the Jefferson Memorial," Savage wrote. "We were so low that it was not difficult to pick out the details."

Wooldridge told Savage to follow the pilot direction indicator, or PDI—an aircraft instrument used by bombardiers to indicate heading changes—for thirty seconds and said they would reach "bombs away" at that point. Savage remembered that *Thirty Seconds over Tokyo* was the title of a book (by Ted Lawson) and a movie (with Spencer Tracy) about the Doolittle Raid on the city now burning beneath him. Knowing that they would be in the center of things so quickly was "a rude awakening to the realities of war," Savage wrote. He added, "As soon as we took up a straight heading, one-by-one searchlights caught us until, just before bombs away, we were in the beam of 10 or 15 of them. Seemed like we were the top of an Indian teepee with all the poles converging on us. Just as bombs away occurred, so did reality. Suddenly a series of 'Whoomp!' 'Whoomp!' was heard all over the airplane. Sounded like many big doors being slammed shut in an acoustic auditorium." *It was 2:15 a.m. Chamorro Standard Time, March 10, 1945.*

"I'm Hit, I'm Hit!"

Japanese shells exploded inside Savage's airplane. Radio operator Cpl. Edward G. Acheson bounded from his seat, leaned into the bomb bay, and confirmed that all bombs had released properly. While Acheson was away from his seat, shrapnel ripped through his compartment and turned the seat to ribbons. When he moved again, as if to return to his seat, a small-caliber shell exploded inside the aircraft exactly where his head had been an instant earlier.

If Savage was an expert pilot, Master Sgt. Gerald P. "Jerry" Kalian was one of the most experienced flight engineers in the B-29 force. Kalian now reported on the interphone that the number four engine had lost all its oil pressure and was losing power. Savage told right-seat pilot 2nd Lt. Ernest E. "Ernie" Dossey to feather the engine. When the crippled engine ceased providing power, Savage put in a little left aileron to hold up the right wing and keep the B-29 in balance. Savage's bomber turned for home in the strangely illuminated night with three engines turning.

"I'm hit, I'm hit," said right blister gunner Staff Sgt. John L. "Buck" Buckley on the interphone. His voice was oddly subdued, as if what he was saying wasn't important. Buckley was clutching one arm with the other, watching blood pour all over his chest and lap, staring in wonder.

"Buck, tell me your condition," Savage said on the interphone. "Somebody back there, tell me Buck's condition." Left blister gunner Pvt. Donald W. Turner was trying to do exactly that. "I don't know, sir," said Turner.

"Buck, are you able to tell me where you're hit? What kind of wound is it?"

Bug-eyed, Buckley stared down at himself and spoke, still in an unnaturally low voice. "Sir," he said, "I don't hurt any. But my arm is bleeding. I have been shot."

He was right. He had a small-caliber bullet or a round piece of metal imbedded in his arm and was bleeding profusely. Crewmembers were supposed to remember one another's blood types and Turner was trying to remember Buckley's. Turner was reaching for a syringe of morphine. Tail gunner Cpl. Pete Wirganis was with Buckley and Turner now, and was certain his fellow gunner was bleeding to death. Turner was distracted. "Boss," he said, "I think number one is on fire."

An Air Corps photographer had hitched a ride at Guam and was taking pictures out of the rear hatch above the auxiliary power unit, the putt-putt. With the aircraft obviously badly damaged and groaning, and Buckley now sprawled in disarray and drenched in blood, the photographer abandoned the open hatch and joined radar operator 2nd Lt. Robert N. Morgan. A few seconds later, a small-caliber shell blew up the putt-putt and severed the cables to the elevator, the bomber's horizontal tail surface.

Wrote Savage, "Jerry Kalian confirms that oil pressure is gone so I tell Ernie to feather no. 1 and he does. I, however, being somewhat less alert, forget to release the aileron pressure I had applied when we lost no. 4.

"I look around to see where we are. As I look out my side window all I see is black, which seemed peculiar considering Tokyo was on fire."

Savage looked up through the overhead windows and discovered Tokyo. His B-29 was upside down, 5,000 feet above the burning capital. Every airplane commander had been briefed that the B-29 couldn't handle the stress of inverted flight. Savage was trying to decide between a bailout and a controlled crash. To himself, he thought, "So this is how an aircraft gets shot down." But then he had a second thought: "Since we ain't dead yet, surely something can be done."

In the fashion of the fighter pilot he had wanted to be, Savage rolled the aircraft to an upright position. Navigator 2nd Lt. William D. Born began giving him headings to take an easterly route away from Tokyo. After some confusion and a few minutes flying in the wrong direction, piloting what was "no longer a four-engine bomber but now a two-engine transport," Savage ordered his crew to jettison all loose and heavy objects from the plane.

He learned later that in addition to flak jackets and such, one of the loose and heavy objects that they so dutifully jettisoned was his pride and joy, his hat, weighing all of eight ounces, with a "fifty-mission crush" on it.

They flew east, the glow of Tokyo falling behind to their right. Savage felt a perverse kind of pleasure about him and his crew being in immediate mortal danger. He wouldn't have chosen this situation, but now that it was here it was a challenge to his piloting abilities, and that was George Savage's reason for being. Relieved that the terrors of Tokyo were now at his tail, Savage settled down and determined to use all of his skill to bring his crew to safety.

That's when Cpl. William S. Brooks, the central fire control gunner who had taken Buckley's place at the right blister, spoke on the interphone and told Savage that three or four Japanese fighters were flying parallel to the B-29.

"Let me know when they make a pass on us," Savage said. To himself, he thought, "This is all I need." *It was 2:20 a.m. Chamorro Standard Time, March 10, 1945.*

Savage wasn't thinking of shooting back. For his crew, that was not an option. "It seems that Twentieth Air Force had decided that if our guns were loaded we might shoot down other B-29s in the dark so we had no ammo on board except for what we carried in our 45 automatics and that is not too effective against fighters," Savage wrote. "It also seemed probable that my decision to jettison all flak jackets might have been a bit premature."

Savage had told Brooks to let him know when the fighters made a pass. "Seems the fighters were very leery of the firepower of our Superfortress but then they were not on the mailing list of Twentieth Air Force," he wrote. The fighters made cautious, quartering attacks from the rear, one-by-one. As they rolled into their attack, Brooks called it out and Savage turned into them to spoil their aim. Tracers from their guns were everywhere around the besieged B-29, but no one heard or felt any more hits.

The fighters kept pressing their conservative attacks until Savage found a high bank of cloud and flew into it. Safely away from the fighters but far from really safe, Savage took stock. He found that his bomber's fuel transfer system had been hit, and that he had no way to use fuel from the number one and number four fuel tanks. This meant that Guam was out of reach.

Airplane commanders had been briefed on the possibility of using the embattled sulphur island of Iwo Jima as an emergency landing spot. Savage struggled now to remember everything he'd been told about Iwo Jima. He knew that the Marines had a foothold on the island and that the island had a working airfield, albeit one with a fairly short runway. At least one B-29 had made an emergency landing on the island already, and this was supposed to be an option today. If he could get there, Savage was confident he had a good chance of bringing the B-29 to the ground safely.

"We couldn't get back to Guam but had to try for Iwo Jima where the Marines had gotten a foothold on the island. That was the good news. The bad news was that when the fuel transfer system had been shot up, puddles of AVGAS [aviation fuel] were left all over the bomb bay. The smell of AVGAS throughout the airplane was quite disconcerting but what really took the hide off the hog was the St. Elmo's fire, which was shooting sparks all over the airplane, inside and out! I could say that the airplane exploded and all aboard were lost but that would spoil a great story. Instead, we endured this situation for what seemed like forever until we finally broke out of the clouds." Savage was now struggling to make the safety of the short runway on a tiny chunk of sulphur and rock that most people would have said had little value as real estate.

The Musser Crew

Hit by antiaircraft fire near Tokyo, an unnamed B-29 commanded by Capt. John J. Musser of the 29th Bombardment Group from Guam disintegrated and burned. The crew was on their first mission—and their last. Radar operator Eugene A. Homyak and central fire control gunner Cpl. Jack D. Krone were able to escape from the Superfortress, heave themselves into the night, and yank on the ripcords of their parachutes.

Almost nothing else is known about the crew led by Musser (not to be confused with Gordon Muster of *Tall in the Saddle*) or of the passenger they were carrying, Capt. Clarence Holman Jr. Perhaps Musser and right-seat pilot 2nd Lt. Robert K. Reger struggled desperately to try to save the aircraft. A "missing air crew report" created after the mission provides no clue.

Killed in action were Musser, Reger, bombardier 1st Lt. Frank B. Whayman Jr., navigator 2nd Lt. John A. Schur, flight engineer Tech. Sgt. Paul J. Simmons, radio operator Cpl. Dean A. Arnold, left blister gunner Cpl. Robert M. Peterson, right blister gunner

Cpl. Reginald T. Rosser, tail gunner Cpl. Donald L. Osterholm, and Holman. Ahead of survivors Homyak and Krone awaited a horrific fate in many ways worse than going down in a burning bomber.

The Johnson Crew

It was a bad night for the Guam-based 29th Bombardment Group and for a crew that arrived over Tokyo just behind Musser's. First Lieutenant Warren F. Johnson was airplane commander of the B-29 named *Tiny Tim*, also called *Dam-fi-no*. With pilot 2nd Lt. George R. Loughborough and the rest of his crew, Johnson—like Musser— was on his first and only combat mission.

Again, a B-29 was hit and went down. Again, almost nothing is known about what happened. *Tiny Tim* fell in flames near Tokyo. Killed in action were Johnson, Loughborough, radar operator 2nd Lt. John T. Puglisi, bombardier 2nd Lt. Edward J. O'Conner, flight engineer Cpl. Wendell R. Vance, radio operator Staff Sgt. David Woll, central fire control gunner Cpl. Rex M. Fifield, left blister gunner Cpl. Spencer Mason, right blister gunner Cpl. John J. Mullin, and tail gunner Cpl. David J. Shaner. Initially, as happened often, the men were listed as "missing in action." Unknown to the American side, Japanese authorities recovered the remains of these crewmembers and interred them.

No one got out of *Tiny Tim*. No parachutes snapped open in the night.

The night was not over for the tortured 29th group, which would lose five Superfortresses altogether on a night when losses to the entire strike force totaled just fourteen. An unnamed B-29 commanded by Capt. Lucas M. Neas was also shot down and lost with eleven crewmembers plus a passenger, Lt. Col. Martin Wheeler. Another B-29 named *Renton's Reck*, after the city in Washington state where some B-29 Superfortresses were manufactured, ditched at sea—one of five planes to do so on this mission—and airplane commander 1st Lt. Gilbert M. Lichte was rescued. As the main strike force passed over Tokyo, the 29th Group's fifth casualty, a B-29 named *Cherry the Horizontal Cat*, was still in the air in the hands of airplane commander 1st Lt. Firman E. Wyatt—but not for long.

The Fling Crew

So did they really see Tokyo alight, as everyone claims, only to fly off in the wrong direction—farther from their target and farther from home—after becoming the first B-29 crew from their group to reach the Japanese coast that morning?

When this narrative was written sixty-six years after the war, fully five members of the crew of *God's Will* were alive and articulate. All agreed that they saw the streetlights of the Japanese capital before the city was set afire, misunderstood what they were seeing, and continued north. They flew over open water paralleling the coast away from their intended run-in location at Choshi Point. The Fling crew had traveled far under considerable stress and reaching Japan was making things worse rather than better.

They "expended extra fuel in searching for the target," an official report would later say. Their B-29 strayed from clear, windy Tokyo to shrouded, snow-spattered skies above open water just off the coast north of the capital. Had they been a few miles inland, they might have been in the same location where three other B-29s, caught in a more intense part of the same snowstorm, would soon fly into the same mountain at the same time.

The crew of *God's Will* was burning precious gas and was lost. Reb Carter had long since become accustomed to the drone of the R-3350s in his ears. He had no guns or ammunition but was peering from his blister trying to discern some distinctive feature, any distinctive feature, in the early-morning darkness. The enlisted men aboard *God's Will*, Carter included, shared a tent with crewmembers of another B-29 commanded by 1st Lt. Murel W. Hardgrave. It would have been little comfort to Fling's airmen to know that, at this very moment, Hardgrave's airmen were in even bigger trouble than they were. A lot of Superfortress crews were having trouble now that the parade of bombers over the center of the Japanese capital had begun.

Over Tokyo, silvery B-29s continued to pass through searchlight beams, incendiary bombs continued to tumble from their bays, and the city burned with such intensity that flyers could smell roasting flesh. The Fling crew continued to struggle to get its location right.

All along, navigator Phillip Pettit and radar operator Baker had been trying to get the radar set to work. Pettit made no attempt at celestial navigation because of poor visibility in a sky now filled with snow and because his attention was focused on the malfunctioning radar. The effort paid off—the radar flickered on and was now working intermittently. Pettit told Fling that he was seeing Choshi Point on his scope.

He was wrong.

Fling made a ninety-degree left turn to head to the west. *God's Will* made landfall over the Japanese home islands for the first time. About fifteen minutes later, Dwyer, looking down from his perch in the nose, saw a mountain covered with snow. Right-seat pilot "Pete" Peterson saw it too.

"There's a snow-capped peak right below us," Dwyer said over the interphone.

"There's not supposed to be a mountain there," Fling said. The men knew that there was no mountain near Choshi Point.

Dwyer would later say that *God's Will* came very close to slamming into the mountainside. Fling threw the aircraft into an abrupt, climbing, 180-degree turn. He pointed the bomber's nose back toward the ocean from which they had just come.

They retraced their route back to the ocean. Fling turned south looking for Choshi Point. The radar went on the blink again. Weary from struggling to get into the right place, the Fling crew was skirting the Japanese coast north and east of Tokyo.

By now, the crew of *God's Will* had been lost for an extraordinary, fuel-guzzling two and a quarter hours, had nearly slammed into a mountain, and was seething with frustration and anxiety. Fling and his crew had now been lost even longer than their squadron mate Bertagnoli had, but they were not going to follow Bertagnoli's example and abort. They were determined to carry out the mission even though, as Carter noted in his journal, "we knew we wouldn't make it back to base because we were low on gas."

And then, finally, deliverance—Tokyo.

"We were eighty miles from the target when we saw the fire," wrote Carter. The bombing of the city had been going on in earnest for more than two hours now.

When *God's Will* began to enter the remnants among the final swarm of B-29s approaching Tokyo, Carter now heard the sounds of other aircraft and of gunfire. He saw the searchlights, the flak bursts, the burning urban sprawl rushing toward him. Carter wrote in his journal that flak was "intense and rather accurate" and that "about 100 searchlights" were stalking the B-29s.

God's Will, far later than anyone ever intended, was now rapidly approaching its drop point. Fling turned the aircraft over to bombardier Red Dwyer. After all this time, after all this frustration, only one man was now fully occupied, and that was Dwyer. The others had time for their thoughts.

Carter was thinking that maybe it was divine intervention, but it was more likely crew skill that brought *God's Will* to Tokyo after so much time on the wrong flight path. Carter wasn't sure that either God or the crew were exhibiting their best skills in those early-morning hours. In the journal that wasn't a diary, Carter recounted in neat, block lettering, "We were in trail with each B-29 about one minute apart from the next. We were supposed to be the number seven ship from our group over the target but due to getting lost we were one of the last to bomb." *God's Will* was now flying parallel to B-29s from a different group, braving the heat thermals with Dwyer hunched over his Norden bombsight, trying to ignore the most spectacular view anyone would ever see of a world capital afire.

In the final moments, Carter peered out and saw a falling bomb. It had come from a B-29 above them at higher altitude. Distances were deceptive, but Carter was certain the bomb was dangerously close. He estimated that it missed the left wingtip of *God's Will* by just ten feet.

After what many in the crew believed had been an eternity, Dwyer said, "Bombs away."

It was 3:01 a.m. Chamorro Standard Time, March 10, 1945.

Group Commander
Col. Henry C. Huglin had taken command of the 9th Bombardment Group on Tinian a few days earlier. This was the same group as the Fling crew, the Bertagnoli crew, the Keene crew, and the Hardgrave crew. Flying with the Capt. Robert A. McClintock crew of a B-29 named *Tokyo-K.O.*, Huglin led his group to the Empire that night after observing shock among aircrews when they learned they would attack at low level. "Until we reached Japan we flew

at around 2,000 feet," Huglin wrote in an unpublished memoir, although the field order specified cruising at 4,000 to 5,000 feet. "We climbed to bombing altitude when we were approaching the mainland. We flew individually in sort of a stream of airplanes. Our group was about one-third of the way back in the stream. [As we got closer to the target we would] then turn to the northeast for about 30 miles before turning on our northwest axis of attack on the industrial center of Tokyo.

"The whole time we're on this dog-leg pattern Tokyo was in view and in flames; it looked to us like we were headed into Dante's Inferno or through an open door of a blast furnace from which we might not come out." *It was 3:05 p.m. Chamorro Standard Time, March 10, 1945.*

Staff Sergeant Carl Barthold was radio operator in the Capt. James M. Campbell B-29 crew. He belonged to the 870th Bombardment Squadron, 497th Bombardment Group and took off from Saipan in the early evening of March 9, 1945, aboard a pathfinder aircraft leading the way to Tokyo. *U.S. Army*

Major Sam P. "Sammy" Bakshas was the experienced officer who filled in as airplane commander aboard *Tall in the Saddle*, a B-29 Superfortress that was shot down over Tokyo. *Bakshas family*

The B-29 Superfortress named *Star Duster* (aircraft no. 42-93858) was originally painted as "A Square 30." This bomber flew the March 9–10, 1945, Tokyo firebomb mission as part of the 497th Bombardment Group, with Capt. Wilfred N. "Bill" Lind as airplane commander. *Star Duster*'s right gunner, Joe C. Swann, is one of the figures in this narrative. *U.S. Army*

This B-29 crew, led by Capt. Percy Usher Tucker, flew in *Lady Annabelle*, named after Tucker's wife. The aircraft and its crew flew the big firebomb mission to Tokyo. Tucker and his crew belonged to the 40th Bombardment Squadron, 6th Bombardment Group on Tinian. *Terry Tucker Rhodes*

This is a ground portrait of a B-29 Superfortress, the biggest, most complex, and most advanced bomber in the world when it carried out a bombing campaign against Japan. No other country had a comparable aircraft. *U.S. Army*

Captain Percy Usher Tucker, taciturn, a taskmaster, cordial to some and cold to others, was the stern airplane commander of the B-29 Superfortress *Lady Annabelle*. This stateside portrait depicts Tucker as a first lieutenant. *Terry Tucker Rhodes*

Believed to be taken December 24, 1942, this portrait depicts two brothers at war: 2nd Lt. (later Capt.) Percy Usher Tucker (right) is a new Army Air Forces pilot. Second Lieutenant (later 1st Lt.) Lee E. Tucker was a cavalryman and wears the army's leather Sam Browne belt, even though the belt was officially discontinued by an army regulation dated June 7, 1942. Percy Usher Tucker became airplane  commander of the B-29 Superfortress *Lady Annabelle* and led his crew on the March 9–10, 1945, assault on what men called the Empire. Lee Tucker was killed in combat in northern Italy on April 17, 1945. *Terry Tucker Rhodes*

This is the Capt. Percy Usher Tucker crew of the B-29 named *Lady Annabelle* in a portrait taken on Tinian on July 15, 1945, three months after the great Tokyo firebomb mission. The pirate emblem signifies the 6th Bombardment Group. In the back row (left to right): left body gunner Staff Sgt. Robert K. Ryan, tail gunner Staff Sgt. Joe Majeski, radar man Staff Sgt. Joseph W. Ryan, radioman Staff Sgt. John W. Pierce, right body gunner Sgt. Carl Schlemmer, and central fire control gunner Tech. Sgt. Edward C. Roach; in the front row: bombardier Flight Officer Joseph Krogman; pilot 1st Lt. John T. "Gummy" Kearney; airplane commander Capt. Percy Usher Tucker; navigator 1st Lt. Robert Rice; J. T. Jones, who may have been a navigator from another crew; and flight engineer 1st Lt. George "Laddie" Wale. Schlemmer and Rice did not fly the March 9–10, 1945, mission to Tokyo. On that mission were two men not shown here: navigator 1st Lt. Edwin J. Koniusky and right body gunner Cpl. John R. Dodd. *Terry Tucker Rhodes*

First Lieutenant Robert "Bud" McDonald learned about the then-secret B-29 Superfortress from his father, who had inside knowledge. He arrived in Guam but was not yet ready to begin flying in combat at the time of the March 9–10, 1945, Tokyo firebomb mission in which his 93rd Bombardment Squadron commander, Major Sam P. Bakshas, was an important figure. McDonald began flying missions to Japan as a B-29 airplane commander later in March 1945. *Nancy Reynolds*

Sergeant William J. "Reb" Carter was left blister gunner on the B-29 Superfortress named *God's Will*, piloted to Tokyo on March 9–10, 1945, by Capt. Dean Fling. *Doug Carter*

Some members of the Capt. Leon M. Keene B-29 crew on Tinian in typical work attire just before the March 9–10, 1945, Tokyo mission. From left to right: flight engineer 2nd Lt. John R. Jewett, an unidentified navy member "who brought us beer," navigator 2nd Lt. Donald E. Nichols, radar operator Sgt. Marshall D. Long, and tail gunner Sgt. James T. Hash. Long was killed when their B-29 ditched at sea at the end of the Tokyo mission. Jewett, Nichols, and Hash survived the ditching and the war. *James T. Hash*

B-29 Superfortresses of the 500th Bombardment Group drop incendiary bombs on Yokohama on May 29, 1945. Sergeant Howard J. Clos, left blister gunner on a B-29 piloted by Capt. Ferd J. Curtis, took the official photo, which was used on a propaganda leaflet dropped on named Japanese cities to warn them in advance of a fire raid. *U.S. Air Force*

The pilots of this 504th Bombardment Group B-29 Superfortress made nine attempts to land at the emergency airstrip on Iwo Jima. When the bomber finally came to earth, it plowed through a P-51 Mustang flight line, destroying four fighters. The crew got out of the B-29 before it burned to cinders. *U.S. Air Force*

Typical billet for a B-29 Superfortress gunner in the tropics: in his Quonset hut to which he was assigned after weeks of living in tents on Tinian, Sgt. William J. "Reb" Carter of the 9th Bombardment Group has an air mattress, blankets, a handmade nightstand, and a helmet. The risqué pinups belong to the airman in the next bunk. Most of Carter's wall photos depict his girlfriend, Phyllis Ewing. *Doug Carter*

With the silhouettes of escorting P-51 Mustang fighters in the far background, B-29 Superfortresses of Brig. Gen. Emmett "Rosy" O'Donnell's 73rd Wing head from Saipan toward the Japanese mainland on a high-altitude, daylight bombing mission. *U.S. Air Force*

Typical of "the thousand kids" who bombed Tokyo was the B-29 Superfortress crew led by Capt. Ferd Curtis (who later changed his name to Fred). *Carl Curtis*

Major General Curtis E. LeMay, alone on Guam, perhaps as he looked when watching B-29s take off for Tokyo in the final daylight hours of March 9, 1945. *Chester Marshall*

B-29 crewmembers. *U.S. Air Force*

The first B-29 to arrive on Saipan: pilot Maj. Jack Catton shakes hands upon arrival at Saipan with Brig. Gen. Haywood "Possum" Hansell on October 12, 1944. *U.S. Air Force*

B-29s on a high-altitude bombing mission over Japan. *U.S. Air Force*

Joe Krogman was bombardier on the Percy Usher Tucker crew of *Lady Annabelle*. *Joe Krogman*

Krogman at his bombardier station while in flight. *Terry Tucker Rhodes*

B-29 crewmembers enjoy a coffee break. *Terry Tucker Rhodes*

A formation of B-29s over the Pacific. *Terry Tucker Rhodes*

Tokyo burns following fire bombing by B-29s on the night of May 26, 1945.
U.S. Army Air Forces

War correspondent Ernie Pyle talks with an unidentified staff officer on Saipan while observing B-29 operations. Pyle wrote eloquently of the fear crews felt about ditching the B-29 Superfortress at sea. *U.S. Air Force*

On a mission to Nagoya on January 3, 1945, left blister gunner Sgt. James Krantz hangs out into the open airstream from a B-29 named *American Maid*. Krantz was badly battered and severely injured, but other crewmembers were able to pull him back inside the plane and he survived the war. *U.S. Air Force*

B-29 Superfortresses over Mount Fuji near Tokyo. *U.S. Air Force*

These P-51 Mustang fighters are receiving help from a B-29 to navigate their way back to their base on Iwo Jima. *U.S. Air Force*

Unidentified member of the Tucker crew in the bombadier's seat of *Lady Annabelle*. *Terry Tucker Rhodes*

B-29s drop firebombs on Japan. *U.S. Air Force*

This is a B-29 Superfortress en route to Japan. *Terry Tucker Rhodes*

Fifi is the B-29 Superfortress demonstrated at air shows today by the Commemorative Air Force of Midland, Texas. It is the only flying B-29 in the world. *Robert L. Burns*

CHAPTER 13

The Way Out

Mission to Tokyo
March 10, 1945, 3:05 a.m.–7:40 a.m.

BRIGADIER GENERAL THOMAS S. "TOMMY" POWER, the leader of the B-29 force flying from Guam and the overall air commander of the mission, stayed over the target for ninety minutes. He was aboard the B-29 named *Snatch Blatch*, alias *City of Los Angeles*, with airplane commander Tony Simeral. Crewmembers, including radio operator Erwin, had taken up stations where they could observe the conflagration beneath them.

Power, who struck many as a mean-spirited man who was even harder than LeMay, was actually quite touched by what he was observing. He was making red crosses on a hand-held map to show blocks where fires broke out. He wore his red crayon down. Winds generated by the fires spread the flames far and wide.

Unlike Power, crewmembers aboard the B-29, including airplane commander Simeral, were becoming impatient and nervous. Red Erwin said something on the interphone about what a prize *Snatch*

Blatch would be for Japanese antiaircraft gunners. No one liked lingering this long over a well-defended target.

Power repeatedly uttered short comments that signified approval at the way the mission was going. Beneath his gruff exterior, Power felt some sympathy for the human beings on the ground. It was not his job to feel it. It was not in his nature to show it.

In an official report, Power later wrote:

> The best way to describe what it looks like when these fire bombs come out of the bomb bay of an airplane is to compare it to a giant pouring a big shovelful of white-hot coals all over the ground, covering an area about 2,500 feet in length and some 500 feet wide. That's what each single B-29 was doing! There must have been well over three hundred airplanes, all of them spewing these white-hot incendiaries. They started fires everywhere. Of course, Tokyo was a highly inflammable city, and as the fire swathes widened and came together, they built up into one vast fire.

Power had been instrumental in persuading LeMay to use the tactics that were destroying Tokyo during this long night. Along with chief of staff Larry Norstad, Power favored incendiaries. Hiding his sympathies, Power would later tell a reporter that those on the ground deserved what they got.

Power might have been the hardest man among the thousands of Americans over Tokyo that morning. But while he kept up his front during and after the Tokyo mission and later in life, Power was not unmoved by the human suffering beneath his wings. As he kept looking down, he occasionally wiped his eyes. One crewmember believes the words "poor bastards" escaped from his lips.

"We can only stay about another ten minutes, General," Simeral's flight engineer Sgt. Vern Schiller told Power, referring to the B-29's fuel state.

"Okay," Power responded, and for once he appeared relieved. *It was 3:05 a.m. Chamorro Standard Time, March 10, 1945.*

Tokyo on Fire

More than two and a half hours after the first B-29s began releasing their firebombs, possibly eighty thousand Japanese had been swept up in those flames. Many, including Asia scholar Mark Selden, who wrote in *Japan Focus*, contend that the widely seen figure of one hundred thousand who ultimately died in the bombing is misleading.

The figure of roughly 100,000 deaths, provided by Japanese and American authorities, both of whom may have had reasons of their own for minimizing the death toll, seems to me arguably low in light of population density, wind conditions and survivors' accounts. With an average of 103,000 inhabitants per square mile (396 people per hectare) and peak levels as high as 135,000 per square mile (521 people per hectare), *the highest density of any industrial city in the world* [emphasis added], and with firefighting measures ludicrously inadequate to the task, 15.8 square miles (41 km square) of Tokyo were destroyed on a night when fierce winds whipped the flames and walls of fire blocked tens of thousands fleeing for their lives. An estimated 1.5 million people lived in the burned out areas.

Aboard the first B-29s to traverse the capital, now heading home, crewmembers were able to see Tokyo burning long after their departure, when they were out at sea two hundred miles away.

The Bakshas Crew

The big bomber carrying Sammy Bakshas, Gordon Muster, and others narrowly missed falling within the perimeter of the firestorm that was enveloping a major part of the city.

In a different B-29 named *Gamecock*, radio operator Trip Triplett, the Oklahoma farm boy who was part Cherokee, was catching his balance and recovering from his own plane being batted all over the sky. Triplett peered down right at about the time *Tall in the Saddle* was hit. "As far as the eye could see, to the east and to the north," Triplett wrote in his personal memoir, "there was a sea of flame, a mass of roaring fire that seemed to cover the city like a boiling cauldron. Intense winds whipped the raging fire and smoke into greater fury. Occasionally a delayed action bomb, dropped by some of the planes along with their incendiaries, blossomed amid the blazing holocaust. How could this fire ever be put out? How could anyone possibly live through the sea of hell?"

The bomber force was more than two-thirds of the way through its destructive mission as Triplett observed the inferno below. *It was 3:20 a.m. Chamorro Standard Time, March 10, 1945.*

Wrote Triplett, "I was suddenly shaken from my trance of awe. The blinding finger of a searchlight snapped on and we were caught, glistening, nude and helpless. Jim [right blister gunner Staff Sgt. James Turner] and I drew back from the gun port instinctively. There was no place to hide from that glaring, probing, blue-white beam. Little red shooting stars came spiraling up from below and filled the sky around us. These were tracer bullets from the ack-ack below.

"As we turned east toward the sea, still skirting the north edge of Tokyo, the light left us. Jim and I continued to gaze with fixation down upon the burning city.

"Out to our right, a thousand feet or more below us, a plane flared brightly in the dark sky. Fuel tanks aflame. It hit the ground and spewed chunks of flaming wreckage for several hundred feet, silhouetting for a brief moment the pines into which it crashed."

Triplett had been granted an extraordinary view of the demise of *Tall in the Saddle*, of Bakshas, of Muster, of Eugene Cook, of Leland Fishback, and of the dreams of twelve men who had hoped to complete the mission, finish the war, and go home to their families. *Tall in the Saddle* ran out of speed and altitude and was obliterated by fire twenty to twenty-five miles northeast of Tokyo. Bakshas circled over the village of Itabashi three times before the damage and the onboard fire were totally out of control.

Triplett was looking down from above. Peering upward from below, in a location almost thirty miles removed from the firestorm in Tokyo, was eight-year-old Hidesaburo Kusama. Accompanied by his brother, Kusama stood transfixed and watched *Tall in the Saddle* crash into the forest of Itabashi-mura. Kusama told himself that the crew were heroes for purposely crashing into the trees to spare the lives of the residents of the village. At that instant, at the age of eight, Kusama told himself that one day he would investigate the crash and write a book about it.

Nine men aboard *Tall in the Saddle* lost their lives on the spot. Sammy, who had Aldora waiting for him back home, was among them—the strapping Sammy Bakshas, whose romance had been like a dime novel and whose love of flying was total. Gordon Muster and Eugene Cook were also among those who perished in the crash. The other crewmembers who died at the scene were radar operator 1st Lt. Theodore R. Homling, bombardier 1st Lt. Earl J. Hake, navigator 2nd Lt. John R. Hagadorn, gunner Cpl. Willard A. Seitz, gunner Cpl. Fred T. Harley, and gunner Cpl. Donald J. Heaney. Bakshas was the oldest at thirty-four, Harley the youngest at twenty-one. When Kusama did write his book, he reported that villagers found nine of the crew dead in the woods and buried them.

Somehow surviving the shootdown of *Tall in the Saddle* were Fishback, radio operator Cpl. Laverne J. Zehler, and tail gunner Cpl. Glen H. Hodak. The tail section of the bomber was intact, and Hodak apparently simply stepped out of the aircraft. All three were injured, Fishback gravely. Considering that Fishback was apparently right at the spot on the flight deck where the Japanese antiaircraft shell struck dead center, the fact that he survived, even with severe wounds, is extraordinary.

Sakae Tomiyama, thirty-five, chief of the community fire defense group, went ahead of the other villagers to the crash site to fight the fire ignited by the B-29. Elderly woodcutters told Tomiyama that "two or three devil-like tall Americans" were alive. The villagers gathered around Tomiyama were afraid. "None of them had ever seen Americans and they did not know what to do or how to speak when they first met them," Kusama wrote. Tomiyama led the way to the wreckage and began yelling, "*Detekoi* (Come out)."

More than one hundred villagers gathered at the crash site. Some showed hostility toward the three Americans when they emerged from the wreck. The view of the sky above Tokyo reflecting the blaze from the air raid was still fresh in their minds.

After he learned they were unarmed and wounded, Tomiyama pleaded with the villagers not to hit the Americans. "If you want to hit them, come and hit me!" Tomiyama shouted at the excited townspeople. One of the Americans—after all these years, there is no way to know which one—pointed to his wristwatch and said to Tomiyama, "I will give you this watch so please help us." For five years Tomiyama had studied English seven hours a week at an elite high school, so he fully understood the first words he'd ever heard spoken by an American. The record is unclear as to whether Tomiyama accepted the watch, but he told the Americans that he would help them.

Without violence, the Japanese took the three—Fishback, Zehler, and Hodak—to a shelter and eventually turned them over to military police. Villagers buried the nine members of the crew killed in the crash and placed a wooden cross atop the mound, though none of the villagers was Christian. It quickly became clear that Fishback could barely walk and a crude stretcher was made for him. Zehler and Hodak walked with some difficulty.

In a 2007 paper, "Allied Aircraft and Airmen lost over the Japanese Mainland," Toru Fukubayashi wrote:

> Fishback was seriously wounded at the time of capture. Tokyo Kempei Tai asked Tobu Army Medical Dept. to hospitalize him, but due to chaos under the air raid, the Medical Dept. refused this request. In the meantime, a medical officer of Tobu Army, 1st Lt. Rokuro Sonobe came to examine Fishback, but he gave no treatment, because he thought the wounded had no chance of recovery. In consequence, Tobu Army was compelled to take him over and quite at a loss [as to] what to do with him. Two days later, by order of Lt. Col. Kimiya Ichinohe, three soldiers of Tobu Army, accompanied by 2nd Lt. Sadao Motokawa and W/O Masao Kuwahara of Tokyo Kempei Tai, took Fishback to an air raid shelter in the schoolyard of Tokyo foreign language school (present Tokyo University of Foreign Studies), and beheaded him, then buried his body under trash and wreckages."

After the war, at the War Crimes Trial in Yokohama, Ichinohe and Motokawa were found guilty of murdering Leland Fishback. They argued that his wounds were so grievous it was a mercy killing. The tribunal sentenced Ichinohe to death. Kuwahara was sentenced to life confinement for helping the execution and burial, and medical officer Sonobe to two years for refusing medical treatment.

The other two survivors of *Tall in the Saddle*, Zehler and Hodak, were taken to a Tokyo military prison. They would not be there long. In the period just after the war, family members of *Tall in the Saddle*'s crew—Aldora Bakshas among them—learned only that the men were declared missing and later dead. American authorities gave them no details. More information did not become widely known until Kusama wrote his account, published in Japanese in 2006.

The Kordsmeier Crew

Morrilton, the town in Arkansas where B-29 Superfortress airplane commander Hubert L. Kordsmeier grew up, hasn't changed much, and the people in the town haven't changed much either. In his white farmhouse on eighty acres of farmland along Route 1, which is still in the family today, siblings, horse, mules, cows, chickens, and a grape orchard surrounded Kordsmeier. The house did yet not have wallpaper, indoor plumbing, or electricity when Kordsmeier was born there on January 27, 1920. Kordsmeier was the oldest among five sisters and six brothers.

Sixty miles northwest of Little Rock on the banks of the Arkansas River, with a population of just under seven thousand and almost in the exact center of the state, Morrilton offers "Old World charm and unsurpassed scenic beauty," according to the town's brochure. It has a certain timelessness like many hamlets in the Deep South that have sent a disproportionate number of their sons to war.

Another native of Morrilton, Navy PBY Catalina pilot Nathan Green Gordon (1916–2008), earned the Medal of Honor for a dramatic rescue mission at Kavieng Harbor in the South Pacific and was later Arkansas's lieutenant governor for fully two decades, from 1947 to 1967. The nearby town of Lonoke produced Arkansas Razorback and Detroit Lion football player Maurice L. "Footsie" Britt (1919–1995), the first man in history to earn all four of the nation's top valor awards in a single war. Britt was awarded his Medal of Honor for repelling a German attack in Italy; the medal was presented to him on the football field where he played. He replaced Gordon as lieutenant governor from 1967 to 1971, but his ambitions to become governor were thwarted—and the region's military tradition broken—when an upstart Bill Clinton won the governorship in 1978.

In an interview with the author of this book, recalling his rescue mission described in a citation as showing "conspicuous gallantry and intrepidity above and beyond the call of duty," Gordon spoke of the American tradition of bringing everyone back from the battle. "Even if they've fallen, you leave no one behind," said Gordon.

He was wrong.

"Even today we have never been told what really happened," said Louis Kordsmeier in a 2011 interview for this book. "They never brought my brother home from the war."

"Other families at least have the satisfaction of having their loved one's remains brought home," said another brother, Clement Kordsmeier. Despite the extraordinary destruction wreaked during bombing missions, the remains of nearly all American aircrew were recovered and repatriated after the war and interred according to family wishes.

Not Kordsmeier. "We didn't get a body," said Clement. "We didn't get anything."

Second Lieutenant Hubert L. Kordsmeier was airplane commander of a B-29 Superfortress of the 498th Bombardment Group flying from Saipan. Hubert Kordsmeier's group commander, other high-ranking officers, and even LeMay wanted at the time, as the Kordsmeier brothers still want today, to know what happened to him. The reason they wanted to know extends beyond Kordsmeier and his crew.

For reasons that may remain forever a mystery, shortly after depositing their firebombs on a burning Tokyo, three B-29s from three different bomb groups, two from Guam and one from Saipan, *flew into the same mountain* in Japan *at about the same time*. Kordsmeier's appears to have been the first. *It was 3:40 a.m. Chamorro Standard Time, March 10, 1945*. There is no official record of the time of impact or how it occurred. The time given here is based on educated analysis.

The other question, apart from how three planes could have flown into the same mountain, is: how did three B-29s end up almost a hundred miles northeast of Tokyo, meaning a hundred miles farther from home than they were supposed to be? Members of the Fling crew, who were similarly lost but later found their way, wondered if the cantankerous radar sets aboard the three B-29s were functioning.

Kordsmeier was piloting a Superfortress so new that the crew had not yet given it a name. It was the tenth combat mission for Kordsmeier and his crew.

Apart from the furious winds at high altitude that would later be called the jetstream, which were not a factor on tonight's low-level mission, and apart from convection currents kicked up by the burning of the Japanese capital, which were not a factor for these three bombers, the weather was unremarkable. These B-29s— Kordsmeier's and two others—"seemed to have mistaken the course due to bad weather on their way to the target and encountered extremely severe turbulence," according to a Japanese report, possibly referring to turbulence caused by the sheer heat in Tokyo. We will never know whether they were hit by Japanese gunfire. A crewmember in another aircraft in Kordsmeier's squadron saw a B-29 that could only have been Kordsmeier's "burning . . . over Tokyo immediately after bombs away."

Kordsmeier and his pilot, 2nd Lt. Claude T. Dean, must have experienced a period when they struggled with the controls before slamming into 5,657-foot Mount Fubo in the Zao Mountains. Shinichi Kanno, a witness on the ground, remembered "the whirr of a B-29." Kanno remembered his neighbors in what he called a "playful" manner as if "having fun," shouting: "Ah! That is a B-29! It is a B-29 air raid!" Why they were amused about American bombers being overhead is not clear. Kanno and his neighbors peered into the night and "witnessed a flame burst halfway up Mount Fubo." "We looked fixedly with wonder as a blue flame flared up," and the B-29 continued burning, Kanno recalled. Other witnesses reported a blue-white fire that persisted through the remaining hours of darkness and into the dawn that followed. Only later in the day would parties of local residents make their way to the spot where the B-29 had dug a furrow 330-feet long in the 10-foot-deep snow before burning, at an elevation of 3,983 feet above sea level.

Aboard the unnamed B-29 with airplane commander Kordsmeier and pilot Dean were navigator 2nd Lt. Leonard Gottleib, bombardier 2nd Lt. Robert L. Owens, flight engineer 2nd Lt. Harold Raybould, radio operator Staff Sgt. Martin Boskovitch, central fire control gunner Sgt. Henry S. Solomon, right blister gunner Staff Sgt. Ernest L. Bretag, left blister gunner Sgt. Martin J. McMahon Jr., radar operator Staff Sgt. Samuel F. Reneau, and tail gunner Sgt. William E. Fry.

The Wyatt Crew

Cherry the Horizontal Cat, commanded by Firman Wyatt of the badly battered 29th Bombardment Group operating from North Field, Guam, was apparently the second of the three B-29s that went into the slope of Mount Fubo northeast of Tokyo and far from home. The second plane impacted at 4,921 feet of elevation.

The pilot of Wyatt's aircraft was Wesley O. Chandler, who'd taken Reserve Officer Training Corps courses in the Clemson University class of 1940. Chandler was married with a baby boy. A page in his honor created by Clemson alumni shows an earnest, boyish face and a full life ahead, and quotes the Army Air Forces as reporting "Aircraft lost as a result of: unknown." It was Chandler's third combat mission. We do not know what he said, thought, or saw during that final moment when exploding antiaircraft fire obliterated the forward fuselage of the B-29.

The availability of a few snippets of information about Chandler, who still has family members in Hickory, North Carolina, is a stark contrast to the faceless images we retain today of so many of the thousand kids. All have names, but most are hard to see because their legend is preserved poorly and in some cases relatives have scattered. The letters home, the love letters, the scrapbooks, the photo albums are all gone today and with them the faces of so many men. Only their names remain.

They are forever young.

We know from others that the third B-29 to fly into a mountain had on board a much-respected, smoothly functioning crew, which is a little piece of knowledge in itself, because a surprisingly large number of B-29 crews were characterized by dysfunction, discord, and dissonance.

We do not know much else about the Carr crew.

The Carr Crew

The 29th Bombardment Group suffered greater casualties than any other group in those predawn hours of Saturday, March 10, 1945, but it was the 19th Bombardment Group, also on North Field, Guam, and it was the group's 93rd squadron, which Sammy Bakshas commanded, that provided the third aircraft in the three-plane mountainside disaster.

Capt. Samuel M. Carr was airplane commander of the third Superfortress to collide with the looming slope in darkness and swirling snow. Carr's B-29, which did not have a name painted on its nose, carried twelve, including a ride-along, Major Ollio J. Laird, who was squadron operations officer, a job that made him Sammy Bakshas's deputy. Laird emulated Sammy Bakshas by displacing the airplane commander Carr in the front left seat, and was probably handling yoke and throttle when the bomber slammed into the ridgeline. It was a swift, abrupt end to a harmonious crew.

Other crewmembers were pilot 2nd Lt. James F. Nudgins; bombardier 2nd Lt. Edward P. Olefirowicz; flight engineer, navigator 2nd Lt. Leon A. Payne; 2nd Lt. Leonard G. Robinson; radio operator Flight Officer Francis E. Tully; radar operator Cpl. Gilbert N. Tice; central fire control gunner Cpl. Joseph Kish Jr.; gunner Cpl. Albert D. Lutes; gunner Cpl. Charles E. Mabry; and gunner Cpl. Robert L. Lott. All perished instantly. There was too little remaining of the smashed B-29 for anyone to have lived for any period of time after it went in. The approximate time the three B-29s smashed into the earth within minutes of each other can only be made on the basis of an educated guess, based on Japanese reports. *It was 3:40 a.m. Chamorro Standard Time, March 10, 1945.*

For the Wyatt, Kordsmeier, and Carr crews, the war was over. But the great firebomb mission was still wrapping itself up. Superfortresses were still careening through the night, most heading toward home now, the last few still exiting the burning Japanese capital.

The Keene Crew

Things could hardly have been worse for the crew of the unnamed B-29 Superfortress that had the unpopular Capt. Leon M. Keene occupying the airplane commander's seat and the much-liked interloper from headquarters, the heir apparent to Keene's job, John C. Conly, struggling in the radar compartment just behind the bomb bay. Riddled by small-arms fire, losing fuel, caught up now in a snowstorm that had engulfed plane and crew for three hours, the B-29 emerged from darkness into a cloudy, gloomy daylight and everybody on board was pretty sure of two things: they were lost and they didn't have enough gas to get home. It did not help that this was one of the crews that did not function like a well-oiled machine. Most of the men had high regard for one another and believed in teamwork, but one or two crewmembers didn't fit in well with the others. No situation demanded teamwork more than the one they were in now.

They were going to have to ditch.

Like dots begging to be connected, ships and planes were lined up all along routes to and from the Empire, eager and ready for no purpose except to rescue B-29 crews that went down in the water. The planes were beefy PBM Mariner flying boats mostly from Navy Rescue Squadron One (VH-1) at Saipan. One of the ships was the seaplane tender USS *Cook Inlet* (AVP 36), responsible for ministering to the PBMs but also for conducting independent rescue operations. Keene's bomber outfit, the Tinian-based 9th Bombardment Group—the outfit of Huglin, Fling, Bertagnoli, and Hardgrave—had thus far never actually lost an aircraft. The *Cook Inlet* had never rescued a crew.

Duty for the sailors aboard the seaplane tenders was reasonably comfortable most of the time, except when they came under attack from Japanese suicide aircraft, the kamikaze. "Our seaplanes and our tender were given a huge responsibility for the safety of B-29 crews," said Milburn P. Sanders, the sailor who had been riding in the Blue Ridge Mountains when Pearl Harbor was attacked. "We knew that every pair of eyes and every set of ears aboard our ship could make the difference when one of those big bombers made a big splash. Those boys were carrying the war to the enemy and if we had a chance to help them we wanted to do it."

Nothing was more torturous to a B-29 crew than knowing they would have to ditch, yet also knowing that they might spend hours more in flight waiting for it to happen. Wrote Ernie Pyle, "'Ditching' out here isn't like 'ditching' in the English Channel, where your chances of being picked up are awfully good. 'Ditching' out here is usually fatal.

"We have set up a search-and-rescue system for these 'ditched' fliers, but still the ocean is awfully big, and it's mighty hard to find a couple of little rubber boats. The fact that we do rescue about a fifth of our 'ditched' fliers is amazing to me."

Added Pyle: "Yes, that long drag back home after the bombing is a definite mental hazard, and is what eventually makes the boys sit and stare."

For the Keene crew, night became day. Swirling snow was replaced by intermittent wet gloom. The unforgiving Pacific slid past beneath. Long before the words were used in the title of a novel, B-29 crews were calling it "the cruel sea." Conly was in an unspeakably cruel situation.

Because of the storm, all of the bomber's navigational aids, including Conly's radar set—there it was again, a problem with the radar—were inoperative. In the radar compartment with the crew's regular radar man, Sgt. Marshall D. Long, Conly had now been struggling for hours to get the radar to work. "We wanted to know where the hell we were," said tail gunner Sgt. James T. Hash, who was too far back to see Conly and Long at work but was able to hear them—and pilot Keene—on the interphone. "It wouldn't be quite right to say we were all feeling desperate, but we were close." In his earphones, Hash heard Keene say that the B-29 would be able to remain aloft for maybe two more hours, but that wasn't enough to enable them to reach friendly ground, so it wouldn't prevent them from having to ditch. The crew had already thrown some equipment overboard to reduce the weight—and fuel consumption—of their bomber, but Keene wanted more.

Accompanied by navigator 2nd Lt. Donald E. Nichols Jr., Conly headed for the bomb bay. The citation for an award later bestowed on Conly tells the story: "Major Conly and the navigator took charge of jettisoning the equipment through the open bomb bay doors. During this operation some of the equipment including two flak suits caught on the extreme lower part of the rear of the forward bomb bay and the doors would not close. Major Conly removed his parachute, lowered himself by his hands down into the bomb bay and dislodged the equipment with his feet. The bomb bay doors were then closed. [Conly] went back to the radar compartment and continued working with his radar set."

A ditching in the Pacific was still a considerable time ahead. Very much in command, Conly could easily have returned to the airplane commander's seat and taken back the flying from Keene. Instead Conly kept working on the radar set and in time picked up an island on his scope. The crew didn't know where they were, and Conly didn't know which island he was looking at.

Tokyo's longest night had ended. The sun was coming up over the Pacific. *It was 7:40 a.m. Chamorro Standard Time, March 10, 1945.*

CHAPTER 14

"What's a B-32 Dominator?"

The B-29 Superfortress in the American Air Campaign, January 1, 1945–March 3, 1945

A T THE START OF 1945, the world was paying little attention to the B-29 Superfortresses that would continue to operate three months longer with XX Bomber Command in India and China. Crewmembers in India and China felt their contribution was being overlooked, and it was. Twenty-First Bomber Command in the Mariana Islands was immediately and totally eclipsing XX Bomber Command in India and China.

On Saipan and Tinian, on January 3, 1945, the command marked a high-altitude firebomb raid on the industrial city of Nagoya, rapidly becoming a familiar target, where the Mitsubishi plant was relentlessly turning out new aircraft. Ninety-seven Superfortresses launched on the mission, including one that crashed at Anatahan Island in the Marianas. Seventy-nine bombers reached the target, but the formation was split up and only fifty-seven dropped on the primary target.

The B-29s encountered swarms of fighters. The fighters made aggressive firing passes on a bomber named *American Maid*. In the

American Maid's left blister, gunner James Krantz was blown out of the airplane by sudden decompression after gunfire narrowly missed him. Krantz was the gunner who had paid attention when Sgt. August Renner was catapulted out of a B-29 named *Mustn't Touch* over Nagoya twenty days earlier. A harness of Krantz's own design prevented him from falling six miles to the ground. Instead, Krantz dangled precariously outside the aircraft in the rushing, frigid airstream.

Other gunners struggled in vain to pull Krantz back into the aircraft. Like an unwanted appendage to the B-29, Krantz dangled there, flapping, being slapped about in a world of noise and wind blast, fortunately with his oxygen mask still attached and working. After a couple of attempts and about ten minutes, a trio of crewmembers combined their strength and succeeded in pulling Krantz back inside. The B-29 returned to Isley Field on Saipan and Krantz was still around to talk about the experience six decades later.

Krantz recovered fully from his subzero ride outside his bomber. Metaphorically speaking, Krantz fared better than XXI Bomber Command boss Possum Hansell, who was under pressure from his superiors. The B-29 campaign in general, and the Nagoya raids in particular, did not seem to be working well. Apart from the loss of two other B-29s over Nagoya, the latest incendiary bombing was determined to have been largely ineffectual. After months of trying, Superfortress crews still had not found a way to cope with winds and weather at high altitude over Japan.

Hansell enjoyed a superb record as a bomber leader in Europe. He was truly a pioneer in the B-29 campaign. On Saipan, he struggled to ease frictions with his 73rd Wing commander, the headstrong Rosy O'Donnell. Hansell had every reason to believe that he was doing a good job and that, as the B-29 force continued to grow in size, he would remain in command.

He was wrong.

Winds, weather, and the simple element of misfortune besieged the Superfortress crews when they returned to Nagoya on January 14, 1945. The B-29s were engulfed in Japanese fighters and most had to bomb through haze. Five B-29s were lost, although one returned to Saipan on two engines and made a shaky landing, the last ever for this bomber that saved her crew.

On that mission, a squadron mate remembered the loss of one aircraft: "Capt. Leonard L. Cox was KIA [killed in action]. The number 3 engine caught on fire on the way to Nagoya. Cox released the bombs and fragments struck the aircraft. Cox attempted to ditch the aircraft and the center section of the plane exploded right before they struck the water. The aircraft crashed northwest of the Marianas about one third of the way to Iwo Jima. Four out of the 11-man crew survived the crash and were picked up by the Navy in life rafts."

On January 19, B-29s from Saipan struck the Kawasaki aircraft plant at Akashi. Of eighty bombers that made it into the air, sixty-two dropped on the primary. No aircraft were lost, and the mission was deemed the first true success of the year.

This happened too late to help Hansell.

Enter LeMay

On January 20, 1945, Maj. Gen. Curtis E. LeMay arrived on Guam from China for what he thought would be a brief visit and a routine meeting with Hansell, his counterpart in the Marianas. But Hansell had a visitor from Washington, and the meeting was not routine. Army Air Forces commander Gen. Henry H. "Hap" Arnold had dispatched key aide Lauris "Larry" Norstad from Washington to tell Hansell that Arnold was firing him. No one on Guam was expecting this. The situation was tragic and heartrending for all: Hansell was an experienced combat commander; he and Norstad had worked together for years, and their families had socialized before the war.

But Norstad was far more than an unwilling hatchet man bearing bad news from the boss. Norstad was, in fact, the engineer of his friend Hansell's downfall. While Arnold viewed Hansell as too slow in achieving success—his extraordinary accomplishment in fielding the B-29 force in the Marianas goes largely unrecognized in the history books—Norstad saw Hansell as the obstacle to using the weapon Norstad favored, the incendiary.

"I had to decide to take the action [relieving Hansell] before we lost the goddamned war," Norstad said later. "The Old Man [Arnold] really had to come to a point where he was torn between his great fondness for Hansell—very warm personal feeling—and what had developed. And surely there were . . . more circumstances in which Hansell had no control, and over those which he did have control, utter absolute complete and irreversible lack of competence." As Norstad said later, Hansell's belief in daylight precision bombing had cost him "the best job in the Air Force."

Everyone involved in the change of command knew that LeMay was an experienced combat commander and more of an operator than an administrator. Hansell himself readily acknowledged that LeMay was superbly qualified to take over XXI Bomber Command. Respect for LeMay was universal, but respect did not mean affection. When LeMay spent a few days on Guam before returning to China to pack his bags, come back, and take over the campaign against the Japanese home islands, St. Clair McKelway wrote:

> He was around a few days, said almost nothing to anybody, was what, by civilian standards, would be called rude to many people. He was a big, husky, healthy, rather stocky, full-faced, black-haired man, thirty-nine years old, from Columbus, Ohio. He apparently couldn't make himself heard even in a small room except when you bent all your ears in his direction, and when you did he appeared to evade your attempts to hear him. He did this by interposing a cigar or pipe among the words that were trying to escape through teeth that had obviously been pried open only with an effort, an effort with which the speaker had no real sympathy and to which he was unwilling to lend more than half-hearted assistance.

Brigadier General Roger Ramey, Hansell's deputy, flew back to China with LeMay to take over XX Bomber Command. Gracious to the last, Hansell wrote to Arnold: "General Norstad arrived yesterday and informed me of your decision to relieve me of this command, and replace me with General LeMay. I was surprised, but I accept your decision." He had but one favor to ask: "I have a request to make. It is this: I should like to be protected against the well-meant efforts of my friends to find me a job that is 'commensurate with my varied experience' or one that will absorb my energies. I am being relieved of the best job in the Air Forces; my energies are, at least temporarily, spent. It has been my lot to prepare for and pioneer both the air offensive against Germany and that against Japan. I should like a job now which will afford me the time and opportunity to rehabilitate myself." Hansell's request was to command a training wing in the southwestern United States.

LeMay was back by late January. A tentative plan to have Hansell stay on Guam in a newly created slot as deputy commander was a bad idea—when a top leader is removed from a job, he should be whisked away as quickly as possible. The idea to keep him there was all the worse because LeMay had been Hansell's subordinate in Europe three years earlier. With a lot of fuzzy thinking going on, Hansell seemed to be the only person who realized this. He explained to his bosses why it would make no sense for him to remain, and he was soon gone—a great airpower leader whose final wartime assignment would have to be called a failure. After a tearful farewell to many, including the Catton crew of the B-29 named *Joltin' Josie*, Hansell departed Guam for the United States on January 20, 1945.

At the end of January, LeMay received a visitor and learned something Hansell apparently didn't know. An Army engineer captain stepped off a plane from stateside and flashed papers that impressed everyone he saw and immediately got him an audience with the two-star general. In LeMay's office on Guam, the captain told him about Groves's Manhattan Project and the supersecret effort to develop a new weapon called the atomic bomb. This apparently was the occasion when LeMay learned that, on orders from Arnold, Col. Cecil E. Combs, Twentieth Air Force deputy for operations, had set aside four Japanese cities not yet bombed and ordered that they were not to be attacked. If the new weapon was to make an impression on the Japanese, it needed to be used in warfare, not shown off in a peaceful demonstration, and its effects would be most apparent if it was deployed to a location where no bomb damage existed already. The cities were Niigata, Kokura, Nagasaki, and Hiroshima. For separate reasons having to do with culture and religion, Kyoto was also off the target list.

LeMay had other things on his mind—Hansell's B-29s hadn't been hitting targets with anything resembling accuracy, and now that they were LeMay's B-29s, they still weren't—so he listened to the briefing with limited interest.

"Generally speaking, I could understand what the Army man was talking about," LeMay said later. "We had a very powerful weapon. But it was late in the war and I was busy."

It is not usual for a captain to make a demand of a major general, but the junior-ranking visitor secured LeMay's written agreement not to fly any more combat missions. With a Distinguished Service Cross in his 201 File, LeMay had no need to prove his courage, but the restriction annoyed him. To the extent possible, he had always led from the front. The stage was now set for an important mission to Tokyo to be led not by LeMay but by Tommy Power.

In retrospect, Hansell faced an impossible task: trying to implement a strategic bombing campaign with green crews and untested aircraft against enemy targets more than a thousand miles away and weather conditions never previously encountered in warfare (in part because bombers had never before flown so high). Add maintenance problems, logistics nightmares, and a unique command relationship (Hansell reporting to the always-impatient and seriously ill AAF chief, General Arnold), and it appears that the seeds of Hansell's dismissal were sown almost from the moment he took command of the fledgling B-29 force.

The Fling Crew

On January 21, 1945, the Fling crew of the aircraft later to be named *God's Will* embarked on the long journey from the United States to the western Pacific. The men left McCook Field, Nebraska, in their own B-29 and paused at Herrington, Kansas. Their subsequent stops in New Mexico and at Mather Field in California were typical of the long, winding path from the training grounds of the American Plains to the war zone of the Pacific islands. Like many before them, the Fling crew proceeded to the island of Oahu in the Territory of Hawaii and from there to Kwajalein, and finally to Tinian.

The long transoceanic trek was anything but routine as another B-29 airplane commander, Bud McDonald, would soon learn when he had to turn back after taking off from Oahu. Concerned that Superfortress crews did not have enough training in long-distance formation flying, Hansell had requested that the Air Transport Command (ATC), which was responsible for the men until they reached the war zone, allow squadrons to make the 2,300-mile journey from California to Hawaii in formation. Permission was denied on the grounds that the aircraft lacked sufficient range to fly that distance in formation. The flight would have been without bomb load and would encounter no opposition, as they would in a few weeks later on similar flights from Guam, Saipan, and Tinian to Tokyo. Still, Gen. Harold Hal George, commander of the ATC and Hansell's friend and mentor, refused to agree to Hansell's plan. There is no indication that LeMay subsequently planned the proposal.

Left blister gunner Reb Carter noted that Tinian offered "short rains nearly every night," an outdoor theater for his outfit, the 9th Bombardment Group, badminton, horseshoes, swimming (including a potentially risky swim into an underwater cave), and a few USO shows. At one such show, Carter met Dixie Dunbar, a vivacious, Kewpie doll–like burlesque performer from his hometown of Atlanta. After a show, the two Georgia natives talked for fifteen or twenty minutes.

The men slept in large tents, any one of which could house the enlisted members of two B-29 crews. They slept on cots on a crushed-coral floor. Carter noted that the enlisted men's club did not initially have refrigeration. The men dipped bottled beer in 100-octane aviation fuel and placed it in the shade to cool. Initially the men had a windmill-like device to wash their clothing.

Carter found a Japanese skull, took out some of the teeth, and mailed them to his girlfriend Phyllis to give to her young nephew. He had come a long way from Atlanta.

Bombing Campaign

In the early part of his tenure, LeMay continued to send B-29s on high-altitude, daylight precision bombing missions of exactly the kind that had gotten Hansell fired. A January 23, 1945, return to Nagoya was made in the face of furious winds and heavy clouds. Seventy-three Superfortresses launched. Only twenty-eight dropped on the primary target. Two aircraft were lost.

A January 27 mission to Tokyo was worse. Fighters were everywhere. The Japanese shot down nine B-29s.

The 313th Wing, commanded by Brig. Gen. John H. Davies, joined the fight from North Field on Tinian in February, bringing to the Marianas the 6th, 9th, 504th, and 505th Bombardment Groups. Soon afterward to Guam came the 314th Wing (Tommy Power's outfit) with the 19th and 29th Groups, to be joined later by the 39th and 330th.

By now, the silvery B-29s had taken on individual personalities with names (often incorrectly called nicknames), pictures (named "nose art" by later generations, although the term did not exist at the time), and plenty of color everywhere. The elaborate scheme of identifying bomb groups and individual aircraft with geometric symbols and numbers on each fin was approaching its zenith. Even from a distance, it was possible to know almost everything about an individual Superfortress merely by scanning it from nose to tail. Some of the pictures on noses would not be allowed in a family publication today, but they reflected the unwillingness of crews to lose their sense of humor, as well as their unconquerable irreverence, even when the bombing campaign was going very poorly.

On February 4, 1945, XXI Bomber Command launched its first full-strength mission under LeMay. It was considered a success. A week later, two combat wings struck the Nakajima plan at Ota, near Tokyo. It, too, was deemed successful. LeMay had not yet instituted changes but appeared to be faring somewhat better than Hansell.

Sulphur Island

On February 19, 1945, the largest force of United States Marines ever assembled—seventy-four thousand Marines of the 3rd, 4th, and 5th Marine divisions under V Amphibious Corps—journeyed to a tiny hunk of coral and slag close to the Japanese homeland. Iwo Jima is just five miles long and two and a half miles wide at its widest point, and it has been described by many as a pork chop when viewed from the air. Located in the Bonin island chain west of the midpoint between Saipan and Tokyo, the island is mostly barren, with a 556-foot extinct volcano on the southern tip of the island, Mount Suribachi. It was a prefecture of Japan and a place of dark caves and smelly sulphur, and it became the site of one of the epic battles of history.

To history-minded Marines, the waterborne attack on this worthless piece of rock "better suited to death than life," as *Life* magazine described it, evoked memories of an earlier American battle on dry land. Watching the landing craft head ashore, one American officer noticed that the order, the neatness, and the inevitability of it, was an exact copy of Pickett's Charge on the third day at Gettysburg—the only American offensive action in which greater casualties were suffered. *Life* magazine noticed that Suribachi was just about exactly the height of Little Round Top at Gettysburg, while a nearby slagheap of volcanic dirt resembled Gettysburg's Cemetery Ridge. "Among Americans who served on Iwo Island," wrote Adm. Chester Nimitz, commander in chief of the Pacific command, "uncommon valor was a common virtue."

For the amphibious assault on Iwo Jima, 880 ships and hundreds of warplanes backed the invasion force. LeMay's B-29 crews were among the Army, Navy, and Marine aircraft that pounded Iwo in the longest sustained aerial offensive of the war, although many in the B-29 groups saw this as a distraction from their primary function. "No other island received as much preliminary pounding as did Iwo Jima," said Admiral Nimitz.

The effort to soften up Japanese defenses helped little. Entrenched in caves, Japanese troops—who were outnumbered by the Marines five to one—fought on for thirty-five days. It was a horrific, point-blank battle. For the men on the ground, it was unspeakable.

Iwo, of course, was the site of the most famous photo ever taken: Joe Rosenthal's immortal image of the second raising of the American flag on Suribachi. When it was over, the Marines had suffered more than 6,821 dead and about 19,217 wounded. Of the eighty-four Medals of Honor awarded to Marines during all of World War II, fully twenty-seven, or almost a third, were awarded for action on Iwo Jima.

After it was over, a former chief of naval operations, retired Adm. William V. Pratt, asked in *Newsweek* magazine about the "expenditure of manpower to acquire a small, God-forsaken island, useless to the Army as a staging base and useless to the Navy as a fleet base . . . [one] wonders if the same sort of airbase could not have been reached by acquiring other strategic localities at lower cost."

The seizure of Iwo Jima almost immediately provided a boon to those who had to fight in the air. Iwo was neutralized as a base for Japanese warplanes. Never again would the B-29 force in the Marianas come under air attack.

Until the island was taken, Superfortresses en route to Japan routinely flew a dogleg-course around the island increasing the already extended distances they were forced to cover. This burned precious fuel, but could not hide the giant aircraft formations of very heavy bombers from radar surveillance. Iwo Jima had been the ideal early-warning site to bolster other Japanese intelligence assets, reporting B-29 formations and giving the Japanese home islands time to prepare for an oncoming bomber stream.

Now in the hands of the Americans, Iwo Jima became a base for escort fighters to accompany B-29s to Japan, not just the proven P-51D Mustang but the yet-untested P-47N Thunderbolt, a new, longer-range variant of a familiar fighter. Iwo Jima now began to host facilities for rescue forces that might save B-29 crewmembers when they ditched.

Iwo had three small airstrips. The airfields were Motoyama No. 1, also called Chidori or Central Field, even though it was located on the southern corner of the island; Motoyama No. 2, also called North Field, even though it was in the center of the island; and Motoyama No. 3, also near the center of the island. Seabees quickly extended runways and expanded facilities. None of Iwo's airfields was large enough to house a B-29 combat group, but they could handle fighters. Most importantly, with quite a bit of tweaking by the Seabees, they could serve as an emergency stopping-over place for battle-damaged B-29s limping home from the Empire without sufficient fuel to reach the Marianas. LeMay told Adm. Raymond Spruance that, "without Iwo Jima, I cannot bomb Japan," although he had been doing so before the invasion started.

The McDonald Crew

The long trek from the United States to the war zone was difficult for all who took part, but never more than for the crew of Bud McDonald, which traveled from Great Bend to Kearney (both in Nebraska) to Albuquerque to Mather and onward to John Rodgers Field on Oahu, Hawaii. McDonald's navigator, 2nd Lt. Alexander L. "Lew" Parry, later wrote that the plan for the next day was to pass over Johnston Island and proceed to Kwajalein. "On takeoff, the oil cooler flap stuck closed on no. 2 engine. This turned out to be eventful. We were carrying a full tank of gas in the bomb bay and were heavy. The engine overheated and failed and then began to windmill (turn backwards due to wind resistance). The windmill placed a very serious drag and took some smart work by Mac and Kit," a reference to airplane commander McDonald and pilot 2nd Lt. William "Kit" Kittrell.

Wrote Parry,

> We dropped the gas tank from the bomb bay and headed back to Hawaii. We were only a few minutes out. We were losing altitude rapidly and I told Mac the shortest route was to fly over Pearl Harbor, which was a "No, no." It was over Pearl or into the drink. Up came the fighters and they were signaling that the engine was trailing lots of smoke. Without further interference, we got over the end of the runway, still too high, and [McDonald] holding on for dear life. Mac told Kit to cut the throttles (he had in mind slowly) and Kit cut them as directed and we plunked down on the runway—so hard I thought the landing gear would go through the wing.

As it turned out, this mishap, all too routine for the trouble-prone B-29, gave the crew a respite from the war: they were forced to spend two more weeks in Hawaii until a replacement engine could be delivered and installed.

On their second attempt, the McDonald crew reached Kwajalein, refueled, and continued to Tinian, where they left their B-29 to be operated by another crew. They were taken to Guam and assigned another B-29, eventually called *The Merry Mac's*.

Fire to Tokyo

Growing constantly as new bomb squadrons joined the force, Twentieth Air Force and XXI Bomber Command attacked Iwo Jima, Truk, Nagoya, and Tokyo (twice) in February 1945, all with few changes in tactics. The largest mission yet came on February 25 when 229 Superfortresses launched for the Japanese capital and 172 dropped on the primary target.

Operation Matterhorn, the separate B-29 war waged from the China-Burma-India (CBI) Theater, was on the verge of wrapping up. Typical of late contributions by India-based airmen was a March 2, 1945, mission staged from bases in China and flown against Singapore, which at this late date was still in Japanese hands. The 468th Bombardment Group lost two Superfortresses of the sixty-four that began the mission. They were the last B-29s to be lost in the CBI.

B-32 Dominator

While the AAF were preparing to pound Japan with wave after wave of B-29 Superfortresses, they also invested heavily in an aircraft that was meant as a backup to the B-29. While the B-29 was developed in great secrecy, the B-32 Dominator seems to have been designed, developed, flown, and taken into combat in almost total obscurity. When he saw something about it in the GI newspaper *Stars and Stripes*, B-29 crewmember Carl Barthold scratched his head and asked, "What's a B-32 Dominator?"

Lieutenant General Barton K. Yount, the wartime head of AAF Training Command, told *Popular Mechanics* magazine, "The B-32 will help us knock out the Japs just twice as quick."

Built by Consolidated and looking much like a single-tailed version of the planemaker's B-24 Liberator, the B-32 employed four of the same troublesome R-3350 engines found on the Superfortress. The first prototype retained a twin tail and lacked a pressurization system, gun turrets, and landing gear doors that appeared on subsequent airplanes. It was prone to—surprise—engine problems and fuel leaks. There were also general stability problems. It crashed after thirty test flights, stalling the program. By that point, B-29s were arriving in the China-Burma-India Theater, and Consolidated had not yet flown an example of the B-32 that had the features of a production-standard airplane.

It would have been appropriate to cancel the B-32. Instead, the AAF placed an initial production order for 1,500 aircraft. This was later reduced to 300, of which just 115 production versions of the Dominator were delivered (although with three test ships), making up just two-tenths of 1 percent of the 50,750 bombers manufactured in the United States during the war. Consolidated built the aircraft at its Fort Worth, Texas, facility where the second production B-32 crashed before it could join the test program.

Project crews—who were far more familiar with the complex controls of the B-32 than a "line" crew would have been—eventually took two aircraft to Clark Field in the Philippines to test them in actual combat where more soon joined them. They found the B-32 to have an unreasonably high noise level, a poor engine layout, and, of course, engine troubles. Author Stephen Harding wrote that the B-32 was "a rugged and stable, although admittedly temperamental, bombing platform."

The high-mounted, 135-foot wing, similar to the narrow wing developed for the B-24 and with about 6 feet less of wingspan than the B-29, would have made the B-32 a poor aircraft in which to ditch at sea, although it appears no crew ever did so. The B-32's fuselage was approximately 83 feet in length, making it fully 16 feet shorter than a B-29. Its armament and bombload were comparable to that of the B-29. Speed, range, and service ceiling were almost identical. The B-32's gross weight of 101,000 pounds was about 20,000 pounds less than that of a B-29. Its crew was eight men compared to the eleven typically on a B-29.

Eventually, officials dropped plans to include pressurization and remote-controlled guns, both features of the B-29, on the B-32. Apparently unaware that Curt LeMay had taken the war to low altitude, Yount told *Popular Mechanics'* Wayne Whittaker, "We can now safely approach Japan at moderate altitudes, climb up over the target for the bombing run, and after the bombs are dropped come back down for most of the trip back to home base." Yount also said with some justification, "tests on the combat model of the B-32 showed more accurate fire control with individual turrets."

By the end of the war, in addition to an expanded presence in the Philippines, a single squadron of B-32s was committed to the effort against the Japanese home islands. After a series of delays involving other B-32s, just two of the planes, named *The Lady Is Fresh* and *Hobo Queen II* and piloted by Col. Frank S. Cook and Col. Frank Paul, reached Clark Field, Luzon, as planned, after a journey that included a stop at Guam where B-29 crewmembers displayed enormous curiosity.

The B-32 crewmembers were good men, but it would be an exaggeration to credit them with much influence on the outcome of the war. They were every bit as irreverent as some B-29 flyers could be (for example, they simply ignored the Pentagon when it decided to change the name of their plane from Dominator to Terminator).

The men who supported, maintained, and flew these heavy bombers had experiences similar to those of B-29 crews and were every bit as dedicated. Among them was an Army aerial photographer, Sgt. Anthony J. Marchione. He was just nineteen. He hailed from Pottstown, Pennsylvania, and played the trumpet in high school. For reasons both poignant and tragic, Marchione was to become the best-known crewmember of the B-32 aircraft.

CHAPTER 15

Flexing the Fire

The B-29 Superfortress in the American Air Campaign, March 4–March 9, 1945

RETURNING TO GUAM FROM HIS OFFICE in the Pentagon, Larry Norstad conferred with LeMay. The two men had known each other for ten years but had never been close. They respected each other but were not friends. Norstad told LeMay the obvious. Just as Possum Hansell had gotten a pink slip, LeMay would be fired too if he did not improve bombing results over Japan. The ordnance depots on Guam, Saipan, and Tinian were now overflowing with incendiary bombs, and Norstad wanted to use them. Both men knew that a change in tactics was in the cards. Before the great Tokyo firebomb mission and the fire blitz to follow, however, one more strike was going to be made against the Japanese capital more or less the old-fashioned way.

LeMay wanted to try one more daylight bombing mission but with several variations. He lowered the altitude of the bombers from a typical 32,000 feet to just 25,000, and he struck Japan at a different time of day—his crews would take off at midnight, fly north in darkness, and arrive over Tokyo in early-morning daylight. This was the plan for March 4, 1945, devised by LeMay with Norstad in attendance and looking over his shoulder.

The date marked the end of two weeks of fighting on Iwo Jima, and Marines were still slugging it out with determined Japanese defenders. The island was nowhere near secure.

At every decision point, LeMay ignored opportunities to have Arnold or Norstad endorse his decisions. LeMay listened to others. He sought advice and took it. He changed his mind when appropriate, eventually becoming an advocate of the incendiary after long favoring the explosive bomb. But LeMay had a personal integrity that made it unnecessary for him to possess the stamp of someone else's approval—a wonderful lesson for a very different generation of brass today. LeMay knew that each time he made a change, if it succeeded, Arnold and Norstad would receive some of the credit. If it failed, LeMay would be fired just as abruptly as Hansell had been.

So it was with the decision to take off at midnight. The B-29s would fly individually to a point about fifty miles off the coast of Japan, assemble there after the arrival of daylight, and turn to approach the capital in formation. It was a small variation on the tactics that had been used so far, but it appeared promising.

To Tokyo on March 4

This was conceived as a "single-wing" mission, with Rosy O'Donnell's 73rd Wing on Saipan doing the honors, but at the last minute some aircraft from John Davies's 313th Wing on Tinian and Tommy Power's 314th on Guam were added to the mix.

One of O'Donnell's key leaders was Col. Samuel Russ Harris Jr., commander of the 499th Bombardment Group and a very accomplished B-29 pilot. O'Donnell and Harris clashed from time to time, as when Rosy derided the group commander's staff for being "too old." Like LeMay and Norstad, they enjoyed mutual respect but little warmth. When historian Robert A. Mann helped Harris publish his diary after the war, Mann wrote that Harris was "opinionated," which put it mildly.

At midnight, some 175 B-29s began taking off in the darkness. According to Harris, they did so at thirty-second intervals (rather than sixty seconds, which many considered the minimum safe separation), and it took a little over an hour for 114 of them to lift off from Saipan. Another 39 bombers went aloft in the dark at Tinian and another 22 from Guam. A handful of airplane commanders reported mechanical problems and aborted before takeoff, but every aircraft that started its takeoff run made it into the air. Some crewmembers felt more than the usual anxiety over possible midair collision as they went skyward into blackness from two islands that were dangerously close to one another, but no collision took place. Harris wrote, "The assembly was fair—although some trouble was experienced because some of the airplanes were at unbriefed altitudes and others milled around looking for a leader of their choice."

Historian Jim Bowman transcribed an account of the mission from the viewpoint of another of McDonnell's groups, the 500th, commanded by Col. John Eugene Dougherty:

> On this date the 73rd Wing flew another high-altitude precision strike against target 357, the Nakajima Aircraft Engine plant in Musashino, near Tokyo. However, there would be a tactical change this time in the hope of fooling the enemy. The B-29s would take off at night, so as to arrive over the target much earlier than before. Because of the night takeoff there would be no attempt to form up by squadrons or groups. Each plane was to fly individually to the Wing Assembly Point off the coast of Japan. By that time, it would be daylight and the planes would assemble there into formations and proceed to Japan. If an aircraft was unable to find its squadron or group formation, it was to join any formation. Any planes unable to locate any friendly planes were to proceed to the coast of Japan individually and bomb the last resort target, the coastal city of Hamamatsu.

Bowman wrote that the bombload for each Superfortress was thirteen 500-pound general-purpose bombs. On takeoff, one 500th Group B-29 ran into a problem when the life rafts popped out of the fuselage compartment above the wing, forcing the crew to abort takeoff and taxi back to have another life raft installed. This crew eventually got aloft and completed the mission.

When dawn rose off the Japanese coast, a familiar scenario replayed itself. The primary target near Tokyo was completely covered with clouds. Accurate bombing of the relatively small factory grounds would be impossible, so nearly all Superfortresses diverted to the secondary target, the central urban area of Tokyo. The city was also cloud covered, but as a large-area target it could be effectively bombed by radar. The aircraft dropped their bombs between approximately 9:45 and 10:15 a.m.

Among the B-29s bombing Tokyo on March 4 was *Texas Doll*, the aircraft in which a bombardier had died in radio operator Carl Barthold's arms on an earlier flight. Replacing the previous airplane commander Carter Arnold was the recently arrived Edward Cutler, who had attended the funeral service for the bombardier on his first day in the Marianas. Arnold and Cutler were both married to women from the Lone Star State, so the aircraft name remained unchanged.

Cutler described the mission:

Japan was under 10/10 cloud cover so we had to bomb Tokyo by radar instead of visually hitting [it]. We saw no fighters and flak. Don [navigator 1st Lt. Don Julin] got us to our rendezvous 50 miles off the coast right on time. If there is safety in numbers, we were secure. Our formation blossomed out into a 27-plane convoy.

About two hours out, on the homeward journey, the trouble started. Our no. 4 engine had lost too much oil and the prop couldn't be feathered. We carried it along for four hours at 150 IAS (indicated air speed). The gunners unloaded the ammunition from the aft turrets by hand. I never saw a man work faster in the thin air at 14,500 feet than Gray [a gunner elsewhere identified as Sgt. Bob Grey]. After thinking that everything would be OK (as we had only 30 minutes to go), it happened. The terrific RPMs of the free-spinning prop started the prop shaft turning and it twisted over toward Andy's direction (right-seat pilot 1st Lt. Bill Anderson). Finally, the prop burned off and flew under the wing and somehow over the tail—thank gosh.

The crew of *Texas Doll* was looking at the amputated stump of the number four engine, outboard on the right wing. Losing an engine was survivable, but the situation was worse than that. A white-hot fire was eating through the metal nacelle of the R-3350.

In spite of it all, Cutler and crew had enough fuel to get home. The fire went out just before Cutler put the aircraft down on Saipan. After fifteen and a half hours in the sky, the B-29 was returning two hours late, to be greeted by a ground crew that had thought it lost. "The ground crew was doing handsprings as we pulled into the hardstand," Cutler wrote. "Quite a crowd gathered as we had erroneously been reported as having ditched"—an experience still universally feared by crewmembers. Another bomber in Cutler's group did ditch, and the airplane commander and pilot died while the nine other men were rescued. It appears that neither Cutler nor the airplane commander who ditched and lost his life ever considered diverting to Iwo Jima, where fighting was heavy.

Also among the B-29s bombing Tokyo that day was *God's Will* of the 9th Bombardment Group, with Dean Fling in the left front seat and Reb Carter at the left blister gun. They must have been among the last aircraft on the mission, because Carter wrote that the first bomber from his group launched from Tinian at 1:15 a.m., fully eighty-five minutes later than Harris's on next-door Saipan. Unlike Harris's bombers, *God's Will* carried ten 500-pound M17-A-1 clusters of magnesium incendiaries, although Carter noted that, "different planes carried different loads." In the dark early-morning hours flying toward the Empire, Carter snuggled up in the padded tunnel over the bomb bay and caught four hours of sleep. The crews carried a standard issue of ammunition, which for Carter meant 750 rounds of .50-caliber cartridges per gun.

Carter wrote that while flak was heavy and accurate for some B-29 crews, it was "meager and inaccurate for us." He also noted that "one boy in our squadron was hit," referring to Sgt. Maurice E. Chrisman, a radio operator on the 1st Lt. Stanley C. Black crew of a B-29 named *Thunderin' Loretta*, although the crew usually flew another ship, *Tinny Anne*. Chrisman was wounded. It was a piece of shrapnel from flak that struck his boot. Chrisman was hurt badly enough to receive a Purple Heart, but not too badly to fight another day—to his misfortune, as it would turn out. Also in trouble over the target was a B-29 called *Dinah Might* commanded by 1st Lt. Raymond F. "Fred" Malo, not because of Japanese gunfire but because of a devilish multitude of mechanical problems typical for the Superfortress. No Japanese fighters appeared.

"An aircraft engine factory was the primary target but there was a thin undercast so we just bombed the city," Carter wrote. "The results were excellent for every element except ours. Our lead ship got screwed up and dropped its bombs outside the city. All the other ships toggled their bombs on the lead ship."

Tense words from Fling and others on the interphone informed Carter that *God's Will* was going to escort *Dinah Might* as it attempted to get home. Malo's host of mechanical troubles seemed to be multiplying. Wrote Carter, "Lt. Malo's bomb bay doors were stuck in the 'open' position, the fuel transfer was out and the radar was out. We led Malo's ship to Iwo Jima. It was the first B-29 to land on Iwo Jima so they had newsreel pictures taken of them and write-ups in the newspapers." Fling and Malo were not sure how they could help each other. Iwo Jima was within reach, but bitter fighting was taking place there. No B-29 had ever saved itself by landing on the sulphur island. Doing so clearly entailed huge risk, which is why XXI Bomber Command had informed crews that Iwo Jima was not yet ready to serve as a refuge.

B-29 to Iwo Jima

Still, the first Superfortress attempt to land on Iwo Jima took place late that morning. *Dinah Might*'s airplane commander Fred Malo acted against orders when he chose to put down on the desolate, embattled island.

Malo was twenty-four and just five weeks out of the United States. He wrote that his auxiliary tanks refused to feed, leaving him without enough usable gas to get home to North Field, Tinian. Like most of the thousand kids, Malo and his crewmates dreaded the idea of plunking their B-29 down in the water. Getting close to his very last drop of aviation fuel, Malo looked over the island that was still the scene of intense ground combat, studied the tiny strip known as Motoyama Airfield Number 1, and told himself that the runway was too short. "We can't land there," he said out loud in a tone that suggested he believed they could. It is not clear whether Malo knew that the Marines controlled only half of the airfield; the Japanese controlled the other half. Malo's fuel state was now beyond desperate, and it was going to be either the Pacific or Motoyama No. 1. It was decision time.

An embattled battalion commander, Maj. Shelton Scales of the 4th Marine Division, watched *Dinah Might* make its first pass circling the peak of Mount Suribachi. The bomber was too close to the mountain, Scales thought. It was going to crash. He had never seen a B-29 before and was impressed by its size, but he was not certain it was under control.

In the cockpit, Malo whipped the aircraft around, missing the slope. On his second pass, he could see more of what was going on beneath him, including Marines and Seabees running for the airfield from all directions but blocking his landing path. Desperately low on fuel now, Malo was forced to make a third pass.

Malo tightened his grip on the control yoke and told himself there was not enough fuel for attempt number four. With help from copilot 1st Lt. Edwin Mockler, he put down the gear and flaps. He made his approach. Aware of the dictum from on high but not of the situation below on the ground, Fred Malo had made up his mind that whatever happened to him on this day, he was not going swimming.

Dinah Might touched down and looked for a moment like it was going to careen off the runway. Mockler stood on the brakes. The aircraft trembled and skidded down the runway. Its left wing knocked over a field telephone pole with a clang that resonated against the roar of the R-3350s.

Seeing their squadron mate on terra firma, the Fling crew in *God's Will* turned for home. During the remainder of the flight, Reb Carter was able to take another brief nap.

Dinah Might came to a halt about twenty feet short of absolute disaster. Despite shooting going on all around them, Marines and Seabees danced and swarmed all over the aircraft. As Malo revved up his engines and turned the bomber around, the Japanese began to zero in on it with mortars and artillery. An artillery shell exploded about fifty feet to Malo's left.

Malo parked *Dinah Might* in open sight, alongside a frail Marine Corps "grasshopper," a Stinson OY-2 Sentinel. Scales came up to the aircraft, which he described as "the size of a monster." Already, troops on Iwo Jima were using "monster" as a radio code word to refer to any B-29 they encountered, although this was the first they ever saw on the ground.

Under fire, a frenetic conversation ensued in which a Seabee agreed with Malo that the runway as it existed was too short for a B-29 landing or takeoff—notwithstanding the landing he had just made—and assured Malo that if he would remain overnight, he would have a thousand more feet of runway by noon the following day. Malo was well aware that a B-29 needed just a little less pavement to take off than to land, and he was not eager to make the acquaintance of the Japanese who were shooting at him.

What happens next is in dispute. A Malo family member later said that Malo had his crew hand-fill *Dinah Might*'s fuel tanks with two thousand gallons, apparently using buckets. A different account says that there was not yet any aviation fuel at the airstrip, (although there would be in less than a week for the March 9–10, 1945, Tokyo mission) and that Malo simply repaired a faulty valve and was able to get his fuel tanks to feed properly. Apparently Malo had little concern about damage inflicted to the wing leading edge by the phone pole. One way or the other, *Dinah Might* ended up with enough fuel in the proper fuel tanks to continue on its way home to Tinian. Malo again turned down the invitation to remain overnight and he and his crew were soon on their way. As Malo predicted, the B-29 was able to take off without mishap.

Apart from the Malo crew's adventure, the March 4 Tokyo mission—the last effort of XXI Bomber Command before the great Tokyo firebomb mission—was a success.

Build-up to the Big One

By now, 314th Wing commander Tommy Power was leading the chorus of voices at LeMay's Guam headquarters that were not merely suggesting but, to the extent they could when dealing with a gruff boss, *demanding* change. Power had a head-to-head with one B-29 airplane commander who said in plain English that he wasn't going to risk the men on his Superfortress unless something improved.

To mix metaphors, Power and the others were preaching to the choir. From his earliest days as a bomber leader in Europe, LeMay had been willing to institute change whenever it would make aerial bombardment more effective. LeMay was a mere group commander when he suggested and won approval for many of the changes in tactics and formation flying that improved the situation for crews in Europe. He knew he was living in a time of change.

The previous month, the largest number of warplanes ever sent to a single target, 1,003 B-17 Flying Fortresses escorted by 948 fighters, hauled their bombs from bases in England to Berlin. As measured in tonnage, this was almost identical in destructive power to the 334 larger B-29s soon to travel to Tokyo. The Berlin mission (on February 3, 1945) was the first ever in which Americans abandoned their policy of precision bombing of military and industrial targets and directed their efforts instead toward the center of a city. Lieutenant General James H. Doolittle, now the Eighth Air Force commander in England and formerly the intrepid Tokyo raider, objected strongly to targeting a city and protested to his boss Tooey Spaatz. The latter officer was sympathetic but overruled Doolittle quickly and decisively. Oddly, Doolittle never mentioned the issue in his autobiography.

Until now, a broad perception had existed that the British bombed cities, while the Americans bombed military and industrial targets. The perception was too simple by half, but it was not completely wrong until the Americans introduced change.

Some associate the change with Dresden. In fact, Dresden came a fortnight after Berlin (on February 13, 1945) and marked the second time Americans targeted a city center—although it was the first time they did so with firebombs. American prisoner of war Kurt Vonnegut Jr., who was working as forced labor in a slaughterhouse in Dresden, wrote of the horrors of the bombing attack, which killed so many that German troops and police had to dispose of bodies using flamethrowers.

Like Norstad, Tommy Power believed incendiaries could be lethal against urban populations in the Japanese home islands. Perhaps more than any other airpower general, Power believed in shifting the battle to low altitude. Power told LeMay that B-29s would need less fuel and could carry more incendiary bombs if they attacked from lower altitude. The large aircraft would be readily visible from the ground, but Japan's defenses were not set up for such an attack. Norstad, Power, and LeMay all believed that the Japanese night fighter force posed a negligible threat to the bombers. Changing the time of day on March 4 had been a good move, but changing the altitude and the ordnance would be even better.

LeMay deserves as much credit as anyone else not only for implementing these ideas but for thinking them up. By the time Norstad and Power were influencing his thinking, LeMay had already begun work toward a low-level firebomb operation. After his visitor Norstad went to sleep, LeMay stayed up at night studying reports of the operations carried out by Harris and Doolittle.

Prelude to Change

Senior officers in LeMay's circle believed a low-level firebomb attack would work, but others, including Lt. Col. Robert S. McNamara and several of XXI Bomber Command's key intelligence officers, thought otherwise. They feared the B-29s would be placing themselves within easy reach of relatively small-caliber antiaircraft weapons. According to LeMay biographer Warren Kozak, LeMay's intelligence officers predicted losses in the range of 70 percent. That would have meant 233 Superfortresses and 2,563 men, or more than half of all the heavy bomber forces stationed at Guam, Saipan, and Tinian.

LeMay had once received a letter from a mother who accused him of killing her son and who promised to send LeMay another letter each year on the anniversary of the son's death. With far more human fragility than anyone around him realized, LeMay believed that the only way to avoid greater losses was to defeat Japan. Told that the United States might suffer a million casualties if it had to make an amphibious invasion of the Japanese home islands, LeMay did not have much regard for the new, secret bomb he had been briefed on, but he believed that even without an atomic bomb he could find a way to use the B-29 to bring Japan to the surrender table.

Wrote Kozak,

> LeMay did not have to take into account the impact on Washington of a tremendous loss of Japanese civilian life and property. He understood the military chain-of-command, and he knew how to get around any issue that could stop his plan.

Although LeMay had good reason to believe that he would get the green light for this mission, he never asked anyone above him directly for permission, but it was there in a variety of circumstantial ways. The [ordnance] dumps on Guam and Tinian were already filled with thousands of tons of incendiaries. They had to be there for a reason. It was almost as if Arnold was waiting for a commander to go ahead with the raid without actually suggesting it himself. But successful mission or catastrophic failure, LeMay would present it as a *fait accompli.*

Air Force historian Michael Sherry wrote, "LeMay's command genius lay in his decision to avoid introducing these methods piecemeal, to take the parts and throw them together at once, producing a whole dwarfing the sum of its parts."

Bomb group commander Samuel Russ Harris Jr. wrote in his journal that he attended a generals' conference on March 5, 1945. The next day he wrote, "A mission is in the wind." At this juncture, plans for the great Tokyo firebomb mission were still tentative. Harris feared something big would be happening on March 7. "It's not allowing us enough time to get the ships in shape and will probably show up in aborts if not losses." Harris apparently believed the target would be Nagoya, but he was wrong about both the date and the location.

In fact, Nagoya was part of LeMay's plan. In addition to the great Tokyo firebomb mission, the XXI Bomber Command boss was developing a concept for a "blitz" that would bring incendiaries to Nagoya, Osaka, and Kobe. The first mission, the big one to Tokyo, would inflict severe damage on the Japanese capital if it succeeded, but LeMay wanted something even bigger, a way of hammering the Japanese so heavily that they would break. There was nothing cosmetic about the plan by the western allies to invade Japan—a million men were being moved from Europe to the Pacific for that purpose in one of the greatest logistics efforts of all time—but LeMay felt that enough fire on enough Japanese cities might win the war. Arnold T. Johnson, commander of the 497th Bombardment Group in Saipan, wrote in his journal that, "If this month is successful, we should deal our enemy a mortal blow."

If Tokyo failed, the "blitz" plan would have to be shelved.

As planning and preparations evolved, everyone was busy. LeMay's staff had to ponder many factors that often were interdependent. Timing was a major challenge, especially given the scattering of the B-29 force among three islands in the Marianas (Guam was about 130 miles from adjacent Saipan and Tinian). Experience had shown that trying to have B-29s take off thirty seconds apart was too unpredictable and too dangerous. An interval of a full minute was needed between each aircraft. This meant that the bomber stream would be four hundred miles long and would take two hours to pass overhead.

Radio operator Carl Barthold remembers flying a training mission of two hours' duration during which his crew practiced a low-altitude approach to an imaginary target. "We were told to rehearse this and we weren't told why." Harris, the 499th group commander, wrote of flying a training mission on March 7, not so much to adjust crewmembers to an expected change of altitude but for the purpose of practicing the use of radar for bombing and navigation. The radar on the B-29 was continuing its habit of frustrating crewmembers at every turn, working perfectly some of the time and not so well more of the time. Another airplane commander, 1st Lt. Gordon Bennett Robertson Jr., wrote of a March 7 "local night mission for the specific purpose of practicing radar bombing runs—an important technique we would use to bomb an obscured target through an overcast/undercast." Robertson may not have known that LeMay required clear weather over the target, if not in the surrounding environs. Bake Baker of the Dean Fling crew of *God's Will* wrote that on March 7, "We went on a practice mission. Radar bombing at 7,000 feet. I think we'll really blast the enemy. Bombing very accurate." Baker's crewmate bombardier Red Dwyer wrote, "Briefed this morning at 0800 for low level radar practice bombing as ordered by Washington." Dwyer added that results were good. His reference to Washington appears to have been speculation.

Other crewmembers remember no practice flights being conducted before the men were tasked to go to Tokyo at low altitude. Apparently, most did not participate in this training. Had all three of LeMay's bomb wings been at full strength, the general would have needed training flights for 720 bombers and crews. At this juncture during the buildup of forces in the Marianas, the real number was more like 480, with O'Donnell's wing on Saipan at full strength, Davies's on Tinian very nearly so, and Power's on Guam still at less than half its intended inventory of men and materiel. Even at the lower figure, it would not have been practical to put every crew and every bomber into the air solely to provide training. "Our pilots certainly knew how to fly the B-29 at every altitude it could reach," said Barthold, who also remembers a mood of "busy-ness and tension" as airmen on Saipan worked to prepare for an upcoming mission.

In fact, more than one mission was on the agenda. LeMay was going to launch a ten-day fire blitz using every B-29 he could put into the air and every firebomb in the Marianas, plus any more that Navy logisticians could deliver in short order. LeMay's staff told him no replacement incendiaries could be available before the second week in April.

Wrote Barrett Tillman,

The effort leading up to the Tokyo raid was immense. Orchestrating the work of as many men as a light armored division was LeMay's operations officer, Col. John Montgomery. In the day and a half before takeoff 13,000 men on three Pacific islands toiled almost without stop. Mechanics brought each plane's four engines to the best possible condition. By hand or by truck, ordnancemen hauled bomb bodies from storage dumps to the hardstands where "bomb builders" attached tail fins, joisted the weapons into the cavernous bomb bays, and inserted fuses. Fuel trucks drove from plane to plane, filling their tanks to the brim. According to Montgomery, preparing a combat wing for a maximum effort was "a helluva lot worse than planning a maintenance schedule for an airline."

Twenty-First Bomber Command's "mission capable rate" (MCR), the number of B-29s that were ready to make a takeoff on an operational mission, had been around 60 percent, meaning that at any given point nearly half of all Superfortresses were useless. With talented supervision and a lot of sweat, ground crews brought the overall MCR up to 83 percent.

On March 7, key officers on Guam, Saipan, and Tinian, including squadron commanders like Sammy Bakshas, received a briefing.

Mission to Meetinghouse

It would have been impossible to keep secret the fact that a major operation was about to occur. At different levels, LeMay's staff expended differing degrees of effort to keep things secret, which explains why Bakshas was protective of information a lot of others knew. According to St. Clair McKelway,

> The need for maintaining secrecy about such an operation, even among staff people and military officers and men of the Bomber Command, was more urgent than might be supposed. The Japs still held the island of Rota, within sight of Tinian, and on all three of the main islands of the Marianas, which had been conquered and converted into B-29 bases, uncaptured Japs still lurked by the hundreds, some of them conceivably with portable radio transmitters that could reach Rota or Iwo Jima [still, in early March, a contested battleground] if not Tokyo. Official intelligence had shown in the past that Tokyo sometimes seemed to know just what we were going to do before we did it.

According to Laddie Wale, flight engineer on the Tucker crew, security was uneven and inconsistent and "our bosses did more talking about it than they did enforcing it." Wale had no doubt that a maximum effort loomed. "I knew as early as March 7 that we were going into something big."

Harris wrote of a generals' meeting on March 7 and of a planned mission against Nagoya, a night attack to take place at 5,000 feet. The next day he wrote that the target was not Nagoya but Tokyo.

McKelway, the public affairs figure, discovered on the morning of March 7 that no operations order had been written. "It was being written by the Operations people, giving detailed tactical procedures for the forthcoming maximum effort. How many of the details did Washington know? . . . In fact, hardly anybody knew about it, especially about the unprecedented, daring, almost unbelievable decision to go in at low level instead of at twenty-five or thirty thousand feet. The Cigar [LeMay] had made that decision [the previous day], it seemed. The field order would go out to the wings this afternoon and to Washington at about the same time." McKelway had been reading a copy of *Lee's Lieutenants* given to him by the now departed Possum Hansell. Knowledgeable about the Civil War, McKelway compared the decision now being made by LeMay to "Grant's, when he let Sherman try his march through Georgia."

The operations order McKelway awaited was issued at 8:00 a.m. on March 8, 1945. It said that XXI Bomber Command "will attack Urban Area of Meetinghouse with maximum effort on 'D' Day. Location: 3541N-13948E." The order was classified SECRET, but the code word and the map coordinates were unnecessary. Every one of the thousand kids knew that Meetinghouse was a *nom de guerre* for Tokyo. This was the order that would send O'Donnell over the Japanese capital at 7,000 to 7,800 feet, Davies at 6,000 to 6,800 feet, and Power at 5,000 to 5,800 feet.

It appears that in some bomb groups, selected officers were briefed that evening on the upcoming mission. Although Reb Carter and other enlisted members would not know the target until the following afternoon, bombardier Dwyer wrote: "[We were] briefed tonight on first low level B-29 raid on Tokyo. *Heavy losses are anticipated* [emphasis added]."

The thousand kids went to bed on the night of March 8, 1945, knowing that the weather forecast was as favorable as any ever got in this part of the world.

Had they known what lay on the public affairs officer's bookshelf, they might have been grateful that McKelway was thinking of Grant and Sherman rather than the analogy to Pickett's Charge that others were attributing to the Marine onslaught at Iwo Jima. Superfortress crewmembers went to bed with the sound of guns being tested in the pits and aircraft engines being revved up in the parking revetments, and it was just as well none of them were thinking about the exceedingly brave and brash Maj. Gen. George E. Pickett at Gettysburg. Pickett's Charge, after all, was a bloodbath.

CHAPTER 16

The Way Home

Mission to Tokyo
March 10, 1945, 7:40 a.m.–12:00 midnight

A T THE CONTROLS OF AN UNNAMED B-29 that had been blasted and battered, Capt. George Savage watched darkness fade and daylight arrive while struggling with his controls and working to save his crew. There would have been ample justification for Savage to tell the crew to bail out. Aviation fuel was sloshing around inside the aircraft. One spark, one recurrence of the St. Elmo's fire that had stalked them throughout the long night, and the Savage crew would be dead. As daylight arrived and every passing second made the condition more dangerous, Savage weighed his options. Fighting was still going on at the north end of Iwo Jima, and even after the Malo crew's successful landing there six days earlier, the sulphur island was anything but an inviting prospect. Savage looked out at the bleak, ominous Pacific and began a conversation with his navigator and flight engineer about whether, and how, they might attempt to reach the embattled island, which was still possibly as many as two hours in front of them. *It was 7:50 a.m. Chamorro Standard Time, March 10, 1945.*

The Simeral Crew

After fifteen hours and four minutes in the air on a grueling marathon that left the crew exhausted and edgy, the great Tokyo firebomb mission's on-scene air commander Brig. Gen. Thomas S. Power returned to Guam's North Field aboard Tony Simeral's B-29. The Superfortress was *Snatch Blatch*, also called *City of Los Angeles*. It had been shiny and silver when they took off; now it was blackened with soot. Perhaps, as *Snatch Blatch* taxied in, reeking with the stench of the firestorm Power may have glanced to one side and witnessed the empty parking revetment to which the Bakshas crew and *Tall in the Saddle* would never return. Radio operator Red Erwin began shutting down his gear, cleaning up his workstation, and reflecting that they were lucky no Japanese gunner had caught them in his crosshairs.

The aircraft came to a halt and two of its engines were still running when Power finally dropped to the ground. Author Wilbur H. Morrison wrote that there were dark circles around Power's eyes and he badly needed a shave.

Curt LeMay, having spent the night listening to sporadic radio reports in his Quonset headquarters, greeted Power with a hint of a smile. St. Clair McKelway looked on and tried to read the two men. Neither general possessed enough information, yet, to say with certainty that the mission to Tokyo had been a success. Both were thinking they'd done the job, but they were eager to learn more. Power told LeMay that antiaircraft fire had been lighter than he'd expected, Japanese night fighters had not been a visible presence, and the fires in Tokyo, which ultimately combined into a single vast conflagration, had been more devastating than he'd expected.

One reason it was too early to be certain: although Power was home, other B-29s were still scattered all over the sky. *It was 8:30 a.m. Chamorro Standard Time, March 10, 1945.*

The Keene Crew

With Leon Keene at the controls and John C. Conly working the radar out back, the exhausted Keene crew prepared to ditch. Putting a sixty-five-ton bomber down in the water was still right up there at the top of things crewmembers feared most. It didn't help that it usually happened after time, turmoil, and fatigue had already taken a toll. Unlike George Savage and Dean Fling, Keene did not have enough fuel even to contemplate making a try for Iwo Jima.

At midmorning the Keene crew had been in the air for more than fifteen hours and had spent more than half of that time trying to coax their bullet-damaged B-29 toward the 9th Bombardment Group's home base on Tinian. It was a troubled crew in the best of times, and now the trouble was worsening.

Having dislodged loose gear in the bomb bay, Conly was back at the radar set and had it functioning. On his scope, he discovered a small island. While the B-29 struggled through a dirty sky filled with low, moist clouds and volcanic ash, Conly worked on the interphone with Keene to plan an offshore touchdown in the water.

Everyone aboard the B-29 believed the island was Anathan in the northern Marianas, which the Allies had bypassed, leaving a small contingent of Japanese soldiers to face possible starvation. All twelve men on the B-29 were wrong. The island was actually Farallón de Pájaros, which was little more than the volcano Uracas protruding from the sea; it was also in the northern Marianas, but was uninhabited. Some discussion took place on the B-29's interphone about ditching, storming ashore with Colt .45 automatics, and having a gunfight with the Japanese. But while Farallón de Pájaros offered white sulphur, yellow smoke, a little scrub, and slopes of lava and ash, it had no trees, plants, food, drinkable water, or Japanese.

Once they were able to see through the undercast and make estimates, bombardier 2nd Lt. William E. Dutrow, who had the best view out the bomber's rounded nose, and plane commander Keene began telling the crew that they would be going down into ten-foot waves. Some in the crew later said they wished it were Conly, not Keene, in the front left seat, but others respected Keene as a veteran pilot. As the aircraft descended closer and closer to the roiling wavetops, tail gunner Sgt. James T. Hash remembered that he had seen a picture of a B-29 that broke in half and took its crew to the briny depths. Now Hash listened as Keene continued briefing the crew on the interphone.

"This will be my last message," said Keene. "We are ditching near an island. The radar operator has identified it as Anatahan Island. Everyone take positions for ditching."

Each crewmember checked in to report being ready to ditch. Hash remembered being told that hitting the ocean could have the same impact as hitting a brick wall.

The tail gunner was supposed to egress the aircraft from a window at his right shoulder (meaning the left side of the aircraft). "Captain," said Hash, "I haven't gotten rid of my window yet."

"Do it now," came Keene's voice.

The rearward-facing Hash popped the window. ("I thought the sound of the engines would break my eardrums.") He put his parachute against his gunsight and tightened his lap belt to brace himself. Hash wondered why the aircraft seemed to be slightly nose-down rather than nose-high the way it was supposed to be in a ditching.

Two more words came from Keene: "Ditching . . . now!"

Hash stiffened. He told himself this didn't seem to be going right. *It was 9:50 a.m. Chamorro Standard Time, March 10, 1945.*

The Savage Crew

"The former Jap airstrip at the south end of the island [Motoyama No. 1 Air Field] was deemed safe to attempt a landing," George Savage wrote. "It had a runway that was just 4,000 feet long. We made our approach and as our landing gear came down bad news came with it. Strange articles fell from the left wheel well. The upshot of it all was that we had no brake pressure and one of the wheels on the left gear was no longer round."

Although stressed and struggling, Savage felt confidence in his piloting skill as he maneuvered to touch down at the extreme end of the runway. The giant Superfortress was just feet off the ground. Savage was pulling back on the control yoke when the control cable snapped and the yoke fell into his lap. Savage swung his head to the right and yelled to his copilot, "Ernie, pull back on your wheel!" Second Lieutenant Ernest E. Dossey did exactly that in what Savage called an "honest to God grease job." The bomber came into contact with the ground at exactly the moment when it went out of control. Savage did not write down the time of his landing, but based on other accounts, it is possible to make an educated guess. *It was 9:50 a.m. Chamorro Standard Time, March 10, 1945.*

Dossey's muscle on the yoke helped, but it wasn't quite enough. Wrote Savage, "With no brakes, and a bad wheel on the left gear; and—wouldn't you know it?—a cross-wind from the left, as soon as rudder control was lost we started to veer off the runway to the left."

Coming the other way on the left side of the empty runway was a Jeep with a lone occupant. Savage waved frantically trying to get him to turn out of the way. The driver gave Savage a broad smile and waved back in a friendly manner. As the Jeep disappeared under the bomber's 141-foot, 3-inch wing, Savage braced for the impact when what was left of the landing gear smashed the Jeep and its cheerful occupant. The "bump" Savage expected didn't come. He learned later that the Jeep driver ducked beneath hood level and that the truck's windshield vanished when the B-29's wing flap scraped it off.

The aircraft came to an abrupt halt against the hill on the left of the runway. Everyone who scrambled out of the Superfortress was miraculously unharmed, with the exception of bombardier Flight Officer Malcolm G. "Mac" Wooldridge. He suffered a bloody nose when the nose wheel came up through the floorboards and smacked him in the face. Right blister gunner "Buck" Buckley, who'd suffered a very bloody yet almost painless wound over Tokyo, was drenched in his own blood now as he nimbly dropped from the plane and ran for safety.

The crew of the bomber consisted of Savage, Dossey, navigator 2nd Lt. William D. Born, Wooldridge, radar operator 2nd Lt. Robert N. Morgan, flight engineer Cpl. Gerald P. "Jerry" Kalian, radio operator Cpl. Edward G. Acheson, central fire control gunner Cpl. William S. Brooks, Buckley, left blister gunner Cpl. Donald W. Turner, and tail gunner Sgt. Pete Wirgianis. Savage later said that an AAF photographer was also aboard. (In his writings, Savage sometimes identified Buckley as the tail gunner).

They were lucky. There was no fire, only one terribly abused B-29. In days to come, Savage would complete thirty missions and would be said to have "left B-29s scattered all over the Pacific," according to an online bomb group history: "One more B-29 to his credit and he would have become a Jap ace."

Wrote Savage, "Later that day I was sitting in what appeared to be a big shell hole. A grungy Marine was there too. He was dirty, grimy, and had eyes like two pee holes in the snow. I felt that in spite of the recent past I wouldn't trade places with him for all the goodies in the world. I started to tell him so but before I could say it he blurts out, 'I wouldn't trade places with you for anything in the world.' I guess that's what makes the world go 'round."

Savage's aircraft was badly battered and never flew again, although in wrecked condition it managed to appear in a two-page spread in the April 9 issue of *Life* magazine. Savage and crew had to be transported home to Guam, where "I expected to be greeted with a hero's welcome. Instead, I was hustled to group headquarters where I was forced to sign a Report of Survey [billing me to pay for] one broken B-29." They never asked Savage to whip out his checkbook.

The Fling Crew
Other crews were beginning to land safely at their home bases. Percy Usher Tucker put *Lady Annabelle* down on Tinian, heaved a sigh of relief, and prepared to light a cigarette. Flight engineer Laddie Wale made a final comment on the interphone: "You know? I think we're going to be doing more of this." In other B-29s that came home safely, radio operator Carl Barthold and radar operator Trip Triplett bounded to the ground and began thinking about food and sleep. All the while, the Keene crew was about to ditch and the Fling crew of *God's Will* was struggling, paying the price for spending a couple of hours being lost.

When *God's Will* appeared in the distance approaching Iwo Jima, the sun had become bright, flying conditions were as good as they would ever get in this weather-wracked corner of the world, and the ground around Motoyama No. 1 airfield looked almost red in its brightness. Crewmembers including left blister gunner Reb Carter took position to give Fling any visual cues he was going to need.

Radar operator Bake Baker wrote in his notes that they had gotten lost for a second time after bombing Tokyo late and that the Marines lost twenty-five miles of terrain and later regained fifty while *God's Will* was settling to earth. Bombardier Dwyer recalled that "bullets were flying around us" as Fling taxied *God's Will* to a halt in front of a cluster of Marines.

In one of the standard reference works on the air campaign, a photo of Savage's wrecked B-29 is identified as "Dean Fling's airplane." In fact, unlike Savage's plane, Fling's—although it sustained two shrapnel holes in a wing—was capable, once it could be refueled, of flying its crew home. *It was 10:30 a.m. Chamorro Standard Time, March 10, 1945.*

The Keene Crew

Ditching: it really was like hitting a brick wall. James Hash was thrown against the cushion he'd created for himself and suffered a broken and bloody nose. The B-29 Superfortress broke in two just behind the wing, exactly where the radar compartment was located. Conly—the interloper and heir apparent to Keene—was killed instantly. Conly was later awarded the Silver Star, the United States' third-highest combat military decoration, but he wasn't ever going to see the medal and he wasn't ever going to replace Keene as airplane commander either.

Up front Keene, pilot 2nd Lt. Richard D. Gordon, Dutrow, and flight engineer 2nd Lt. John R. Jewett were all battered. Navigator Donald E. Nichols Jr. apparently took refuge in the padded tunnel over the bomb bay, which was not a ditching position according to the manual, and escaped through the astrodome above the tunnel. The others were able to get out of the aircraft at the nose. With an enormous amount of physical exertion while battling the churning sea, they inflated a crew-sized yellow rubber dinghy. Several of the men had their Colt .45 automatics in big, waterproof cellophane bags. They looked toward a short stretch of beach surrounded by sheer volcanic cliffs that could easily smash their life rafts to pieces. They wondered why they saw no Japanese.

Hash climbed out of his tail gunner's window and staggered, trying to hold his balance standing on the vertical stabilizer. He saw radio operator Sgt. Leon B. Namoff bouncing up and down on the wavetops with his personal life raft deployed and central fire control gunner Sgt. Joseph Carroll struggling to stay afloat without one. Hash tossed his own life raft to Carroll.

Hash saw a bloody T-shirt that belonged to left gunner Sgt. Bernard T. Ladd. Torn from his body, the shirt was floating ashore. Neither Ladd nor radar operator Sgt. Marshall D. Long was ever seen again (this was the same Marshall Long who'd been at Clemson and was friendly with Bake Baker of the Fling crew). Among those who got out of the aircraft safely and occupied another crew dinghy was right gunner Sgt. Edward M. Collins. The men did not fully appreciate it yet—they did not even know which island they'd reached—but Conly, Ladd, and Long were the first combat fatalities of the Tinian-based 9th Bombardment Group, which was completing only its seventh mission in the combat zone.

It was a stroke of luck that the men were able to come ashore on the only stretch of beach on the island. Bombardier Dutrow, a .45 dangling from his hand, was first to realize their mistake. "I know which island this is," Dutrow told them, excited. "This is Pájaros. It's uninhabited. Sometimes we bomb it for practice. If we stay here, our own guys may bomb us."

Thinking they knew where they were—they didn't—the Keene crew went ashore. Nobody believed Dutrow. "This is Anatahan," someone said. The surviving members of the Keene crew huddled together wet, weary, stunned, and surveyed the volcano above them. "I would never have guessed at that point," said Hash, "that we would be on this island for more than 24 hours." *It was 10:45 a.m. Chamorro Standard Time, March 10, 1945.*

The Hardgrave Crew

The second of three B-29 crews to ditch after the mission to Tokyo was aboard *L'il Iodine*, with 1st Lt. Murel W. Hardgrave as airplane commander. His pilot was 2nd Lt. Ernest P. Deutsch. *L'il Iodine* ran out of fuel during the long trek toward home and put down at sea. *It was 11:55 p.m. Chamorro Standard Time, March 10, 1945.*

Other crewmembers aboard *L'il Iodine* included navigator 2nd Lt. Donald Reed, bombardier 2nd Lt. William V. Brabham Jr., flight engineer Master Sgt. David C. Nesmith. In the rear fuselage were radar operator Sgt. Thomas A. Cero, radio operator Staff Sgt. Robert W. Driscoll, central fire control gunner Staff Sgt. John R. Schoonmaker, right blister gunner Sgt. Eroy C. Albrecht, left blister gunner Sgt. William T. Cooke Jr., and tail gunner Sgt. Richard A. Gilman. They all made it into crew rafts and were feeling pretty good about the whole situation even as the sun drew higher in the sky, the tropical heat bore down on them, and a PBM Mariner flying boat passed nearby, apparently without sighting them.

Albrecht was one of several in the *L'il Iodine* crew who shared a tent with members of the crew of *God's Will*, including left blister gunner Reb Carter. "I wonder how Reb and his guys are doing," Albrecht thought. He did not know they were on the ground at Iwo Jima, refueling.

The McCaskill Crew

Of 334 bombers launched against Japan in the early evening of March 9, 1945, some 279 aircraft actually arrived on target after midnight on March 10 and passed over the primary aiming point at Meetinghouse, the center of Tokyo.

That morning, fourteen of the bombers failed to return, including three that flew into the same mountain and three that ditched. The last of the fourteen aircraft lost appears to have been *Hope-full Devil*, a bomber of the 484th Bombardment Squadron, 505th Bombardment Group, piloted by Capt. Bernard "Barney" McCaskill Jr. and flying from North Field, Tinian.

McCaskill's crew had the good fortune to be in mostly clear weather (although with storms off the starboard wing) and to be in radio contact with the seaplane tender USS *Bering Strait* (AVP 34) on lifeguard duty twenty miles north of Pagan Island. The radio operator aboard *Hope-full Devil* was a blue-eyed youngster from Livingston County, Michigan. Staff Sgt. Galen J. Westmoreland enjoyed tinkering with things and was a natural with radio gear. Today he was earning his pay.

It would appear that McCaskill carefully scrutinized the pages in the pilots' manual that explained how to ditch a B-29. Putting a B-29 into the water was a fearsome prospect under the best of circumstances. These were not good circumstances at all. Although slightly less severe than the conditions faced by the Keene crew two hours earlier, the white-capped Pacific was churning up ocean swells of about six feet, making a smooth ditching impossible. A 16mm film taken by a sailor on the *Bering Strait* shows that McCaskill performed by the book. The ship vectored the *Hope-full Devil* to its position. McCaskill lined up abeam the *Bering Strait*, descending exactly parallel to the ship. *It was 12:38 p.m. Chamorro Standard Time, March 10, 1945.*

The B-29 made a flawless, nose-high entry into the six-foot waves and generated an enormous splash. Even though McCaskill had done everything right, the impact was shattering as the B-29 went from one hundred miles per hour to zero in the space of one plane-length. Just off the surface, a swell caught the tail, pitching the rear up and the nose down. The tail section snapped off. As trained, all *Hope-full Devil* crewmembers except the pilots were at ditching stations, each with his back against a bulkhead of some kind. McCaskill was slammed around and suffered a broken back. As the bomber sank nose-first, its shattered rear fuselage pointing at the sky, one crewmember clung to the flap on the right wing and attempted to inflate a dinghy. Two men who exited the tail section were flapping around. Neither knew how to swim.

"I was pushing down on the rudder pedals for the landing, and doing that and handling the wheel made my body pretty stiff for the impact," McCaskill said later. "That's why my back got broken. I couldn't stand up afterwards and I looked up and the copilot [deputy group commander Lt. Col. Clifford Macomber, who was filling in for a pilot sidetracked by dengue fever] was already getting out."

By the time the plane touched down, the whaleboat from the *Bering Strait* was in the water and headed for the wreckage. The dazed and battered crewmembers struggled to get their bearings, follow emergency procedures, and escape the flooding airplane. Those in the rear cabin deployed life rafts then escaped through the rear cabin exit. Up front, engineer Tech. Sgt. Robert J. Aspinall and bombardier 2nd Lt. Carl R. Gustavson crawled out the engineer's escape hatch. Navigator 2nd Lt. Joseph A. Ptaszkowski crawled into the tunnel above the bomb bay and poked his head up into the astrodome, hoping it would work as advertised. The astrodome was made to pop out in emergencies. There was a lanyard or thong handle used to pop the seal. But the thong had broken. Ptaszkowski pried and pried and finally the dome came loose. He climbed out, rolled over on the wet fuselage, and landed on top of the wing.

By the time the pilots had come to their senses and unbuckled their harnesses, the front of the B-29 was pointed downward, with the nose of the aircraft well below the surface. The cockpit was flooding rapidly. "The water was rushing in, "said McCaskill. "It washed me back to my seat." But McCaskill managed to grab hold of the window and pull himself outside. In squeezing his way out through the window despite the pain of his broken back, McCaskill had to struggle so furiously that the canteen was pulled loose from his belt.

A whaleboat from the *Bering Strait* arrived. Two crewmen were drifting free of the wreckage and the boat maneuvered to pick them up first. Ptaszkowski was the only crewmember not in the water. From his slippery perch on the wing, he counted heads and ascertained that all the crewmembers were out of the plane.

A drama was unfolding on the side of the bomber nearer the ship. Left blister gunner Cpl. Marvin L. Binger was shaken up and having trouble inflating his Mae West. McCaskill inflated it for him and then helped him climb into the crew-sized dinghy. Right blister gunner Cpl. Julius R. Rivas couldn't swim and was desperately trying to hold on to the wing. Each time the plane was caught by a wave, Rivas was slapped back into the water.

Amid much yelling and flapping, the others persuaded Rivas to turn loose. A big wave grabbed him and he went under. McCaskill was able to grab him, inflate his Mae West, and help him hold on to the bobbing dinghy. To keep the crew raft from being tossed against the wing by waves, the men maneuvered it to the lee side of the aircraft. Macomber swam in front of the raft to pull it while McCaskill and Rivas pushed from behind.

The rescue took ten minutes. The *Bering Strait* took survivors on board. Bare-chested, dixie-hatted sailors struggled to lash McCaskill, in excruciating pain, into a litter. The ship's medical officer Lt. James N. Sussex, shirtsleeves rolled up—he never liked long sleeves, a family member later recalled—stood over McCaskill and directed sailors as they moved the litter to the medical bay. Sussex had written a letter home saying that at one point his ship was "the closest U.S. Navy unit to Japan."

The sailors picked up all nine of the B-29 crewmembers, including radar operator Cpl. Leon L. Melesky. McCaskill had taken seriously the order to leave ammunition behind and had left two gunners from his eleven-man crew—Cpl. John C. Edwards and Cpl. Dorsey L. Riddlemoser—on the ground.

As the day wore on, PBM Mariners were busy in the skies of the Marianas region, but it was a B-29 flying the "Super Dumbo," or rescue mission, that belatedly spotted the life rafts holding an exhausted, sick, hungry, and thirsty Hardgrave crew. Sadly, Dumbo provided an incorrect position report because of a navigation error.

Instead of making steam immediately to the right rescue coordinates, *Bering Strait* conducted a search. She picked up the eleven-man crew of the ditched Hardgrave B-29 crew. Hardgrave and his men, fatigued and frightened, began to cheer and to sing the praises of the United States Navy. *Bering Strait* had pulled off her second rescue of the day and was suddenly very crowded, with twenty Superfortress crewmembers on board.

Three days later, *Bering Strait* would relieve *Cook Inlet* at another lifeguard station, enabling the latter ship to return to port with the Keene crew. In the meanwhile, the McCaskill crew would be safely aboard a Navy ship but out at sea for another three days.

Scorched City

"It was worse than anything in Germany," Radio Tokyo announced in the aftermath of the March 9–10 firebomb attack. The Army publication *Impact*, which was classified "confidential" but widely disseminated among troops, ran a bleak aerial image of "the whitened sepulchre of what was once a tremendous area of Tokyo." B-29 Superfortress crews brought home with them the stench of burnt death. Back from the mission, in the sunlit morning, 1st Lt. Bill Lind of the 497th Bombardment Group taxied into his parking slot, pulled back the window next to his seat, and yelled down to me in his ground crew, "Hey, boys! Come over to this aircraft and *smell* Tokyo!"

Hours later, when everyone else on the mission was either killed, captured, safely home, or safely aboard a ship, the Keene crew had not been heard from. As darkness settled over the Marianas, intelligence officers analyzing the events of the day assumed the Keene crew was lost. A vast air-sea rescue apparatus remained on duty but was useless at night, and darkness was falling, too, over the men who'd survived the Keene ditching and were alone on an uninhabited island. One crew was still out there, but the great firebomb mission to Tokyo had ended. The fire blitz of Japan had just begun.

CHAPTER 17

The Fire Blitz

The B-29 Superfortress in the American Air Campaign, March 11, 1945–April 12, 1945

MORE THAN TWENTY-FOUR HOURS after the fire came to Tokyo—it was now March 11, 1945—battered survivors of the Keene crew were huddled together for warmth on the dismal little slab of beach on Farallón de Pájaros.

They'd built slit trenches in the sand. The officers slept on one big life raft and the enlisted men on another. Above them was a volcano, moist scattered clouds, and for many hours no sign of anything else. Leon M. Keene did his best to oversee first aid and survival preparations, but Keene had cut his' leg on glass escaping from his B-29 and had to pause frequently to receive medical help while at the same time presiding over the rationing of drinking water.

That morning, a PBM Mariner flew over and dropped food, orange juice, cigarettes, and malted milk tablets. The supplies fell into the water nearby and the Keene crew fought their way out into the surf to retrieve the materials. Inside one of the packages was a note: "Seaplane tender will arrive within one hour . . ."

It is almost impossible to imagine the exhaustion, frustration, and seething dissent that gripped the Keene crew that late afternoon, some thirty-six hours after bombing Tokyo, when they were still stranded and stuck. That is when the men saw a ship. To Hash, it looked like a battleship. He wondered why Curt LeMay's command thought this crew was important enough to send a battleship.

In reality, it was the seaplane tender *Cook Inlet* (AVP-36). Keene's was the first crew the ship had ever picked up. Hash noticed the steepness of the ship's side but was determined to climb up to it, with help from eager sailors. Said Hash, "They gave me a shot that knocked me out while everybody but me went to the officers' mess." The Keene crew would be aboard the *Cook Inlet* for fully three weeks while the ship remained on patrol. "I would like to see pictures that show how haggard we were," Hash said.

They were the last members of the great Tokyo firebomb mission to be recovered.

The March Fire Blitz
On the night of March 11–12, 1945, XXI Bomber Command carried out the second mass low-altitude incendiary strike in what became known as the March Fire Blitz. Three hundred ten Superfortresses took to the air over Nagoya. This time, the operations order permitted Superfortress crews to carry "small" amounts of ammunition. Once again, many crews ignored the prohibition and went into action with a full load of guns and gunners. On this night, however, no Japanese fighters were fired upon.

They usually hated Nagoya because of the flak. It was better defended than any the Japanese city, not excluding Tokyo. Nagoya was the first mission for Bud McDonald, who'd watched B-29s take off for the great Tokyo firebomb mission but hadn't participated. Now called Mac, but still Bud to close friends and family, McDonald had not yet received the B-29 that his crew would call *The Merry Mac's* (dubious apostrophe and all). They traveled to Nagoya in an unnamed aircraft.

They were among the first over the target. The bomb run went smoothly. Bombardier 2nd Lt. Alvin W. Dillaber called, "Bombs away."

Nothing happened.

McDonald pulled the pilot's emergency salvo switch, which overrode the bombardier's.

Still, nothing happened.

Their aircraft was over a hostile city, being stalked by searchlights, flying with bomb bay doors open, and eating up fuel. McDonald and right-seat pilot "Kit" Kittrell faced every challenge to airmanship possible. After a confab between Dillaber and flight engineer Staff Sgt. John S. "Red" Henrickson, the Superfortress made a second bomb run, Dillaber said, "Bombs away," and again, nothing happened. McDonald pulled his salvo switch again and still, nothing happened. After Henrickson crawled into the bomb bay to check the rack switches, McDonald made a third bomb run, an unheard-of tactic in such a dangerous situation.

"With the bomb bay doors open and the lights shining it, it felt like we must be the biggest thing in the sky and they couldn't miss us," remembered navigator 2nd Lt. Alexander T. "Lew" Parry, referring to Japanese gunners. On the third try, Dillaber was again unable to drop, but when McDonald activated the salvo switch, the bombs finally fell away.

Wrote Parry, "I set course for Iwo Jima and asked Red, the flight engineer, how we stood on gas as we had spent a lot of gas on three runs at rated power. Red said we were fine with enough gas to get back to Guam." The McDonald crew understood that Marines held only about half of Iwo Jima. The men were prepared to land there if necessary, but glad to be told they wouldn't need to.

Midway between Iwo and Guam, when a landing at the sulphur island was no longer a possibility, Parry looked over and saw Henrickson with his head in his hands weeping. Parry asked if there was a problem. Henrickson did not answer. He got up and went forward to talk with the airplane commander.

Mac called me saying that Red had made an error in his log of 1,000 gallons of gas! The gauges still showed some gas but for all practical purposes we were nearly out. I gave Mac our position report and he and the radio operator [Technical Sgt. Wallace L. Oldford] began sending emergency messages regarding our imminent possibility of having to ditch. We cut back power and went into a glide with prop RPM at about 1,450. It looked as if the props were hardly turning. We talked about whether we would ditch or bail out as there wasn't too good a record for ditching a B-29. We threw out every bit of gear and anything of weight to lessen our load. In about an hour we had fighter escort.

The B-29 was still in the air. Bud McDonald diverted to Saipan, which was closer than Guam. The front-deck flight crew saw Saipan ahead, and as the aircraft began to descend for a landing, all four engines quit. McDonald pulled the nose up, which fed the last remaining drops of fuel to the engines. He decided to leave flaps up and to land at faster than normal speed. The Superfortress came in "hot" and because they had thrown out the emergency power putt-putt earlier to save weight, they didn't have enough power to apply brakes. McDonald had to ground loop the bomber to bring it to a halt. A ground loop happens as a result of locking the brake on one side or speeding up the outboard engine to cause the plane to sharply rotate around on one wheel and spin.

Edward Cutler, the airplane commander of *Texas Doll* and now a veteran of what he called "the big one" over Tokyo, wrote that the trip to Nagoya was uneventful, the radar was working fine, and that "on this night at least, flak and searchlights were not as heavy as Tokyo." Cutler used muscle to avoid a midair collision over Japan's great industrial city when a B-29 passed "just feet below us."

As Cutler saw it, LeMay's goal of razing Japan with fire wasn't advanced very far that night. While *Texas Doll* dropped incendiary bombs squarely in the center of town, and Cutler saw a lot of smoke, he recorded that the bombs were too widely spread apart to ignite a large urban fire. When Saipan was socked in by weather on the way home, Cutler had to overfly his home base and land at Guam, where officers treated his crew badly, he thought. At one point, he and his crew had to be taken fifteen miles away for a postmission interrogation. "The brass can have Guam," Cutler wrote, a reference to the place being home to LeMay's XXI Bomber Command and a lot of bigwigs. He even wrote that *Texas Doll* bombardier 1st Lt. Stan Erickson "now knows where to kick out any bombs that hang up."

During the Nagoya strike, radio operator Carl Barthold, a veteran of both *Texas Doll* and the great Tokyo firebomb mission, was part of the Campbell crew on a B-29 named *Thumper*, assigned to Super Dumbo, or rescue patrol duty. "We had a rather rough trip because we flew low," Barthold wrote later that day. "I did more work than I have done since leaving the states. I got in contact with a sub via C.W. [continuous wave, meaning Morse code] and later had a nice voice talk with Iwo Jima. As we got to Saipan it was closed in [by weather] so we went to Guam." Barthold didn't notice any bureaucratic problems at Guam and his crew made it safely home to Saipan by the end of the day on March 12. No fewer than fifty-six Superfortresses landed at locations other than their home base that day, all of them apparently from socked-in Saipan.

Cutler's assessment of the Nagoya mission was about right. Reporter Vern Haugland, the Associated Press's man on Guam, wrote that, "the raid did not appear as destructive as Saturday's [March 10] devastation of the heart of Tokyo," but Haugland quoted LeMay as saying, "It apparently was a very good raid."

LeMay's bombers scorched two square miles of city, a result an intelligence report called "disappointing." The mission had little impact on the main Mitsubishi plant and other assembly facilities responsible for 40 to 50 percent of Japan's aircraft production; they continued assembling planes without any break in their output. While it was only the fourth-largest urban area in Japan, Nagoya had the best civil defense and firefighting infrastructure, prompting Superfortress pilot Col. Earl Johnson to write that the city "didn't burn too well." Another intelligence report noted that "Nagoya had an adequate water supply, well-spaced firebreaks, and an efficient fire department which adopted excellent tactics."

Having hauled incendiaries to Tokyo and Nagoya within forty-eight hours of each other, B-29 crews learned that evening that the next blitz target would be Osaka. A mission to Kobe was already scheduled after that.

On March 12, 1945, Bake Baker of the Dean Fling crew learned that a friend from Baker's days at Clemson had died in the Keene crew ditching. "I got some bad news today," Baker wrote, sitting in his tent. "Marshall Long was reported killed today. [Long had died on March 10]. I guess that's about all you can say about it. He sure was a swell fellow."

On to Osaka

The third blitz target on the night of March 13–14, 1945, was Osaka, Japan's second-largest city, with harbor, highway, and rail targets, as well as an arsenal that accounted for 10 percent of the ordnance used by the Japanese army. Flying a mission every other day was draining the crews. "I have tired crews, tired mechanics and tired airplanes," 499th group commander Harris wrote. Two hundred seventy-four B-29s used radar to spray incendiaries on Osaka, destroying 8.1 square miles in the city center. Twenty-First Bomber Command lost two B-29s and thirteen more were damaged.

The frequent journeys to the Empire continued with a mission to Kobe that was scheduled for March 15 and subsequently postponed to the night of March 16–17, 1945.

In keeping with the new LeMay policy, on the Kobe mission the crew on *God's Will* carried ammunition, but only for the tail gun. *God's Will* was the last B-29 to take off from Tinian for Kobe because of problems with its number four engine.

Fling dodged moderate and mostly inaccurate flak. Reb Carter described the crew's arrival over Kobe: "The fire looked even bigger than the Tokyo fire to me. An area with a diameter of about thirty miles over the target was as bright as day but it had a reddish color. The sky was full of B-29s, Jap fighters, phosphorus flak, shrapnel flak, rockets, tracers and the blackest smoke I have ever seen. It was enough to scare the devil."

Carter wrote that when *God's Will* flew into the smoke over Kobe, "it threw our ship around like a canoe on the ocean during a storm. We thought it was going to tear the wings off." After bombardier "Red" Dwyer dropped the bombs, night fighters equipped with radar and powerful searchlights began pursuit. Carter wrote, "I saw as many as five on our tail at one time. Pete [Peterson, the right-seat pilot] was flying our ship like it was a P-38 [fighter] and they never did get a chance to fire at us. They followed us until we were 100 miles from Japan." Carter predicted that because such a large area of Kobe had been completely destroyed, "Kobe probably will never need to be bombed again."

He was wrong.

Some 2.9 square miles of Kobe were burned to the ground, making up about one-fifth of the city's area. About 3,000 people were killed, with about 140,000 injured or made homeless. Some B-29s were caught in searchlight beams for as long as fifteen minutes, and three of the bombers were lost on the Kobe strike.

The fourth and final mission in the great fire blitz, the one that exhausted the last incendiary bombs in inventory, took B-29s to Nagoya again on March 19. By this time, stocks of firebombs were so low that many Superfortresses carried explosive bombs. Just one B-29 was lost.

The blitz involved 1,595 sorties (a sortie is one flight by one aircraft) and used 9,373 U.S. tons of bombs to burn about thirty-two square miles in four cities. Hap Arnold sent a message to XXI Bomber Command saying that the blitz was "a significant example of what the Jap can expect in the future. Good luck and good bombing." Japan's Lt. Gen. Noboru Tazoe, a key leader of the nation's air defenses, said that as a result of the fire blitz he knew, finally, that Japan could not win the war. After long months of trial and error, frustration and fury, B-29 Superfortress crews finally were beginning to believe they were accomplishing something.

On March 21, AAF boss Arnold, now wearing a fifth star at the rank of general of the Army, was back at the Pentagon after being away for several weeks fighting health issues. Arnold followed up on his congratulatory cable with a classified letter to LeMay.

Air operations are colorful and consequently the actual operation is normally the only phase of a command's work that receives public recognition. Your recent incendiary missions were brilliantly planned and executed, but appreciate that behind the successful missions there are thousands of men who do not participate actively as combat crews. The individual abilities of all of these men, welded into a well-organized and ably led team, account for the success of Twenty-First Bomber Command.

I ask that you convey to all members of your command this expression of admiration and appreciation.

I am convinced that Japan is going through a critical period, the seriousness of which will be greatly increased at the time Germany capitulates. This fact imposes a great responsibility on the Army Air Forces, since we alone are able to make the Japanese homeland constantly aware of the price she will pay in this futile struggle.

I am not unmindful of the importance [of] training, maintenance and other problems—in fact, I urge you to continue to recognize that these fundamentals are essential—but I want you to put the maximum weight of effective bombs on Japanese targets, consistent with sound operating practice.

A study of the effect of the Tokyo attack of March 10 and knowledge of the fact that by July you will have nearly a thousand B-29s under your control, leads me to the conclusion that your results are impressive even for old hands at bombardment operations. Under reasonably favorable conditions you should then have the ability to destroy whole industrial cities should that be required. The entire subject of incendiary attacks is, as you know, being carefully analyzed here. It is apparent that attacks similar to that against Tokyo have a most significant effect on industrial production, but further study is being made so that we can give you additional guidance.

Arnold had been in Florida recovering from his second major heart attack (suffered on January 17). Nominally, he was LeMay's boss, both as commander of Twentieth Air Force and as commanding general of the AAF. Both men had been briefed on supersecret United States efforts to develop a new kind of bomb, and Arnold had ordered LeMay not to fly over Japanese territory with this knowledge—not on March 9–10, not ever—but in other areas it's unclear whether Arnold gave LeMay any orders at all.

To biographer Dik Alan Daso, Arnold was "like a nickel-cadmium battery—running on full power all the time until rapidly losing its charge at the end of its lifetime." The once-robust, energetic Arnold was declining into frail health. He would make a visit to the Pacific later in the spring and meet personally with LeMay, but except when Norstad intervened, LeMay increasingly felt he had no direct supervision and made many decisions on his own. It was time now to give weary bomber crews, and especially maintenance crews, a bit of a rest, but LeMay still knew plenty of explosive bombs and more incendiary bombs were coming.

The Bertagnoli Crew
On March 22, 1945, a routine change of crew assignment took place in the 9th Bombardment Group on Tinian. Dean Fling moved

from the cockpit to a staff assignment. Bert Bertagnoli, until now of *Queen Bee*, now changed cockpits and became airplane commander of *God's Will*. Left blister gunner Reb Carter routinely noted the change in his journal.

As the air campaign against the Empire went on, a mission to Nagoya on March 24, 1945, exacted its price. The Murel Hardgrave crew of a new B-29 named *L'il Iodine II*, the men who'd survived the ditching of the original *L'il Iodine*, did not return from Nagoya. The crew and their new Superfortress were lost to an unknown cause.

While the thousand kids in the Marianas continued to press the war against Japan, B-29 crews in India prepared to join them. On March 29, 1945, B-29s from India bombed Singapore, which was still in Japanese hands. On March 31, XX Bomber Command in India went out of business and the 58th Wing moved to Tinian, commanded by "Blondie" Saunders.

In less than ten months, XX Bomber Command had flown forty-nine missions and suffered only thirty-seven combat losses. Under Kenneth Wolfe (until July 1944), Saunders (until August 1944), LeMay (until January 1945), and Roger Ramey (until dissolution), the command had done an excellent job in a pioneering environment. Thanks to these veterans paving the way with the very first B-29 operations, the job would be easier now that all of Twentieth Air Force's bombers were in the Pacific with LeMay's XXI Bomber Command.

Okinawa Invasion

On March 26, 1945, the U.S. 77th Infantry Division landed on Kerama Retto, fifteen miles west of Okinawa. Kerama Retto would soon become the largest seaplane base in history, housing the big PBM Mariner Dumbos that rescued many B-29 crews. The seizure of the small island was prelude to one of the most horrific land battles of the war.

The battle began with the largest amphibious assault carried out in the Pacific war, the invasion of Okinawa on April 1, 1945. The date was both Easter Sunday and April Fools' Day, and in these hot climes it was dubbed Operation Iceberg. American forces in the invasion included soldiers of the Tenth Army, commanded by Lt. Gen. Simon Bolivar Buckner Jr., and the XXIV Corps under

Maj. Gen. John R. Hodge, and Marines of the III Amphibious Corps under Maj. Gen. Roy Geiger. Buckner was what might have seemed a demographic impossibility: he was the son of a general who had fought in the American Civil War. During the campaign, Buckner would lose his life under enemy fire, becoming the highest-ranking American killed by enemy fire in World War II (although not as high as Lt. Gen. Lesley J. McNair, who was killed by a U.S. bomb in Europe and posthumously awarded a fourth star). Back in the Pentagon, they were already planning to use Okinawa as a base for the Eighth Air Force, which was expected to make the long transfer from Europe in time to support the invasion of Japan.

By now, Japan's defenses included a growing force of pilots called *kamikaze*, named for a divine wind that had destroyed another foe's naval armada and saved the homeland in the distant past. The fleet gathered around Okinawa—and the western allies' airpower swarming overhead—was challenged now by Japanese pilots willing to commit suicide to defend their homeland.

To support the landings on that hard-fought island, the 73rd and 314th Wings struck airfields on Japan's westernmost island of Kyushu in late March and early April. The 313th Wing took on a new chore when it began dropping aerial mines into the Straits of Shimonoseki between Kyushu and Honshu, in an effort to tie up what remained of Japanese shipping and naval forces. In what was to become known as Operation Starvation, 181 B-29s dropped 1,830 mines; four aircraft were lost on the first two missions.

All three of XXI Bomber Command's B-29 groups made a return visit to Tokyo on the night of April 3–4, 1945. No fewer than 242 Superfortresses took off, of which 152 struck their primary. Again, LeMay seemed blessed. Only one B-29 failed to return from the Japanese capital. Results were also good on a subsequent visit to Nagoya on April 7, 1945, the first time a bomber formation was escorted by fighters. Altogether, B-29s flew eighty-two missions in April, ranging over Japan as if they owned the place, on occasion encountering furious resistance but producing good bombing results.

The Simeral Crew

On April 12, 1945, in the Marianas—because several events occurred on this date, it should be noted that it was still April 11 in Hawaii and Washington—Superfortresses struck Koriyama. Tony Simeral, now promoted to captain, was flying *Snatch Blatch*. Approaching the initial point, radio operator Red Erwin prepared to drop parachute flares and a phosphorus bomb to mark the assembly point for other B-29s. The phosphorus smoke bomb was a 20-pound canister with a six-second delayed action fuse to enable it to fall some distance from the Superfortress before igniting.

Suddenly, the bomber came under attack by fighters. One crewmember said later that the fighters were like yellowjackets swarming out of a disturbed nest.

Erwin launched the phosphorus bomb, but the device clattered down the exit pipe, balked, and failed to fall through its release gate at the bottom. The bomb shuddered, bounced back at Erwin—and exploded. Searing flame shot back into Erwin's face. Burning at 1,300 degrees Fahrenheit and threatening to blow the B-29 to bits, the loose bomb bounced around the inside of the fuselage. Another crewman tried to catch it and smother it with parachute packs, without success.

Red Erwin grabbed himself a handful of hell. Smoke now filled the cabin. Erwin clutched the burning bomb, his eyes a mass of blisters, others choking and vomiting around him. *Snatch Blatch* went out of control, Simeral fighting in vain to prevent the bomber from hurtling earthward. Erwin struggled toward the flight deck.

Copilot 1st Lt. Roy Stables peered through the smoke in disbelief as a burning human being approached him shouting, "Open the window! Open the window!" The heat could be felt from one end of the aircraft to the other, and it seemed certain the bomb would turn the B-29 into a blazing torch at any instant. Simeral screamed, "Get it out the window!"

Somehow copilot Stables overcame his shock at seeing Erwin, afire, doing what no human being should be capable of accomplishing, and managed to open the window. "Excuse me sir," Red Erwin said through his pain, and then threw the flaming canister to the wind before collapsing to the floor in flames. Only three hundred feet from the ground, Simeral pulled *Snatch Blatch* out of its dive to head for Iwo Jima, the nearest landing site affording medical aid.

The crew turned fire extinguishers on the prostrate, burning body of Red Erwin. Stables administered morphine to dull the pain.

Through it all—the trip back and days of surgery following—Erwin remained conscious.

The doctors gave it their best shot: whole blood transfusions, internal surgery, antibiotics to fight infection. For hours they labored to remove embedded white phosphorus from his eyes. The chemical spontaneously combusts when exposed to oxygen, and as each fleck of incendiary was removed it would burst into flames, torturing the airman once again. Through it all Erwin has said, there was an angel by his side saying, "Go, go, go. You can make it." Everyone expected Red Erwin to succumb to the pain, if not the wounds. That night the officers of Erwin's unit prepared a recommendation for the Medal of Honor. At 5:00 a.m. the next morning they awakened LeMay at his headquarters in Guam. LeMay took a personal interest in Erwin, sending his recommendation to Washington, D.C., and arranging to fly Red's brother, who was with a Marine Corps unit in the Pacific, to his deathbed.

LeMay's command flew Erwin from Iwo to Guam, where he could receive better medical care in his final hours. Eager to present Erwin his nation's highest award before he died, LeMay canvassed the Pacific region and learned that there was only one example of the Medal of Honor anywhere—in a glass display case in Hawaii. An aircraft and men were dispatched. No one could find the key to the display case so the men smashed it, grabbed the medal, and rushed back to Guam.

There, just one week after his B-29 had nearly burned up from the inside, Erwin was rolled out in a stretcher. He was wrapped entirely in white, with slits for his eyes and mouth. With his B-29 crew and Maj. Gen. Willis Hale watching, LeMay handed Erwin the medal—surely the only time an American was awarded a medal snatched from a showcase—and told him, "Your effort to save the lives of your fellow airmen is the most extraordinary kind of heroism I know." Through his bandages Erwin replied, simply, "Thank you, sir." LeMay had been certain the award would become posthumous. Erwin surprised everyone by refusing to die. Erwin became the only Superfortress crewmember to be awarded the Medal of Honor for action aboard a B-29 (although one of LeMay's B-29 pilots, Michael Novosel, would later receive the award for action as a Huey helicopter pilot in Vietnam).

The Bertagnoli Crew

On April 12, 1945, the crew of the B-29 named *God's Will*, now commanded by George Bertagnoli—his predecessor Fling, now a major, had been made group assistant operations officer—was enjoying rest camp in Hawaii. They were the first crew from the 9th Bombardment Group selected for rest camp because they'd flown more combat missions than any other crew. It took them two days to reach Hawaii aboard a Navy PB2Y Coronado flying boat.

Bombardier Red Dwyer recalled visiting a volcano, playing softball, and meeting a movie star named Marsha Hunt. He also remembered that the food was tasty, even though it was served by waiters who were Japanese prisoners of war. Bake Baker and Tom Sulentic, the radar and radio operators, respectively, spent a little time enjoying Waikiki Beach, but most of the time explored the big island of Hawaii, where they stayed with a family named Bruce.

Reb Carter spent nearly of all of his time sampling what Honolulu had to offer. Not surprisingly he made time on April 12 to write his girlfriend Phyllis. He began, "My Dearest Phyllis," and described the activities available, including golf, tennis, swimming, surfing, sailing, and apparently his favorite, eating. "The food is delicious and we can eat all we can hold. The past two days I have drank six quarts of milk and eaten about two quarts of ice cream not counting the steaks and ham." On a more serious subject, he said that since he last wrote, his crew had returned to both Tokyo and Nagoya. "On the latter mission [on April 7] we had more flak than on any other mission and it was more accurate. It was bursting all in our formation. We flew right on through it but I don't see how." Of course Carter tells her how much he wishes they were together—"this place would be Heaven if only you were here, darling." He closed with "Always remember how very much I love you. . . . All my love, Bill."

Carter failed to mention several details: the flak at Nagoya had put dents all over *God's Will*, a Japanese fighter had rammed one of the B-29s on the mission, and he'd watched another B-29 explode over Nagoya. He did not explicitly mention that he and his crewmates would be heading back to the inferno over Japan.

Carter also left out something else. Given the time difference, he could have heard the news from Warm Springs, Georgia, before he wrote the letter. But apparently he hadn't.

President Truman

That day, Thursday, April 12, 1945, it was raining in Washington. Not yet aware of what the day would bring, the vice president of the United States, Harry S Truman, dictated a letter to a family member in his hometown of Independence, Missouri. "The situation back here gets no better fast," Truman wrote. "It looks as if I have more to do than ever and less time to do it, but some way we get it done. If I don't get this letter dictated to you, I will never get it written."

The House of Representatives wrapped up its business early. Speaker of the House Sam Rayburn invited his longtime friend, Truman, for a drink in Rayburn's office. Bourbon and branch water was the usual choice. In Rayburn's office, Truman took a telephone call and arranged to proceed immediately to 1600 Pennsylvania Avenue.

When Franklin D. Roosevelt died suddenly in Warm Springs that day, Roosevelt had been in office for so long (since 1933) that most living Americans could remember no other president. When he arrived at the executive mansion, Truman asked Eleanor Roosevelt if there was anything he could do for her. "Is there anything we can do for you?" she responded, "for you are the one in trouble now."

Truman was unknown to many Americans and to all almost everyone abroad. Many quickly learned trivia about him, for example the fact that there was no period after his middle initial, but most knew so little that they might well have uttered Truman's own words on taking office: "I feel like I have been hit by a bolt of lightning." Not until many years later would historians notice that Truman was the only combat veteran—he had been an artillery officer in the Great War, as most were still calling it—to reach the White House in living memory.

Truman wrote in his memoir about a cabinet meeting that day. It was late in the day (the meeting began at 7:08 p.m.), and the meeting was short. When it adjourned, everyone stood silently and left the room with the exception of Secretary of War Henry Stimson. Wrote Truman, "He asked to speak to me about a most urgent matter. Stimson told me that he wanted me to know about an immense project that was underway—a project looking to the development of a new explosive of almost unbelievable destructive power." He added, "The next day Jimmy Byrnes [a longtime Truman confidante] who until shortly before had been Director of War Mobilization for President Roosevelt, came to see me, and . . . with great solemnity he said that we were perfecting an explosive great enough to destroy the whole world." Truman would later write to himself, "I have to decide Japanese strategy—shall we invade Japan proper or shall we bomb and blockade? That is my hardest decision to date. But I'll make it when I have all the facts."

Army Air Forces deputy commander Lt. Gen. Barney Giles, filling in for the ailing Hap Arnold, went with other top military leaders to brief Truman in the White House on April 13, the first morning of his presidency. They apparently did not follow Stimson's example, but instead chose not to mention Groves, Oppenheimer, Tibbets, or the Manhattan Project. The new commander in chief would not receive a full briefing on the atomic bomb for another fortnight.

CHAPTER 18

Air Campaign

The B-29 Superfortress in the American
Air Campaign, April 13, 1945–June 5, 1945

ONCE SMALL IN NUMBERS AND mostly ineffectual, B-29 Superfortresses were now ranging all over Japan. Altogether, B-29s flew eighty-two missions in April. On occasion they encountered furious resistance, yet they produced good bombing results.

The loss of President Roosevelt was news on April 13, 1945, in the Marianas (where the date was one day later than in Washington). As if to avenge the loss of Roosevelt, another firebomb mission was sent to Tokyo that night. In the context of secret weapons then being developed in secret programs, that mission had a consequence the American bomber crews could not foresee.

But first came an unusually tough mission on the night of April 15–16, 1945, when 194 B-29s attacked Japanese industrial facilities in the Tokyo suburb of Kawasaki. It was a tough night for bomber crews. It was a clear evening in the area, and the searchlights, enemy flak, and fighters were particularly effective. Twelve B-29s were lost.

"Here we were on another night strike to the Tokyo area," wrote bombardier 1st Lt. William C. Atkinson, who was certain the Japanese were learning how to defend themselves during the nocturnal hours.

This time we didn't know what we were getting into after having been pretty well shot up on the first two strikes. I was told later by one of the boys in Squadron Operations that after our two first raids they really were worried about our safe return on this night.

The IP [initial point for the bombing run] was made at Manazuru-Misaki and we made a 'precision' radar turn [a 1/4 needle-width turn] on to the bomb run heading. We were reported to have had P-51 fighter cover but we never got so much as a look at any such comforting element in the battle.

It seems that since the last time we pulled a 'nighty' the Japanese had by no means been out of practice with their damned lights. The long bluish beams groped around and finally caught us! Ow! Not again! Our props were desynchronized to throw off sound directed lights but there was no foiling the radar controlled ones. We climbed, turned, and twisted in a vain attempt to escape the lights. Not this time were we going to stick to the bomb run and get shot to hell. It sounded as if all the flak in Nippon was exploding in the bomb bays. [The flak produced] icy fear as it had on the first strike to the same target.

All this evasive action was doing my bomb run no good. I had a fixed dropping angle set on the bomb pip and was to wait, make course corrections at the radar I was connected to the Norden sight and the autopilot, and finally tell Max [the airplane commander] to drop when the pip touched the mouth of the Tama river at Kawasaki. Every time the captain racked the ship up on a wing to dodge a light the [radar] scope picture would blank out. It was awful.

'Bomb bay doors coming open,' and that was the end of my efficiency [in radar bombing] on that trip. The bomb bay doors reflected the radar energy and produced an 'H' indication on my scope. 'Hell's bells!' I thought. Target, coastline, and aiming point completely disappeared. The resulting confusion and maddening casualness of my intercom conversation with Max was humorous but nonetheless effective. Lucky? The bombs tacked right on to the end of a large fire and walked on through the city.

Atkinson wrote that a night fighter chased his crew on its way out of the Empire. The men saw a burst of gunfire behind them.

Max and crew were not hit that night—but Mac and crew was another story.

Bud McDonald, also called Mac, was on just his fourth mission, and every one of them was tough. His aircraft belonged to the 19th Bombardment Group and was supposed to be officially named *City of Philadelphia*, but the crew called it *The Merry Mac's*, a sign of how much they liked their Jackson, Michigan, airplane commander, who was now twenty-three years old. They planned to paint the name on the nose but never got the chance. They'd had engine problems all the way from the heartland of America to Guam and on all three of the combat missions that they'd completed since arriving from stateside. Probably, they never knew that in Japanese culture the number four is considered unlucky.

After the war, the United States did an extraordinarily good job of retrieving the remains of its dead, even crewmembers who perished high over the center of Tokyo while it was white-hot with fire. But it did not always succeed. No trace of *The Merry Mac's*, of Bud McDonald, or of his crew has ever been found. But four other Superfortress crews thought they witnessed McDonald's crew in distress, making it possible to guess where the B-29 went down.

McDonald's former navigator, Lew Parry, who'd been replaced on this flight by 2nd Lt. Wilfred M. Flesher, would later spend many years trying to reconstruct what happened but would never reach a conclusion. Japanese fighters were behaving aggressively in the area, so a fighter could have shot down *The Merry Mac's*. Witnesses thought they saw Mac's number four engine windmilling, and this particular bomber had a long history of problems with that engine, so the crew could have been lost to the all-too-familiar mechanical failures that continued to blight the thousand kids. Or, Parry decided, they could have been shot down by antiaircraft fire. But nobody really knew. No one ever has.

Lost with Bud McDonald were pilot Kit Kittrell, Flesher, bombardier Alvin Dillaber, radar operator 2nd Lt. Carl J. Kleinhoffer, flight engineer Red Henrickson, radio operator Wallace Oldford, central fire control gunner Sgt. Andrew M. Evans, left blister gunner Sgt. Glenn E. Weesner, right blister gunner Sgt. Richard X. Walling, and tail gunner Sgt. Norman H. Wells. Also lost was an observer, 1st Lt. Oscar J. Groft. Parry was not on this mission and survived the war.

The mission to Kawasaki also took the life of Fred Malo, who just four weeks earlier had piloted the first B-29 to land on Iwo Jima. This time, Malo and his crew were aboard a different aircraft, not *Dinah Might*. Of the eleven men aboard his B-29, ten lost their lives immediately. The sole survivor was later to perish in a prison fire that would claim many Superfortress crewmembers.

Briefed on the Bomb

It was not until April 25, 1945, almost two weeks into Harry S Truman's tenure as president, that Secretary of War Henry L. Stimson and Leslie Groves gave Truman a thorough briefing on the Manhattan Project. Stimson wrote that to get to the White House meeting Groves "had to take a secret road around because if the newspaper men, who are now gathered in great numbers every morning in the President's anteroom, should see us both together there they would be sure to guess what I was going to see the President about."

With the war in Europe over but fighting in the Pacific continuing, Truman clearly understood the potential of the atomic bomb to assist in the defeat of Japan. But he also grasped, immediately, what having a bomb would mean for American power in the world. "If it explodes, as I think it will, I'll certainly have a hammer on those boys," said Truman. Historians disagree on his meaning, but many believe he was referring not to the Japanese but to the Soviet Union.

In later years, revisionist historians would portray Truman agonizing whether to use the bomb. In fact, both Roosevelt and Truman routinely expected to use the weapon. Apart from a small cabal of scientists in Chicago, no one seriously contemplated not using it. When Truman took office, the 509th Composite Group, headed by Paul W. Tibbets, was working in the United States and preparing to go to Tinian.

Army Air Forces leaders had selected the Glenn L. Martin assembly line in Omaha, Nebraska, to produce a batch of

Superfortress bombers code-named "Silverplate" aircraft. Martin modified these special B-29s by deleting all gun turrets except for the tail position, removing armor plate, installing Curtiss electric propellers, and configuring the bomb bay to accommodate either the "Fat Man" or "Little Boy" versions of the atomic bomb. The AAF assigned fifteen Silverplate ships to Tibbets's 509th group. These aircraft had a distinct bomb bay shape, but except for Tibbets almost no one in the unit knew why.

On the day Truman became president (April 12 in Washington, April 13 in the Marianas), and before he absorbed details about the new American weapon, the April 13 Superfortress incendiary raid on Tokyo had the unintended consequence of wiping out the Nishina research facility—unintended because the facility was unknown to the Americans.

A separate B-29 mission destroyed a centrifuging separator. These two acts of destruction put a halt to a little-known Japanese program that had never received sufficient funding anyway and had always faced significant obstacles. One Japanese scientist called it a program to develop a "man-made meteor," but he was speaking metaphorically. The Nishina project was Japan's program to develop its own atomic bomb.

This was almost the end of Japanese efforts to construct an atomic bomb, but not quite. The German submarine U-234 left Norway in April bound for Japan. The U-boat was transporting two Japanese officers, a disassembled Messerschmitt Me 262 jet fighter, and numerous blueprints and parts for antiaircraft shells and rockets. By far the most interesting thing found on board when the U-boat surrendered to United States forces in May 1945 were ten lead boxes containing a total of 1,200 pounds of uranium-oxide. The U-234 and its cargo were escorted to Portsmouth, New Hampshire. A complete inventory of the sub's contents was taken at the time, but no paper trail exists that details what became of the uranium. The U.S. apparently added this extremely valuable and rare resource to its existing uranium supplies to be enriched for use in atomic weapons.

In May, Lt. Gen. Barney Giles went to Guam to work with LeMay in planning the strategy of bombing industrial and petroleum targets in Japan. The move was the first step toward setting up a command called U.S. Strategic Air Forces in the Pacific, with its headquarters on Guam, in anticipation of the invasion of Japan. It was eventually to be commanded by Tooey Spaatz. Giles told the press that Japan's 148,000 square miles would receive more bombs than had Germany's 215,000 square miles. An early step by Giles was to support Vice Adm. Charles A. Lockwood's plan to hold airman-submariner conferences with the goal of improving air-sea rescue operations.

The Gray Crew

As the thousand kids pressed the growing air campaign against the Empire, with the size of bombing missions growing every day, more than a few B-29 crewmembers learned that being downed once was no insurance against being downed again.

On May 7, 1945, the crew that had ditched in *Hope-full Devil* after a mission to Tokyo two months earlier was flying without their previous airplane commander, Barney McCaskill Jr. His broken back ended his participation in the war and he was already back in the United States convalescing. Also missing from the original *Hope-full Devil* crew was radar operator Leon Melesky, who'd been badly injured in the ditching and was still undergoing surgical care. Today, airplane commander 1st Lt. Richard A. Gray headed the former McCaskill crew with 1st Lt. Edgar K. Grempler as his right-seat pilot. Yes, they were going to Tokyo again, an increasingly frequent target.

A brace of Japanese Shiden fighters attacked the Gray crew's B-29 at dawn. In the first firing pass, the number two engine and then the entire left wing of the B-29 were set ablaze. The great bomber seemed to fold in upon itself and to crumple, engulfed in flames. Killed in the fighter attack were Gray, Grempler, and radar operator 1st Lt. Mutt C. Myers (replacing Melesky), plus the following veterans of the earlier *Hope-full Devil* ditching, several of whom had been promoted since being snatched out of the water by the seaplane tender *Bering Strait*: bombardier 2nd Lt. Carl R. Gustavson, navigator 1st Lt. Joseph A. Ptaszkowski, radio operator Staff Sgt. Galen J. Westmoreland, right blister gunner Sgt. Julius R. Rivas, and left blister gunner Sgt. Marvin L. Binger. Two members of the original crew who'd sat out the great Tokyo firebomb mission and the ditching now lost their lives as well: central fire control gunner Sgt. John C. Edwards and tail gunner Sgt. Dorsey L. Riddlemoser.

Exactly one man got out of the aircraft and parachuted to the ground. He, too, was a survivor of the earlier ditching—flight engineer Robert J. Aspinall. When he descended to earth in a heavily populated area and was quickly captured by the Japanese, he must have thought he was the lucky one. He wasn't.

That day, another B-29 named *Empire Express* and led by 1st Lt. James McKillip was lost when a Japanese Nick fighter piloted by kamikaze Master Sgt. Tsutomu Murata rammed it. This was apparently not a suicide attack, but rather a frontal attack that either was misjudged or was too aggressive for the high closing speeds. The horrendous midair collision took about ten feet off the left wing of the B-29 and both aircraft went down. The Japanese pilot and all but three of the *Empire Express* crew were killed. The three men bailed out of the Superfortress, descended by parachute, and were captured by the Japanese. They were engineer Tech. Sgt. Edgar McElfresh, left blister gunner Sgt. Ralph Romines, and right blister gunner Sgt. Otto Baumgarten. Like Aspinall, McElfresh, Romines, and Baumgarten may have thought they were the lucky ones. They weren't.

A third aircraft named *Mary Ana* was lost on May 7 when it ditched and everyone in the crew was rescued.

Three days later on May 10, 1945, George Savage, who had cracked up on Iwo Jima after the great Tokyo firebomb mission, got into another jam. Savage was known for his singing voice and for being unkind to B-29 airframes. There was little reason for song as he nursed his aircraft home from a medium-altitude attack on the Otake oil refinery and Kure urban area. With bomb bay doors stuck in the open position and his fuel tanks all but dry, Savage settled into an approach for landing at Guam. "I would have made it," Savage wrote, "but on my first approach another aircraft cut in front of me and I was too close to him to land. So I went around and my engines started to quit on downwind leg. I probably could have made it but I turned onto the final about 50 feet behind another B-29 and when I hit short of the runway and bounced I got into his prop wash which turned me sideways and I didn't have enough control to straighten out the airplane. They do smash up when landing sideways." Savage broke his B-29 in half and everybody walked away from it. The government by now had stopped sending Savage bills for broken B-29s.

On May 14, 1945, Samuel Slater replaced Phillip Pettit as navigator on *God's Will*, commanded by George Bertagnoli. Back from rest camp, Reb Carter wrote in his journal that the mission that day was to mine the harbor at Niigata. "Fighters followed us for two and a half hours but didn't attack us," he wrote.

Tokyo Again

On the night of May 25–26, 1945, an extraordinary 498 Superfortresses were launched on the third all-out firebomb mission to Tokyo. Some 464 of them reached the Japanese capital. Once again, they burned down some sixteen square miles of what remained of the city.

Twenty-six B-29s did not return, the highest single-day loss of B-29s in the war. Although air-defense efforts by Japanese fighters rarely produced dramatic results against nocturnal B-29s, this night was different. A single Japanese fighter pilot, Master Sgt. Isamu Sasaki, a Burma veteran working at the Japanese army flight test center, flying a new Ki-84 Hayate "Gale" fighter (called a "Frank" by the Allies), was credited with shooting down three B-29s in a matter of minutes. "Flying above the American formations, he would select a target silhouetted against the burning capital, then dive at it head-on," wrote historian Jon Guttman.

The men flying this mission could not know it, but on that day (May 25 in Washington, May 26 in Tokyo), the Joint Chiefs of Staff established a date five months hence (November 1, 1945) for the amphibious invasion of Japan's westernmost island of Kyushu. Had they known that very real and serious plans for the final invasion were taking shape, the men who went to Tokyo that night might have found it easier to accept their heavy losses.

No one would ever be able to accept the atrocity that took place on the ground. The mission proved fatal for sixty-two B-29 prisoners of war held in a wooden Tokyo prison in the western suburb of Shibuya. "Flames engulfed the jail," said 2nd Lt. Raymond F. "Hap" Halloran, a B-29 crewmember who was a prisoner of war in a different, nearby location. In the Shibuya facility, the Japanese took a separate group of civilian prisoners and escorted them to the comparative safety of open field shelters. However, prison officials left the Allied prisoners of war, nearly all of whom were B-29 crewmembers, locked in their cramped cells with no way out. Generally, sixteen to nineteen men, sometimes piled on top of one another, would be placed into these filty, vermin-infested cells, which were approximately six feet square.

Among the prisoners who lost their lives were radio operator Laverne Zehler and tail gunner Glen Hodak of Sammy Bakshas's *Tall in the Saddle*. Also lost in the fire was Walter Grubb, right blister gunner from Robert J. Auer's *Zero Auer*, who had made a spectacular bailout during the great firebomb mission, and Eugene A. Homyak and Jack Krone, the only survivors of a crew commanded by John J. Musser of the 29th Bombardment Group that had been shot down on the great Tokyo firebomb mission.

This was neither the first nor the last time the Japanese murdered prisoners of war in violation of the Geneva Convention. The deliberate killings amid the prison fire, however, appear to have eluded prosecutors who conducted war crimes trials for other offenses in the immediate postwar era.

Ongoing Air Effort
The overall effort by the XXI Bomber Command—still part of the Washington-based Twentieth Air Force but operating with considerable autonomy—included the 58th, 73rd, 313th, and 314th Wings (soon to be joined by the 315th) and had produced a stunning transformation. At the beginning of the year, Superfortress crews were still struggling mightily to achieve results on each mission, sometimes involving only a couple of dozen bombers. However, by the middle of April, the B-29 Superfortress was laying waste to Japan's military installations, industry, and cities. Still, soldiers and Marines were wondering what they would find when they went in on the ground.

The final wing to join XXI Bomber Command was the 315th Wing, commanded by Brig. Gen. Frank A. Armstrong Jr. On May 27, 1945, the first bombers of the wing's 16th Bombardment Group touched down at Northwest Field, Guam.

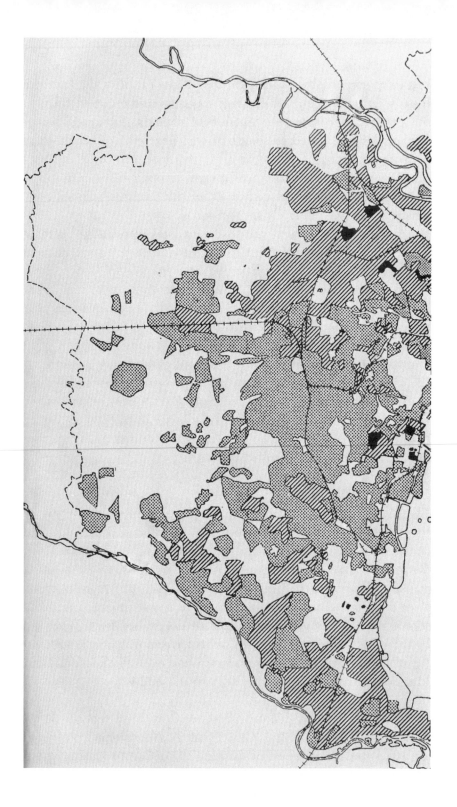

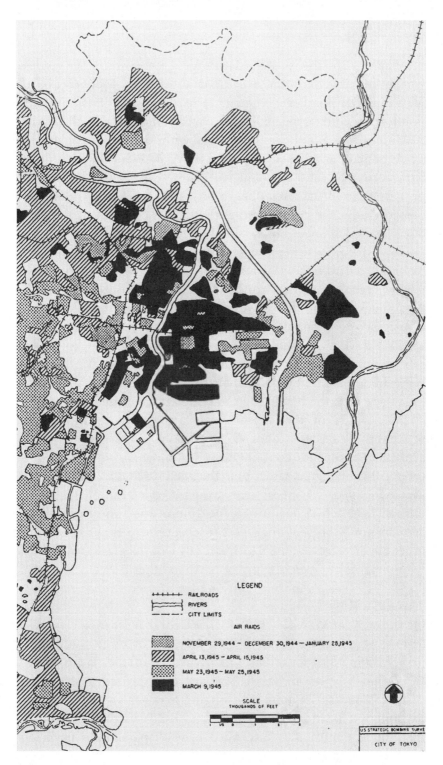

LEGEND

RAILROADS

RIVERS

CITY LIMITS

AIR RAIDS

NOVEMBER 29,1944 — DECEMBER 30,1944 — JANUARY 28,1945

APRIL 13,1945 — APRIL 15,1945

MAY 23,1945 — MAY 25,1945

MARCH 9,1945

SCALE
THOUSANDS OF FEET

US STRATEGIC BOMBING SURVEY

CITY OF TOKYO

A 1947 bomb damage plot of Tokyo covering a handful air raids between November 29, 1944, and March 9, 1945. *U.S. Strategic Bombing Survey*

The Superfortresses of the 315th Wing, known as B-29B models, were different in important ways from those of the four other bomb wings in XXI Bomber Command. The wing's sole mission was to bomb petroleum targets under the cover of night and in all weather conditions. The B-29Bs were equipped with AN/APQ-7 Eagle radar, a new system far more capable than the AN/APQ-13 radar of other Superfortresses. The unit dangled distinctly beneath the fuselage of a B-29, in effect resembling a tiny additional wing. Though it provided a higher state of resolution than its predecessor, the Eagle also required a longer bomb run of up to seventy miles from initial point to drop, meaning that that newly arrived wing would have to be limited to nocturnal missions or to bad weather conditions when Japanese defenses would be degraded. The members of the wing quickly found themselves dubbed "the Gasoline Alley Boys," a reference to a popular cartoon strip by Frank O. King. In the weeks ahead, they were going to deal a mighty blow to Japan's refineries and storage and distribution centers. They were doing a type of bombing that required hair-trigger coordination among the radar operator, the bombardier, and the airplane commander.

The B-29s of the 315th Wing, apparently in anticipation of LeMay's rules for low-level operations, were stripped of all armament except for the tail gun position, which was armed with three .50-caliber guns rather than the two .50s and a 20mm cannon that were aboard a Superfortress when it rolled out of the factory (although in actual operations, the 20mm was almost completely gone by now). At locations on the fuselage where guns appeared on other Superfortresses, the 315th aircraft had the glass area filled in with metal. They were slightly faster than other B-29s.

Three in a Row

On the night of May 28–29, 1945, the George Bertagnoli crew with Samuel Slater as navigator began a stretch of three consecutive, nerve-racking missions. The first was part of the 313th Wing's Operation Starvation. The U.S. Navy had devised a scheme to destroy Japanese shipping by dropping mines from B-29s into the harbors and inland sea of Japan. The B-29s used radar to drop the 2,000-pound mines suspended beneath parachutes from low altitude at night.

On this mission, for the first and last time, the Bertagnoli crew flew a B-29 named *Battlin' Bonnie* instead of their usual *God's Will*. Their target was the Shimonoseki Straits, located between Kyushu and Honshu Islands. They were armed with their full complement of .50-caliber guns and carried seven 2,000-pound mines.

During this low-altitude nocturnal mission, Japanese searchlights bracketed *Battlin' Bonnie* and the aircraft came under intense and accurate fire from flak batteries. Reb Carter wrote, "The flak was very, very, very intense and very, very, very accurate. They were firing at us with about 40 heavy guns plus one hundred 20- 40- and 75-mm. guns. It was bursting so close you could hear it and it sounded like hail on a tin roof when it hit the ship. The small arms were all shooting tracers. They had us bracketed by 25 to 30 searchlights for fifteen minutes. I didn't think we'd make it."

In addition to the flak and small arms, *Battlin' Bonnie* faced another threat. "When we were in the lights," Carter wrote, "a Nick came at us head on, firing 20-mm. cannon rounds and rockets at us. He went about 50 feet below us and was turning around to make a pass at the tail when Wyatt [central fire control gunner Noah Wyatt] let him have two bursts. He went down and exploded when he hit the ground."

Carter concluded, "P.S. Number one engine was cutting out the entire mission." Yet in spite of the fighter, the flak, the small arms, and the engine trouble, *Battlin' Bonnie* dropped the mines from 7,500 feet by radar and they were "right on the target," according to Carter.

The Black Crew

"The Stanley Black crew, the only other plane from our squadron, went down over target," wrote Carter. The crew—including radio operator Maurice Chrisman, who had sustained a minor wound over Tokyo on March 4—had resumed flying its usual aircraft, a B-29 named *Tinny Anne*. Hit by flak, the bomber went down near the city of Fukuoka. The entire crew was killed. In addition to Black and Chrisman, the losses included right-seat pilot 2nd Lt. Charles S. Frank, navigator 2nd Lt. Forrest A. Lee, bombardier 2nd Lt. Robert C. Atlas, flight engineer Master Sgt. Ernest Palasick, radio operator Staff Sgt. Nicholas Bonack, central fire control gunner Tech. Sgt.

Charles Siddens, right blister gunner Staff Sgt. James A. Bowers, left blister gunner Staff Sgt. Joe D. Mann, and tail gunner Staff Sgt. Charles S. Palmer.

It was a heartbreaking loss, but for the time being there was no relief for the Bertagnoli crew. Four days later on June 1, 1945, they were making their first foray in a newly assigned B-29 they called *Sweet Sue*, after Bertagnoli's girlfriend. Her name had not yet been painted on the fuselage. *Sweet Sue* was the lead bomber in a nine-plane formation for this daylight incendiary mission to Osaka. Lieutenant Colonel Leroy V. Casey, commander of the 1st Bombardment Squadron, 9th Bombardment Group, was aboard.

Flak was intense and accurate on this mission, too. Carter wrote, "You could hear it burst and it had to be within 75 feet of you to hear it. It also shook the plane." Unfortunately, it was deadly too. Carter recalled, "I saw one plane take a direct hit in the nose which blew about six feet off the nose. The plane was about four hundred yards from me when it was hit. It went down in a flat spin and three chutes came out of it." Carter concluded his journal entry by writing, "All the other guys in the formation were sweating us out since the flak was bursting so close to us. They thought for sure some of us had been killed." Despite the flak, *Sweet Sue* dropped her load of incendiaries from 19,000 feet on target.

On June 5, 1945, the Bertagnoli crew, aboard *Sweet Sue* for the second time, was speeding toward Kobe. Altogether, 473 Superfortresses were committed to this mission; the now very experienced Tony Simeral was again at the controls of *Snatch Blatch*. Resistance from Japanese fighters was fast and furious. After the fighters withdrew, flak guns shot down a B-29 piloted by Simeral's deputy lead early in the bomb run. The antiaircraft fire damaged Simeral's number four engine and tore a three-foot hole in an outer wing panel through which a torrent of precious fuel began to escape. Still two minutes from the bomb release point, his wing and engine on fire, Simeral kept in mind that he was carrying the lead bombardier, 1st Lt. William Loesch, and that the Superfortresses following him planned to drop on his cue.

Simeral kept power on the burning engine, greatly increasing the risk of an explosion, and led the squadron until Loesch intoned,

"Bombs away." After that, he began a long and difficult fight to save his crew—the same crew that had received deliverance weeks earlier at the hands of Medal of Honor recipient Red Erwin.

For three terrible hours, during which time the Superfortress could have become a blazing torch at any instant, Simeral and his crew fought their way to Iwo Jima. The only airfield available was a short fighter strip and a fuel-starved P-51 Mustang was in the approach pattern with them. Because of the terrain, Simeral would not be able to see the runway until the last moment. In the midst of making the perilous approach, Simeral found that while the flaps on the left side of the aircraft extended properly, those on the right went down only halfway. With help from right-seat pilot 1st Lt. Roy Stables, Simeral muscled the B-29 to its landing and to a welcoming committee of firefighters. He was awarded the Distinguished Service Cross, the second-highest U.S. award for valor.

Simeral's harrowing experience had much in common with that of the Bertagnoli crew. As *Sweet Sue*, the lead B-29 of an eight-plane formation, began its bomb run over Kobe, flak began bursting so close that the crew could hear explosions. Undeterred, lead bombardier Red Dwyer continued flying straight through.

Dwyer released thirty-one 500-pound incendiary cluster bombs 14,000 feet above Kobe. Minutes later, he sighted a swarm of fighters. "Fighters at twelve o'clock level!" he yelled as a single-engine fighter headed directly toward *Sweet Sue*'s nose. "I think he was trying to ram us," Dwyer recalled. As he lined up his gunsight, the sight collided with his steel flak helmet, knocking his helmet rearward and leaving his forehead and scalp unprotected. Dwyer fired two bursts from the forward gun turrets at the fighter trying to ram them. "Each time I fired," said Dwyer, "I saw pieces of it coming off but then we got hit and I didn't see anything for awhile."

They'd been hit, all right—hit at virtually the same instant with two 20mm cannon rounds fired by the onrushing and seemingly suicidal fighter pilot.

The first round exploded when it struck the Plexiglas nose just above and to the right of Dwyer's head. It sprayed shrapnel and Plexiglas into the cockpit. The second round traveled through the hole in the nose created by the first and exploded against the upper forward gun turret at the rear of the cockpit, knocking out the turret.

Dwyer was been momentarily rendered unconscious and was lying motionless across the top of his gunsight, bleeding profusely from the Plexiglas and shrapnel wounds to his forehead and scalp. The heat from the explosion of the 20mm round when it struck the Plexiglas near his head had fused pieces of a baseball hat that he'd been wearing under his helmet to the top of his head.

When Dwyer regained consciousness, he awoke to a chaotic scene. Pete Peterson, who had been piloting *Sweet Sue* when the attack began, and Bertagnoli were bloody and wounded, Peterson with shrapnel wounds in his shoulder and belly and Bertagnoli with shrapnel wounds in the back of his neck and in his forearm. The soundproof insulation that had been wrapped around the upper forward turret was on fire. Smoke filled the cockpit. Bertagnoli, who remembered the smoke was so thick he "couldn't tell if we were right side up or upside down," cracked open a side window. Mercifully, this drew out most of the smoke.

Slater quickly extinguished the fire. Dwyer, Peterson, and Bertagnoli received first aid treatment from Slater and radio operator Tom Sulentic, who applied sulfa powder and bandaged their wounds. Fortunately, none of the wounds were life threatening or incapacitating.

Dwyer began using adhesive tape from the first aid kit to repair wiring that had been damaged, restoring use of his interphone and radio. The crew's radio and Peterson's and Bertagnoli's interphones and radio remained inoperative.

The swarm of fighters continued to attack. They knocked out the lower forward gun turret and two of *Sweet Sue*'s engines: number one, located closest to the wing tip on the left wing, and number three, located closest to the fuselage on the right wing.

The gunners fought back. Reb Carter wrote, "Shorty [tail gunner Norman Fortin] got one and the pilot bailed out. Emershaw [right blister gunner John Emershaw] got another one and he crashed into the ocean. Wyatt [the central fire control gunner] got another that was headed down leaving a trail of smoke with his wings wobbling, when he last saw him. Shorty and I got another. He was leaving a trail of smoke with his wings wobbling when we had to turn our attention to other fighters."

Including the fighter hit by Dwyer, which unknown to him at the time exploded one hundred feet beneath *Sweet Sue*, the gunners were credited with three confirmed and two probable kills of Japanese fighters. With only two engines running, the crew knew they did not have enough power to maintain altitude all the way back to Tinian. They hoped they had enough to reach Iwo Jima. *Sweet Sue* began a very gradual controlled descent toward Iwo. Peterson looked at the cowlings of the two functioning engines—number two, located closest to the fuselage on the left wing, and number four, located closest to the wing tip on the right wing—and saw virtually no vibration. He was thankful their only two engines were running so smoothly.

Peterson, the most devout member of the crew, knew they were in a new airplane today, but he still felt he was seeing God's will. "Maybe," he thought, "we can reach Iwo in spite of it all." To improve their chances, the crew jettisoned everything they could to lighten the load.

As *Sweet Sue* neared Iwo Jima, Dwyer radioed the tower requesting permission to make an immediate landing, but was denied due to other damaged B-29s on the runway or ahead of them in the pattern. *Sweet Sue* then made one or two go-arounds and descended through a hole in the undercast. Four and a half hours after being attacked by fighters, the stricken B-29 touched down halfway down the five-thousand-foot runway near the base of Mount Suribachi, where Simeral's B-29 was battered and blackened. Bertagnoli and Peterson forcefully applied brakes, blowing both tires on the left side and causing *Sweet Sue* to veer off the runway.

The aircraft halted. The crew piled out. As Peterson's gear was being removed, his parachute ripcord fell to the floor. A large piece of shrapnel embedded in the armor plate in the back of Peterson's seat had severed the ripcord and his parachute shroud lines. "God's will, indeed," he said aloud, standing on terra firma.

When the crew examined *Sweet Sue*, they were shocked to discover the propeller on the number four engine, one of the two running engines that delivered them to Iwo, had sustained extensive damage from the fighters. A metal piece the size of a human hand had been blown off of the tip of one blade and three projectiles had penetrated all the way through other areas of the blades. Fortunately the thickest portion of the blades, which had been spinning directly in front of the radius of the engine, had stopped three more projectiles from striking it. Somehow, despite all the damage, the propeller had remained balanced during the long flight from Kobe to Iwo Jima. Had it become unbalanced, the engine would have been shut down, leaving *Sweet Sue* with only one engine and no hope of reaching Iwo. Carter recalled his prediction months before that Kobe would probably never be bombed again. He'd been wrong. He'd come close to being dead wrong.

We need something to happen to bring this war to an end, Carter told himself.

CHAPTER 19

"Destroyer of Worlds"

*The B-29 Superfortress in the American
Air Campaign, June 6, 1945–July 18, 1945*

IN EARLY JUNE 1945, GEN. DOUGLAS MACARTHUR, the western allies' commander in the Pacific, looked back at a month in which a remarkable fifty-four B-29 Superfortress missions had been completed, albeit by men who were not under his command. Now, MacArthur tasked Lt. Gen. Walter Krueger, commanding the U.S. Sixth Army, to develop detailed plans for the invasion of Japan. The brass envisioned a two-step assault, code-named Operation Downfall. The first phase, designated Operation Olympic, called for amphibious landings in Kyushu by Krueger's veteran army on November 1, 1945. If, as expected, Japan continued to resist during the Kyushu campaign and into the winter, the second step, Operation Coronet, was projected for March 1946, and would consist of an amphibious assault upon the beaches of the broad, sweeping Kanto Plain before Tokyo. In combination, Olympic and Coronet would be carried out by a naval, air, and land force greater than any other ever before assembled. A total force of five million men, all American except for the inclusion of three British Commonwealth infantry divisions, a contingent of air support, and the British Pacific Fleet, would be engaged in the land campaigns and on the waters around the Japanese homeland.

Army Col. Robert Dwan, a West Point officer who expected to lead a battalion ashore, remembered it this way. "We planned to take Japan by fighting block to block, street to street, house to house. Even given the damage they'd suffered during the B-29 attacks, we believed that every last Japanese was ready to resist to the bitter end."

The invasion of Japan was still half a year away, at least, as the B-29 force stepped up operations in June 1945.

More Murder

On June 20, 1945, in the unlikely setting of a girls' high school in Fukuoka on the western island of Kyushu—and only hours after a heavy firebombing strike by B-29s—the Japanese marched eight B-29 prisoners of war to a schoolyard and made them stand in a stiff posture. The Japanese then used swords to behead the men. It was an ugly and awful incident, made worse because the first attempt with a blade did not always do the job. Among the prisoners was Robert Aspinall, who'd survived the ditching of *Hope-full Devil* during the mission to Tokyo, resumed flying, and later become the only survivor of the Richard A. Gray crew. Also beheaded were Edgar McElfresh, Ralph Romines, and Otto Baumgarten from the McKillip crew of *Empire Express*. One of the perpetrators was a Japanese army lieutenant who said his mother had been killed in the bombing that morning. At least one junior officer refused to participate and was not punished for refusing; he was the only man in that schoolyard not targeted by U.S. war crimes prosecutors after the war.

Operation Starvation

The 313th Wing continued the aerial mining of Japan through June. It was a tough, thankless job for Superfortress crews, carried out at night with little recognition or feedback. By laying traps for any shipping that might enter Japanese waters, Superfortress crews were, in effect, carrying out an aerial blockade, attempting and preventing the import of food and raw materials into the besieged island nation. Japan was uniquely vulnerable to aerial mining, and intelligence reported that the 1,000-pound and 2,000-pound aerial mines were extremely effective. Although the term was not in use then, these were smart mines that could ignore some ships—minesweepers included—and detonate under others. By the time the campaign stretched into July, it had been through five distinct phases and had dropped tens of thousands of mines, producing "phenomenal results," as LeMay said.

The last time all four B-29 wings went against a target together until August was on June 15, 1945, when Superfortresses struck the combined Kobe-Osaka urban complex again. On the night of June 19–20, 123 Superfortresses of the 314th Wing traveled to Shizuoka, arrived amid heavy antiaircraft fire, and used firebombs to wipe away the industrial city center.

The fledgling 315th Wing with its Eagle radars mounted its first mission on the night of June 26–27, 1945, striking the Utsube oil refinery near Yokkachi. Going into July, the Gasoline Alley Boys flew larger and larger missions against petroleum targets. Striking the Kawasaki petroleum center on the night of July 12–13, the 315th Wing lost its first two B-29s in combat. The wing hit Ube on July 23–24. Kobe-Osaka received more attention in July as B-29 raids went after different industrial facilities in the port city complex.

Earth-Shaking Change

On July 16, 1945, an important change took place when the redundant XXI Bomber Command was phased out, and the headquarters of the Twentieth Air Force was shifted from Washington to Guam. Now, Curt LeMay became the Twentieth commander. As before, his outfit operated independently of Douglas MacArthur and Chester Nimitz. Although he now reported to Tooey Spaatz at U.S. Strategic Air Forces in the Pacific, with headquarters on Guam, LeMay remained largely independent and was now at the helm of the most powerful striking force ever assembled.

Though it went unannounced, U.S. scientists detonated the first atomic device at what was later called the Trinity Site in the New Mexico desert just fifteen seconds before 5:30 a.m. on July 16, 1945 (when it was already July 17 on Guam). A brilliant flash of light, followed seconds later by a shattering sound, swept over observers. The surrounding mountains were illuminated "brighter than daytime," one scientist said, for one to two seconds, and the heat was reported as "being as hot as an oven" at the base camp. The observed colors of the illumination ranged from purple to green and eventually to white. The roar of the shock wave took forty seconds to reach the observers.

The 18.6-kiloton, tower-mounted device (equivalent in destructive power to 18,600 pounds of TNT) was a ball-shaped, early version of the "Fat Man" plutonium bomb later to be dropped on Nagasaki. The very different, gun-type uranium bomb dropped on Hiroshima, the "Little Boy," was never tested in advance.

The detonation in New Mexico had an indelible impact on Manhattan Project boss Leslie Groves and his scientists. The best-known reaction is from chief scientist J. Robert Oppenheimer, who'd studied Sanskrit many years earlier and who now quoted a Hindu scripture from the *Bhagavad Gita*: "Now I am become death, the destroyer of worlds." In more practical language, sensing that the new weapon meant uncertainty for mankind, Trinity Site director Kenneth Bainbridge said, "Now we are all sons of bitches."

Not well known is the fact that the ground detonation was observed from a B-29 Superfortress. Scientist L. W. Alvarez described it:

> I was kneeling between the pilot and copilot in B-29 No. 384 and observed the explosion through the pilot's window on the left side of the plane. We were about 20 to 25 miles from the site and the cloud cover between the ground and us was approximately 7/10. About 30 seconds before the object was detonated the clouds obscured our vision of the point so that we did not see the initial stages of the ball of fire. I was looking through crossed Polaroid glasses directly at the site. My first sensation was one of intense light covering my whole field of vision. This seemed to last for about 1/2 second after which I noted an intense orange red glow through the clouds.
>
> Several seconds later it appeared that a second spherical red ball appeared, but it is probable that this apparent phenomenon was caused by the motion of the airplane bringing us to a position

where we could see through the cloud directly at the ball of fire which had been developing for the past few seconds. This fireball seemed to have a rough texture with irregular black lines dividing the surface of the sphere into a large number of small patches of reddish orange. This thing disappeared a few seconds later and what seemed to be a third ball of fire appeared again and I am now convinced that this was all the same fireball, which I saw on two separate occasions through a new hole in the undercast.

When this "third ball" disappeared the light intensity dropped considerably and within another 20 seconds or so the cloud started to push up through the undercast. It first appeared as a parachute, which was being blown up by a large electric fan. After the hemispherical cap had emerged through the cloud layer one could see a cloud of smoke about 1/3 the diameter of the "parachute" connecting the bottom of the hemisphere with the undercast. This had very much the appearance of a large mushroom. The hemispherical structure was creased with "longitude lines" running from the pole to the equator. In another minute the equatorial region had partially caught up with the poles giving a flattened out appearance to the top of the structure. In the next few minutes wind currents at various altitudes broke up the symmetry of the structure so the shape of the cloud cannot be described in any geometrical manner. In about 8 minutes the top of the cloud was at approximately 40,000 feet as close as I could estimate from our altitude of 24,000 feet and this seemed to be the maximum altitude attained by the cloud. I did not feel the shock wave hit the plane but the pilot felt the reaction on the rudder through the rudder pedals.

Carter's July 18

A flash in the sky in New Mexico did nothing to slow down the momentum of the war the thousand kids were waging from the Marianas. Nor did it prevent the men from occasionally having some kind of life when they weren't strapped into a metal cocoon listening to the drone of R-3350s. With the size of the Superfortress armada always increasing and new men arriving from stateside every day, some bomber crews felt a bit of release from what had been long weeks of constant stress.

On July 18, 1945, Reb Carter was feeling frustrated and bored. Lately he'd been manning his left blister gun position on the Bertagnoli crew only once every six or seven days. At that rate it would be a long, long time before he would have enough "points" to return home to Atlanta, home to his sweetheart Phyllis Ewing.

To pass time the previous couple of days, Carter had been playing lots of cards, particularly pinochle, losing a little change to his best friend Bake Baker in the process. He'd also been reading, reading a lot, reading a whole lot. Fortunately, the 9th Bombardment Group had a small but comfortable library with books, magazines, and tables and chairs. Today, after he tired of reading, he left en route to the Quonset hut that he shared with the enlisted men of his crew, plus enlisted men from three or so other crews.

As usual, whenever he was walking this route this time of day, he made two pit stops. The first stop was the mess hall, where he devoured two slices of freshly baked, piping-hot loaf bread with butter, a treat even for Carter, who had been born without the sense of smell. His second stop was the enlisted men's club for a six-ounce bottle of Coca-Cola, never available at the mess hall. At the club, enlisted men could play a game of Ping-Pong, and within the last couple of months, thanks to refrigeration, consume free ice cream and ice-cold beverages, beer or soda. To Carter there was only one soda—Coca-Cola. He loved Coca-Cola, especially in the six-ounce bottles—unaware that Curt LeMay did too.

Today he wasn't in the mood for ice cream, so after opening the Coca-Cola he left, making a beeline to his Quonset hut, indulging in an occasional sip as he walked. He was now in a hurry to get to his hut—he had a headache and thought a nap might help. As he neared his destination, he saw several Quonsets with silhouettes of rats painted on them. The silhouettes represented the number of rats the Quonset's occupants had killed with their government-issued .45-caliber sidearms. Great sport; there weren't many quail on Tinian.

Carter was in an unusually reflective mood. The silhouettes brought back a rather unpleasant and embarrassing memory. A month or two earlier, after the crew moved from tents to Quonset huts following their return from rest camp in the Hawaiian Islands, he, Baker, and Red Dwyer built a darkroom beneath the Quonset hut that Dwyer shared with the officers from his crew and five or six other crews. Among the three of them, they had scrounged all the supplies and equipment needed to develop photos. The darkroom was roomy, but was somewhat cramped, height-wise. If Carter stood erect, the top of his five-foot-eleven frame struck the support beams beneath Dwyer's floor. So whenever Carter was in the darkroom, he was careful to stay in a stooped position.

One night as Carter worked in the darkroom, a small photo slipped from his grasp and fell beneath the worktable to the dirt floor. Carter got on his knees to it. When he was about to grab the photo, he saw something close to his hand. For an instant he didn't comprehend what it was; after all, the only light source was a red light bulb. A split second later, shock: it was a rat, a huge ugly wharf rat, and it scared the hell out of him. Instinctively he jumped up to run—Wham! His head slammed into one of the beams. He saw stars, lots and lots of stars. Thankfully, Carter had not had any more encounters with rats in the darkroom.

Now, as he arrived at his destination, Carter paused before he entered and marveled at the colorful flowers on each side of the pathway at the front door. Baker's mother had sent snapdragon and phlox flower seeds, which Shorty Fortin, the Bertagnoli crew's official green thumb, planted and nourished with help from Baker, Carter, and the Tinian sun and rain. The result was a vibrant, cheerful addition to their home away from home. Carter smiled. Phyllis's mother had a patch of snapdragons too.

When Carter entered, Coca-Cola in hand, Baker asked if he wanted to play pinochle. Carter said, "No thanks, Bake, I'm still hurting from losing last night and this morning; besides, my head aches a little." Baker chuckled as he teased, "Has Big Bad Reb been attacked again by the little bitty mouse?" Baker grinned, and so did Carter.

"Bake could you spare an aspirin?"

"Sure, Reb." Baker handed one over.

Carter walked to his cot a few feet away, sat on its edge, and swallowed the aspirin with the rest of his Coca-Cola. The beverage reminded him of home and of course Phyllis. Carter loved Coca-Colas, but Phyllis *really* loved them. She and her family drank so many that each week a red Coca-Cola truck delivered a stack of four wooden cases to her front door, only a mile or so from the former residence of Asa Candler, who in 1887 purchased the formula for Coca-Cola from its inventor, John Pemberton, for $2,300. By the time of his death in 1929, Candler had transformed Coca-Cola into one of the largest companies in the United States. Carter had met Phyllis at a public swimming pool located on Candler's former estate, in the summer of 1942. Carter was working there as a lifeguard. Phyllis was there working on her tan.

After finishing his drink, Carter laid down, hoping the aspirin would kick in soon. Maybe music would help.

"Bake how 'bout some music from your radio?"

"Good idea, Reb."

Baker's father had shipped Baker a radio, record player, amplifier, and speaker, which Baker kept next to his cot in a plywood cabinet built by the Navy Seabees on Tinian. Carter specified music from the radio because he had tired long ago of listening to the only three records in Baker's collection. Besides, they were pretty scratched up.

Baker turned on the radio but kept the volume low, not wanting to disturb the other men in the hut. Carter could hear just fine because his cot was next to Baker's.

The "DJ" on the station Baker selected was none other than Tokyo Rose. Carter and Baker didn't care for her commentary, but they enjoyed the music. They had no choice anyway. Baker's radio could only pick up one station that played music; like it or not, they were stuck with Tokyo Rose.

When Baker turned on the radio, Tokyo Rose was playing Glenn Miller's "Moonlight Serenade." This evoked memories of parking in a cemetery behind an old church in Atlanta, smooching with Phyllis, steaming up the car windows while listening to hits by Miller, Tommy Dorsey, and Les Brown, among others.

Carter tried to nap. He couldn't. He kept thinking about Phyllis, always Phyllis. He sat up, reached into the makeshift nightstand next to his cot, and removed the two small photos of Phyllis he'd received the day before. She appeared to have gained a pound or two, but was still slim and gorgeous, he thought. He put the pictures aside and looked up at the dozen photos, all of Phyllis, taped to the wall above his cot. His eyes focused on his favorite, the largest one in his collection. In it he was wearing his issued khakis, standing behind Phyllis's home, carrying her the way a groom carries his bride across the threshold.

Carter lay down again, closed his eyes, and tried one more time to get a little shut-eye. He couldn't quit thinking about Phyllis. After a few futile minutes, he gave up.

He retrieved his fountain pen, an almost-empty bottle of ink, a few pieces of American Red Cross stationery, and his small wooden lapboard from the nightstand. Just before his pen touched the stationery, he thought, "Years from now someone may care what I wrote when I was here on this island in this war at this time." Prior to arriving at Tinian, he had written all of his letters in difficult-to-read cursive, and he had only written the day of the week, never the date, at the beginning of each letter. This time, Carter printed, slowly, deliberately, in easy-to-read block letters:

Wednesday
July 18, 1945

My Dearest Darling,

Honey, I am so homesick, I don't know what to do. The only thing I have done yesterday and today is read and play cards. Gosh! I wish they would let us fly so I could hurry home to you.

Darling, I received the two pictures you sent me yesterday. I think the added weight is very becoming and I want you to keep all of it except maybe a few lbs. off the waistline.

They keep playing songs over the radio, which get under my skin, since they remind me of you. I daydream about you enough without having that to remind me, even more, of the wonderful times we have had together. Every time I think of you, I feel so lonely. Darling, I love you so very, very, very much and always will. I don't think it is possible for anyone to love and miss anyone any more than I love and miss you.

Honey, I can't think of anything else so I will close. Always remember how very, very, very, very much I love my little devil.

All my love & kisses
                                        Bill

X X X X X X X X

Carter placed the letter in an envelope, addressed it, and affixed a six-cent airmail stamp. "I'll mail it later," he thought. Finally, with "Sentimental Journey" playing in the background, he lay down, closed his eyes, and drifted off to sleep. Soon he would be in the air again in a B-29, and while the thousand kids pressed on against the Empire, a million men were being moved from Europe to the Pacific and preparing for the amphibious invasion of Japan.

CHAPTER 20

Mission to Hiroshima

The B-29 Superfortress in the American Air Campaign, July 19, 1945–September 2, 1945

THE WAR CONTINUED. On July 27, 1945, the Bertagnoli crew went to Tokuyama, where Reb Carter watched helplessly while three fighters jumped a B-29 and shot it down. "It exploded and fell in a mass of flames," he wrote.

The antipetroleum effort by the 315th Wing continued on the night of July 28–29, when seventy-six Superfortresses assaulted the Shimotsu refinery. Before the end of hostilities, the nocturnal raids by the wing's B-29s also touched the Mitsubishi and Hayama refineries at Kawasaki and the Nippon refinery at Amagasaki.

Tibbets on Tinian
A new and different band of brothers began arriving at North Field, Tinian, in that summer of 1945, hauling duffel bags out of transport planes, staking out a sequestered cluster of buildings that had been set up for them in a purposely remote location, and giving the cold shoulder to anyone who wasn't one of their own.

The reclusive 509th Composite Group had arrived. It was supposed to be a combat group, just like the other bombardment groups on Guam, Saipan, and Tinian, yet it had only two flying squadrons—one with B-29 Superfortress bombers, the other with C-54 Skymaster transports. No one else among the thousand kids at the B-29 bases in the Marianas had enjoyed the luxury of arriving aboard their own transport planes.

The man who left no doubt that he was in charge of the 509th was Paul Tibbets, born in Illinois but a product of an Iowa upbringing, serious, earnest, and deadpan. Like Curt LeMay, Tibbets understood little of the science behind the secret weapon that Groves's Manhattan Project had wrought, but he knew bombing and bombers. He was no philosopher, but he had to have some sense that nothing less than the fate of the world rested in the hands of his 1,760 men and fifteen specially configured Superfortresses. The bomb bay of each Silverplate Superfortress had been reconfigured to suspend, from a single point, a weight of ten thousand pounds. A lot of work had gone into forming and training the 509th, much of it from the sweat of Tibbets's brow, and the aircraft were kept in shiny, pristine condition.

Tibbets got to work immediately and started building barriers between his men and everyone else on Tinian. Members of other groups within the 313th Wing found Tibbets's troops reluctant to converse, clannish, and tight-lipped.

"They stuck to themselves," said Charles G. "Chuck" Chauncey, a B-29 pilot with the 9th Bombardment Group. "Their aircraft were different from ours. With their tight security, we couldn't find out anything." Far from relying on others at the Tinian base, Chauncey noticed, "They brought all their stuff over with them. You never co-mingled with them or anything like that. Some of our gunners knew their gunners, but their gunners didn't seem to know why the 509th was different or what it was doing."

While other B-29 crews trudged back and forth to the Empire, dropped bombs, came home, or didn't, blew up in midair or ditched at sea, with crewmembers fighting and bleeding and dying, Tibbets's 509th seemed to be on another planet. Other

B-29 crewmembers resented the fact that they seemed not to be part of the war, not taking the same risks as the mere mortals in the traditional Superfortress units. Men like Chauncey began to observe the newcomers flying small, seemingly ineffectual milk runs to easy targets—the crews familiarizing themselves with weather and conditions in Japan. Some of Chauncey's battlemates seethed with resentment. Everybody else was going to the dangerous targets and Tibbets's boys were enjoying the best real estate on the island and fooling around. One of them wrote a poem deriding Tibbets's outfit:

Into the air the secret arose,
Where they're going, nobody knows,
Tomorrow they'll return again,
But we'll never know where they've been.
Don't ask about results or such,
Unless you want to get in dutch,
But take it from one who is sure of the score,
The 509th is winning the war.

The razzing from the members of other bomb groups was not especially good-natured, and it was taking a toll. Most members of the 509th still did not know why they were on Tinian, why they had special aircraft, or why they were sitting out big missions being flown by hundreds of B-29s. Airplane commander Capt. Robert Lewis was more than upset. Exercising his role as commander of the group, Tibbets appropriated Lewis's aircraft. The plane Lewis had thought was his own would eventually wear the words *Enola Gay*, named for Tibbets's mother.

When they arrived in the Pacific, the B-29s of the 509th wore a tail marking designed for their special unit, consisting of a forward-pointing arrowhead enclosed in a circle, both in black paint on the fin. When they began flying missions over Japan, Tibbets's bombers took on bogus markings from other units. *Enola Gay*, for example, wore the circle R that really belonged to the 6th Bombardment Group.

Not yet given its name, *Enola Gay* arrived on Guam from the United States. After technicians completed additional modifications, a crew flew it from Guam to Tinian. The aircraft and its crew began formal training in the combat zone.

On July 29, 1945, Tooey Spaatz arrived on Guam from Europe to take command of Strategic Air Forces Pacific. On the night of August 5, 1945, only hours after Tibbets christened the bomber, ground crews began loading the "Little Boy" weapon aboard *Enola Gay*. They moved the big bomber into position straddling a bomb-loading pit. Not really little at all but actually twelve-feet long and weighing nine thousand pounds with a twenty-eight-inch-diameter belly, the Little Boy was hoisted by hydraulic lift and slipped through the bomb bay with two inches to spare.

Tibbets's crew included four who had flown with him in Europe: bombardier Maj. Thomas W. Ferebee, navigator Capt. Theodore J. "Dutch" Van Kirk, tail gunner Staff Sgt. George R. Caron, and flight engineer Staff Sgt. Wyatt E. Duzenbury.

It was unseasonably cool in the Marianas that night. Tibbets would later recall feeling a chill as he contemplated writing a new chapter in the war waged by B-29 Superfortress crews against the Empire. Later, armchair historians would argue that it was the March 9–10 firebomb mission to Tokyo that marked the turning point in the effort to defeat Japan. None, however, would ever say that the mission to Tokyo and the incendiary blitz that followed was enough to bring down a world power that was dug in and seemingly willing to fight to the last man. The mission to Tokyo would have to share the history books with Tibbets's mission to Hiroshima.

Enola Gay at War

The predawn launch from Tinian involved a number of other 509th Group B-29 bombers. Besides the *Enola Gay*, six aircraft were to participate. Three were weather planes, launched beginning at 1:17 a.m. or more than an hour ahead of the others: *Straight Flush*, commanded by Maj. Claude Eatherly, covered the weather at Hiroshima; *Jabbit III*, with Maj. John A. Wilson in charge, performed the same duty at Kokura; and *Full House*, piloted by Maj. Ralph R. Taylor Jr., headed for Nagasaki. Hiroshima was the prime target, but if clouds prevented visual sighting of landmarks, Kokura and Nagasaki were alternates.

All three of the weather reconnaissance aircraft were well out of the area in and around Hiroshima before *Enola Gay* arrived. Similarly part of the overall effort but never anywhere near the target was *Top Secret*, piloted by Capt. Charles F. "Chuck" McKnight. McKnight's was the backup aircraft in case *Enola Gay* encountered mechanical problems and needed to land at Iwo Jima. His plane was to fly to Iwo Jima and stand ready to take over the mission from *Enola Gay* if necessary.

Two other aircraft, raising the total to three in and around the target, also had key roles. *The Great Artiste*, piloted by Maj. Charles Sweeney, carried special instrumentation to measure the magnitude of the detonation. Sweeney was of Irish descent, brash, and edgy, seen by everyone in the 509th as a foil to Tibbets's calm, straightforward persona. Unnamed aircraft number 91, later to be named *Necessary Evil* and piloted by Capt. George W. Marquardt, carried cameras.

Names had been apparently been chosen already for all of these Superfortresses except *Top Secret* and *Necessary Evil*, which were christened later. However, on August 6, 1945, only *Enola Gay* had a name painted on her nose. The others were painted after the mission.

Most historical accounts have three Superfortresses going to Hiroshima, but two others were in the air and one may have been over or near the target. As historian John Bybee put it, "Nobody else was supposed to be in the air during the Hiroshima mission. Everybody in the Twentieth Air Force knew that. But nobody told the Eighth Air Force." Newly arrived in theater from Europe, the Eighth was responsible for the 3rd Photo Reconnaissance Squadron at Harmon Field, Guam. The squadron launched an F-13 and an F-13A, both photo-reconnaissance versions of the B-29, on August 6. The F-13A *Quan Yin Cha Ara*, apparently piloted by Willis "Bud" Rohling, made a photo run over Tokyo. Its crew may have witnessed the Hiroshima atomic cloud from hundreds of miles away. The unnamed F-13, piloted by Jack Economos, may have actually passed over or near Hiroshima.

To the Target
Shortly after 2:30 a.m. on August 6, 1945, *Enola Gay* taxied out

from its Tinian parking spot with its unique cargo. There was anxiety over the takeoff run. John T. Correll wrote,

> Tibbets had already decided to make use of every inch of the runway. The aircraft was heavily loaded with fuel and the 9,000-pound bomb, and was 15,000 pounds over the usual takeoff weight. He released the brakes, advanced the throttles, and rolled down the long runway, gathering speed. Tibbets resisted the urge to attempt takeoff before the aircraft reached its best speed possible.

"I held firm until we were a little more than one hundred feet from the end of the pavement," Tibbets said. "Thanks to our extra speed—we were at 155 miles an hour—the plane lifted off easily and climbed steadily."

Tibbets was group commander and airplane commander of *Enola Gay*, but another figure, Navy Capt. William S. "Deak" Parsons, was in some sense the leader of the world's first atomic bomb run. Weaponeer Parsons began his day by ignoring the orders from Groves, who had specifically forbidden the midair arming of the bomb, saying it was too dangerous. Parsons, who had seen countless B-29s crash on takeoff since taking up residence with the 509th, felt that if he armed the weapon on the ground, and *Enola Gay* suffered the slightest mishap, the mission would end in disaster for the Manhattan Project, and death for thousands of sailors and airmen on Tinian.

At 3:00 a.m., with the *Enola Gay* safely thousands of feet up and hundreds of miles away, Parsons began carefully inserting the explosive charge that gave the "Little Boy" its teeth. Early in the process, he cut his finger badly on the sharply machined edges of the bomb's tail. Blood glistened on Parsons's clothing and on the surface of the bomb.

At 7:00 a.m., Japanese radar detected aircraft heading toward Japan and broadcast the alert throughout the Hiroshima area. Soon afterward, a weather B-29 circled over the city. At 8:09 a.m., the crew of the *Enola Gay* saw the city appear below. The target was the T-shaped Aioi Bridge that was located in the heart of Hiroshima. At 8:15 a.m., bombardier Ferebee—who did not know what kind of ordnance he was dropping—released the "Little Boy."

The detonation occurred near the central section of the city. The crew of the *Enola Gay* saw a column of smoke rising fast and intense fires springing up.

"Little Boy" went off at a height of 1,800 feet above Hiroshima, an altitude calculated to make the most of the blast effect. Seventy thousand people, including some American prisoners of war, died instantly. Sixty thousand buildings, out of Hiroshima's total of ninety thousand, were completely destroyed. The yield was approximately fifteen kilotons, or equivalent to fifteen thousand tons of TNT. The March 9–10 mission to Tokyo had wiped away a larger urban area and killed more people, but had taken 279 aircraft dropping bombs to do the job. The mission to Hiroshima took just one plane with one bomb, for one city.

A twelve-year-old Japanese student who survived the great Tokyo firebomb mission spoke years later about Hiroshima. "It was a shock of course, but at the time, initially we didn't know what happened," Yoko Ono said. "I heard about it from somebody in my village. It's a very, very different kind of bomb, they said, we have to immediately stop the war. It didn't make sense to me at all, in any way. We didn't understand. . . . It was something that you just could not understand. It was just so bad." Referring to the larger bombing campaign against the Japanese home islands, Ono said, "Well you see, it was because of Pearl Harbor, and so the rest of the world was very, very cold to us when the bombs dropped. Like, 'Oh, they deserved it'—that kind of thinking. For America to have bombed civilians was something that most people accepted. But women and children, old and young, they all suffered. If it had happened not to Japan but in a Western country, maybe the West would have felt differently about it."

The Second Bomb

If the bombing of Hiroshima went flawlessly, the second atomic bomb mission became a fiasco.

Early on August 9, 1945, the effusive Charles Sweeney—the only pilot to fly both atomic bomb missions—took off from Tinian at the controls of the *Bock's Car* carrying the "Fat Man" weapon. Sweeney had commandeered Capt. Frederick C. Bock's bomber, while Bock went along as an observer at the controls of Sweeney's bomber, *The Great Artiste*.

Sweeney launched even though *Bock's Car* had a fuel system problem that rendered a portion of its fuel supply unavailable. The fuel problem should have meant aborting, but to cancel the takeoff, or to return the "Fat Man" to Tinian after takeoff, would have required some disassembly and recharging of batteries that would have taken about three days. The batteries required recharging every three days, and after nine days from the start of assembly the batteries would have to be replaced. The pit, or central core, could only be left in the bomb for about ten days from start of assembly before heating caused degradation of the high-explosive lenses, and there was no other usable set of high-explosive lenses available on Tinian. Of course, the bomb could have been dropped into the ocean, but construction of the "Fat Man" had taken a crew of forty to fifty men three years to accomplish. The Manhattan Project and the 509th would have serious problems if Sweeney could not drop the bomb as planned.

So *Bock's Car* proceeded toward its primary target, the great industrial city of Kokura, its crew possibly—or possibly not—remembering that the rules required a visual drop. The 509th crews had been sternly warned not to drop an atomic bomb by radar. The stakes were too high. What almost no one knew—fortunately, least of all the Japanese—was that, for now at least, there was no third atomic bomb. One additional bomb had reached Tinian, but key components of the third bomb had been damaged in transit and could not be repaired. There was no fourth bomb anywhere, not on Tinian, not en route, and not even in the United States.

Visual conditions did not exist at Kokura. The city was obscured by smoke, much of it left over from a nearby B-29 mission of a day earlier. Unable to see the bombing point, Sweeney turned *Bock's Car* toward its secondary target, the port city of Nagasaki.

Given that the Japanese had had little time to respond to Hiroshima, given the fuel-flow problems aboard *Bock's Car*, and given the smoky conditions at the primary, was this mission too hasty? Group Captain Leonard Cheshire, the British observer with the 509th who was aboard *Bock's Car*, later said this: "As a matter of fact, I may well confess that we were so keen on dropping this bomb on Nagasaki, and would have been so disappointed if the war had ended without our doing so, that some of us jokingly suggested, if Japan did surrender before we flew to Nagasaki, that we might even fly there and drop the bomb just the same!" Another observer described the critical moments of the mission this way:

> When the primary could not be attacked due to cloud cover, they diverted to Nagasaki, where cloud cover again intruded. All told they stooged around for an hour burning reserve fuel they didn't have trying to make the mandated visual attack.
>
> As they lacked the reserve fuel to return the bomb to Tinian, the bomb was dropped in a poorly executed radar attack which was switched to a visual through a sucker hole at the last minute, and which essentially missed the intended aiming point by sufficient distance to reduce the effects on the target of the much more powerful "Fat Man" to far less than that accomplished by the "Little Boy" at Hiroshima. Then, lacking fuel to make it back even to Iwo Jima, the bomber had to divert to Okinawa, where it landed on fumes.

As it turned out, the Nagasaki drop was a radar drop with no visual cues available to the bombardier, in violation of the rule.

Unlike the blast at Hiroshima, a reporter witnessed the Nagasaki detonation from the air. In a bizarre marriage of government and press, Groves had hired *New York Times* science reporter William L. Laurence to write press releases, all of which were kept behind lock and key until the atomic bombings began. Unaware that Sweeney and Bock had switched aircraft and confused about which bomber he was aboard, Laurence later wrote that *The Great Artiste* dropped the second bomb, a mix-up of fact that persisted in official dispatches for years afterward. Laurence was flying with Bock as an observer that day, believing that he was aboard *Bock's Car* when he was actually a passenger on the *Artiste*.

Laurence has often been accused of allowing his insider status with the Manhattan Project to render him bereft of critical judgment. His writings about the atomic bombings were always upbeat and positive. He described the Nagasaki weapon thusly: "It is a thing of beauty to behold, this gadget. In its design went millions of man-hours of what is without a doubt the most concentrated intellectual effort in history. Never before had so much brain-power been focused on a single problem."

Laurence's unqualified praise for nuclear weaponry was especially galling to Bill Lawrence of the *New York Times*, who later wrote balanced stories about the atomic bombings. For decades, just as historians confused the identities of the two B-29s over Nagasaki, they also confused the two reporters—in Lawrence's view, to the detriment of himself.

Firsthand Account

Laurence, the uncritical witness, wrote of Nagasaki as follows:

> We removed our glasses after the first flash but the light still lingered on, a bluish-green light that illuminated the entire sky all around. A tremendous blast wave struck our ship and made it tremble from nose to tail. This was followed by four more blasts in rapid succession, each resounding like the boom of cannon fire hitting our plane from all directions.
>
> Observers in the tail of our ship saw a giant ball of fire rise as though from the bowels of the earth, belching forth enormous white smoke rings. Next they saw a giant pillar of purple fire, 10,000 feet high, shooting skyward with enormous speed.
>
> By the time our ship had made another turn in the direction of the atomic explosion the pillar of purple fire had reached the level of our altitude. Only about 45 seconds had passed. Awe-struck, we watched it shoot upward like a meteor coming from the earth instead of from outer space, becoming ever more alive as it climbed skyward through the white clouds. It was no longer smoke, or dust, or even a cloud of fire. It was a living thing, a new species of being, born right before our incredulous eyes.
>
> At one stage of its evolution, covering missions of years in terms of seconds, the entity assumed the form of a giant square totem pole, with its base about three miles long, tapering off to about a mile at the top. Its bottom was brown, its center was amber, its top white. But it was a living totem pole, carved with many grotesque masks grimacing at the earth.
>
> Then, just when it appeared as though the thing has settled down into a state of permanence, there came shooting out of the

top a giant mushroom that increased the height of the pillar to a total of 45,000 feet. The mushroom top was even more alive than the pillar, seething and boiling in a white fury of creamy foam, sizzling upwards and then descending earthward, a thousand old faithful geysers rolled into one.

It kept struggling in an elemental fury, like a creature in the act of breaking the bonds that held it down. In a few seconds it had freed itself from its gigantic stem and floated upward with tremendous speed, its momentum carrying into the stratosphere to a height of about 60,000 feet.

Finally, in his florid prose written in the public domain for the AAF, the much-impressed Laurence noted that, "As the first mushroom floated off into the blue it changed its shape into a flowerlike form, its giant petal curving downward, creamy white outside, rose-colored inside. It still retained that shape when we last gazed at it from a distance of about 200 miles."

With the only nonmilitary observer perhaps unaware that gas was at a premium or that the Nagasaki drop had been badly botched, Sweeney did a superb job of coaxing *Bock's Car* to Okinawa. He later said that if the island had been ten miles farther, the world's second atomic bomber and its crew would have gone into the sea. Not hindered by a fuel problem, *The Great Artiste* made it directly back to Tinian from the mission, its arrival perhaps contributing to the myth that it had dropped the bomb.

The Nagasaki raid killed about thirty-five thousand people, nearly all civilians. Included were a few Allied prisoners of war. In fact, the devastation would have been at least twice as great had the bomb not missed ground zero by nearly three miles, or about five kilometers.

To Twentieth Air Force commanders, B-29 bomber crews, and especially ordinary Americans of the era, the atomic bombing was an inevitable part of war. Few on the Allied side doubted it was necessary. But fewer still were as one-dimensional as Laurence, who wrote: "Does anyone feel any pity or compassion for the poor devils about to die [at Nagasaki]? Not when one thinks of Pearl Harbor and of the Death March on Bataan." Laurence, incidentally, was awarded the Pulitzer Prize after he put his experiences into a book. Only many years later did some critics—among them, novelist James Agee—carp about the human suffering inflicted by the atomics bombings. A few called the bombings war crimes. These critics never noticed that a mission to Tokyo inflicted more death and destruction than both atomic bombings combined.

Through the final moments of the fighting in the Pacific, Twentieth Air Force B-29 crews continued their conventional assault on the Japanese home islands. Two hundred forty-five B-29s went to Yawata on August 8, 1945. On August 10, B-29s returned to Tokyo while others flew a thirty-one-aircraft mining mission.

Final Mission

The 315th Wing's final mission came on the night of August 14–15, the final night of fighting.

What must have been the final B-29 mission of the war was flown by, among others, *Boomerang*, a Bell-manufactured B-29B Superfortress. First Lieutenant Carl Schahrer was airplane commander; 1st Lt. John Waltershausen the pilot; 1st Lt. Dick Marshall, bombardier; Staff Sgt. Hank Gorder, engineer; 1st Lt. Tony Cosola, navigator; 1st Lt. Dick Ginster, radar operator; Sgt. Hank Carlson, a scanner, occupying what would have been a blister gun position on any other B-29 model; Sgt. Henry Leffler, another scanner; Sgt. Sidney Siegel, tail gunner; and Sgt. Jim B. Smith, radio operator. Smith was a last-minute replacement when the original radio operator was hospitalized.

Although bombing missions were initially canceled when hints appeared that there might be a settlement with the Japanese to end the fighting, on August 13, 1945, Superfortress crews were placed on standby to strike more targets. *Boomerang* radio operator Smith recalled, "It was like being in a ball game. You thought you'd won it. Then, you were told [to go] back in and continue playing." On August 14, notwithstanding expectations of a Japanese surrender, Smith and his buddies were alerted for a maximum effort, a 143-aircraft mission.

"This will be the longest B-29 mission ever attempted from the Marianas [logged time was seventeen hours total]," the briefer told crewmen. "You will be carrying a full 10-ton plus bomb load with no bomb bay fuel tanks. Your assignment is to bomb the Nippon Oil Company Refinery at Akita. [Akita represented 67 percent of Japan's remaining annual oil refining capability.] Your target is located approximately 275 miles northwest of Tokyo.

"The Japanese do not believe we can reach Akita from the Marianas, and fortunately have not built large defenses there. You shouldn't encounter much opposition unless they figure out your B-29Bs have been stripped of armament. The mission to Akita and back will take you almost 3,800 miles. You'll be going to the end of your cruise control envelope since you'll be carrying a minimum of fuel for that distance (a rock bottom 6,300 gallons) and an absolute maximum allowable bomb load of 20,500 pounds. You will be carrying high explosive, general purpose bombs of 100 pound and 250 pound sizes with non-delay tail fuses."

The crew of the *Boomerang* had flown nine combat trips over Japan. They knew that if this mission went as planned, they would not only be testing cruise control to the maximum, but they'd also be testing worn-out engines and worn-out crews who had been flying all-night missions that averaged close to fourteen hours. The briefing officer explained that the word "Apple" would be sent in Morse code if the United States received word of a Japanese surrender. That would be the order for the 315th Wing to salvo their bombs and return to base. The radio operators were ordered to monitor their frequency from the time engines were started.

"It's my guess you'll receive the scrub word 'Apple' before you reach Iwo [Jima] en route to Japan," the briefing officer added.

On to Japan

Boomerang's pilot John Waltershausen remembered, "There were a number of men of different crews that were far from sober when it came time for takeoff. I still can see one of the pilots that needed someone on each arm to help him walk to the plane."

1st Lt. Dick Marshall, bombardier of *Boomerang*, said, "After the order came to start engines we were idling for a while and nothing was moving. The thought went through my mind, 'those suckers out there are really consuming a hell of a lot of fuel.' About that time an order came through to cut engines. We were all thinking the mission had been scrubbed. Soon thereafter, we got the order to start engines again. This time when those engines kicked over they were really laying down a smoke screen from having idled so long, but everything was checking out fine. This time it was for real."

The crew of the *Boomerang* didn't know that at 3:49 p.m. their time (2:49 p.m. in Tokyo), fifty-three minutes before they were ordered to fly, the Japanese Domei News Agency broadcast an urgent message to the United States and Pacific Theater that was picked up by an American radio operator on Okinawa: FLASH FLASH TOKYO AUGUST 14—IT IS LEARNED THAT AN IMPERIAL MESSAGE ACCEPTING THE POTSDAM PROCLAMATION IS FORTHCOMING SOON. It was later assumed Japan wanted to keep the United States informed of its imminent surrender to deter any further bombing.

In Tokyo at 4:00 p.m. on August 14, 1945, Lt. Col. Masataka Ida and Maj. Kenji Hatanaka were plotting a revolt. They planned to occupy the Imperial Household Ministry, cut off the palace from outside contact, and protect the emperor from "traitorous" advisors to help him preserve Japan. Hatanaka's whole army would soon follow. The emperor's name was Hirohito, of course— just one word—but no Japanese would ever have spoken it aloud. In Japanese, he was called *tenno haika*, meaning roughly "his royal majesty."

Emperor's Action

At 8:30 p.m., the emperor signed the rescript. The Imperial seal was affixed. The date given next to the Imperial signature and seal was "The fourteenth day of the eighth month of the twentieth year of Showa [the term for Hirohito's reign]."

The *Boomerang* crew was filled with anxiety, waiting moment to moment for the mission to be canceled. The airplane commander asked the radio operator every few minutes if he'd heard the word "Apple." The answer was no.

In Tokyo, Hatanaka spoke of his fear that if the emperor recorded the rescript and it was broadcast, the revolt would not be able to prevent surrender. The recording team for NHK Radio waited for Hirohito to record the rescript. Prime Minister Suzuki Kantaro signed the rescript at approximately 10:00 p.m. *Boomerang* was boring toward the Empire with a nervous crew, four hundred miles south of Tokyo. They had not heard the word "Apple."

The emperor was getting ready at 11:05 p.m. to be transported to the Imperial Household Ministry where he would record the surrender message. But an advisor, worried that Tokyo might be hit with an atomic bomb, urged the emperor to wait in the bomb shelter until they could learn what target the Americans were aiming at. The emperor went to the underground bomb shelter.

When *Boomerang* was forty miles west-northwest of Tokyo, thirty-six fighters came looking for the B-29. After twenty minutes in shelter, the emperor completed his recording after a second taping, unaware of plans for a mutiny. Two sets of records containing the emperor's surrender were put into metal cases. The lids didn't fit tightly, so they were put into two eighteen-inch khaki-colored cotton bags, originally designed to hold uniforms. Chamberlain Tokugawa locked them in an office safe used by a member of the Empress's staff.

Boomerang was still coming. Bombardier Marshall recalled, "I went back into the bomb bay to arm the bombs. I crawled out onto the catwalk and proceeded to pull the cotter pins from the detonating fuse on each bomb. When I finished, I returned to my bombsight in the nose of the plane, and prepared it with the data I was going to use on this run. Once we crossed the coastline at the predetermined point, we would have about one hundred miles or roughly twenty minutes to target."

When *Boomerang* reached its drop point and Marshall called, "Bombs away," the B-29 was 1,800 miles from base, with about three thousand gallons of fuel left. At that time, a palace uprising seemed to be underway in Tokyo. Hatanaka went back to the Imperial Household Ministry Building where he learned the emperor had indeed recorded the rescript and left the premises. The rebels swept through the Imperial Household Ministry building and the palace grounds in search of the emperor's recorded rescript. With the recordings in hand, they could cancel the emperor's planned broadcast at noon. That would give them time to keep the war going.

The search became frantic and violent. Soldiers kicked in doors and scattered contents of drawers. They were too late. Hatanaka lost control. With tears in his eyes, he told officers it was all over. He added almost inaudibly, "We have given everything to save Japan. We have no more to give."

At 8:21 a.m. by the Americans' clocks (7:20 a.m. in Tokyo), NHK broadcasted a special bulletin. "His Imperial Majesty, the emperor, has issued a rescript. It will be broadcast at noon today. Let us respectfully listen to the voice of the emperor."

The bulletin was repeated over and over. The crew of the *Boomerang* yelled and whooped.

War's End
The surrender of Japan became official at noon on August 15, 1945. Superfortress radio operator Smith wrote,

> If the palace revolt had succeeded, our naval forces would most certainly have come under attack hours after President Harry S Truman received the official Japanese note of surrender. A third atomic bomb was being readied to be shipped to Tinian, and could have been dropped on Japan on the first good weather day after August 17 or 18. [Smith is incorrect about this; the third bomb was not ready to be assembled]. Those of us who remember Truman [once an obscure senator with doubts about the military potential of the B-29] know he would have responded promptly to any Japanese military action coming after Japan's cabled surrender.

On August 15, 1945, the western allies insisted that they were getting the unconditional surrender they'd sought. In reality, they'd acquiesced to preserving the institution of the emperor. Once fighting ended, B-29 crews began flying supply missions to prisoner of war camps.

What many consider to be the true final mission of the war had not been flown yet. The bomber designed as a backup insurance to the B-29, the lesser-known Consolidated B-32 Dominator, was the protagonist.

Three days after the surrender, on August 18, 1945, two B-32s took off from Yontan, Okinawa, for a mission to Tokyo. The B-32s belonged to the 386th Bombardment Squadron.

The two B-32s reached the capital where they were fired on by antiaircraft batteries and then attacked by Japanese fighters. In a Japanese-language memoir, fighter ace Lt. Saburo Sakai wrote of engaging a bomber he initially thought was a B-29 Superfortress. "What I saw was a completely different aircraft. The single vertical stabilizer was enormous and swept upward

toward the rear. I had never seen this plane before but later learned it was a B-32."

Sakai also noted that, "Apparently, this action was legal and we were never questioned about it by [Douglas] MacArthur's forces."

1st Lt. Richard E. Thomas, copilot of the B-32, said that the antiaircraft fire was ineffective, but that the Japanese fighters pressed home their attacks. "A Japanese aircraft came at the B-32 as if to ram us," Thomas said. For reasons unclear, pilot 1st Lt. J. R. Anderson apparently was not in the cockpit during the engagement. Thomas pushed the yoke forward to increase air speed and "pulled the aircraft up into a very steep climb"—but Sakai and another Japanese fighter pilot opened up with cannon fire. They hit the B-32 in the wings and fuselage.

Staff Sgt. Joseph Lacherite, an aerial photographer, heard unusual radio traffic on his headphones. According to Lacherite, copilot Thomas asked the other B-32 to slow down so the damaged bomber could keep up. Then, said Lacherite, an attacking Japanese pilot came on the radio and in English said, "Yes, please slow down so I can shoot you down, too." Lacherite was wounded and was being assisted by photographer Anthony J. Marchione when a new burst of cannon fire struck Marchione.

Members of Marchione's family remember him as typical of the era's citizen-soldiers. Born in Pottstown, Pennsylvania, he played the trumpet in high school according to his sister, Theresa Sell. "He became a photographer after joining the military and took hundreds of pictures," his sister said. Marchione flew three combat missions before the surrender. Now, after the official cessation of fighting, Marchione failed to respond to medical aid aboard the B-32 as it limped back to Okinawa. He succumbed to his wounds before the bomber landed. It was just a month before his twentieth birthday and he was, as far as anyone could tell, the last American to die in combat in World War II.

Superfortresss Scoreboard

Because it introduced atomic fission to war, the B-29 Superfortress evokes all manner of emotions. Some of these feelings suffocate any dispassionate analysis of what was really accomplished, and what wasn't, by the B-29 and its American pilots, crewmembers, and maintainers. Some of those who flew the mission to Tokyo on March 9–10, 1945, believe their contribution to America's war effort has been overlooked, kept forever in the shadows of the Hiroshima and Nagasaki attacks that followed.

Whether it happened on the mission to Tokyo or later, the efforts of all those involved with the B-29 defeated Japan, wiped away any need for an invasion of the Empire's home islands, and bolstered the argument that long-range, land-based airpower is the essential force in warfare. By the time the guns went silent, B-29s had dropped 104,000 tons of bombs on Japan and reduced to rubble 169 square miles in sixty-six cities. The bombing missions left homeless 9.2 million civilians, including 3.1 million in Tokyo. Between June 1944 and August 1945, Twentieth Air Force's B-29 force in the XX and XXI Bomber Commands flew 380 missions, mounted 31,387 bomber sorties, were credited with shooting down 871 Japanese aircraft, and lost 402 bombers. Tokyo, Osaka, Kobe, Nagoya, and Yokohama had been razed.

The men who flew the B-29, and the men who turned wrenches to keep it flying, loved the airplane. It was, after all, a thing of beauty. Wrote Stephan Wilkinson, "From the symmetrical cigar of a fuselage, unbroken even by a conventional stepped windscreen to the tips of its impossibly long, gracefully tapered wings, the B-29 was the antithesis of the locomotive-like British four-engine bombers and the gawky German monstrosities." It was also far more pleasing to the eye than its clunky backup, the B-32 Dominator.

The argument has been made that the B-29 was so dangerous that in peacetime it would never have been placed into production. Four hundred and two B-29s were lost bombing Japan—147 of them to Japanese flak and fighters and 255 to engine fires, mechanical failures, and takeoff crashes. In most wars about half of all aircraft losses have noncombat causes, but the ratio was higher with the B-29. By war's end most of the technical glitches, including problems with the engines, were being solved and the B-29 went on to serve for many more years and to fight in one more war. That did not help the World War II pilots and crewmembers, including some on the March 9–10, 1945, mission to Tokyo, who did not come home from the war because of mechanical failure.

Formal Finish

The formal surrender was inked aboard the battleship USS *Missouri* (BB 63) in Tokyo Bay, on Sunday, September 2, 1945. Speaking to Allied and Japanese officers, Gen. Douglas MacArthur, now the supreme Allied commander for the occupation of Japan, said, "The issues, involving divergent ideals and ideologies, have been determined on the battlefields of the world and hence are not for our discussion or debate." He later added, "It is for us, both victors and vanquished, to rise to [a] higher dignity." Even MacArthur's loudest detractors—and there were plenty in both the Allied and Japanese delegations—admired the grace with which he oversaw the formal end to the war.

A 2,400-aircraft flyover was supposed to begin during the signing—the largest aerial formation ever assembled. Many of the thousand kids who'd flown to Tokyo on March 9–10, 1945, were slated to pass over the capital and Tokyo Bay once again, in a dramatic show of force by the conquerors. It was a mixed formation of Army and Navy aircraft, including carrier-based aircraft, and it was having difficulty getting into position. The weather in and around Tokyo was poor and the beginning of the flyover was delayed.

The Japanese signed first. Observers looked around for the planned flyover and saw no sign of it. The great gaggle of warplanes was out there in the distance beyond eyesight, getting into formation for the final pass over the *Missouri*. The delay was causing some irritation on the part of those who were orchestrating the ceremony. After the Japanese finished, MacArthur began signing as the supreme Allied commander. Because this was such a historic event, MacArthur used several pens, each of which was destined to become a treasured artifact.

Columbia correspondent Webley Edwards was providing a real-time radio report of the surrender ceremony. "General MacArthur is using a fifth pen," Edwards spoke into his microphone. "Everyone is going to get a pen out of this surrender document and here comes one of the big B-29s which I suppose is the leader of the flight which was to put on a demonstration of airpower here over the bay this morning."

But it wasn't. The planned aerial formation hadn't arrived yet. The lone B-29 now being observed wasn't the leader of anything.

Not chosen to participate in any of this was B-29 airplane commander George Bertagnoli, who'd replaced Dean Fling and who was going to fly over the ceremony whether LeMay, MacArthur, or anyone else liked it or not. Bertagnoli was a "really good man," left blister gunner Reb Carter said, but he had a rebellious streak too. Before the planned aerial formation could arrive, Bertagnoli detoured from an assigned supply flight to a different location and, without permission, set his B-29 up for a straight, flat run over the moored *Missouri*.

Bertagnoli and left blister gunner Reb Carter looked down from their B-29. Today, the one-time crew of *God's Will* and later *Sweet Sue* was flying *T-n-teeny II*. As they passed overhead, Bertagnoli, Carter, and other crewmembers saw MacArthur sitting at the signing table on the ship's deck. The Edwards broadcast was playing on the plane's interphone. They heard Edwards say, "here comes one of the big B-29s," and then they heard the sound of their own engines in their earphones, conveyed by the broadcast.

As the Bertagnoli crew flew overhead, Edwards continued: "The weather was miserable for a demonstration of airpower. The maximum ceiling is not more than fifteen hundred feet, but everything is going to plan. General MacArthur has finished signing. Lieutenant General Jonathan Wainright and General Percival have saluted him and MacArthur is back to the microphone."

MacArthur announced that representatives of each of the victorious Allied nations would begin signing. Six minutes after the Bertagnoli crew came and went, Edwards stated that observers aboard the battleship were still waiting for the massive flyover. Three minutes later, the sun that had hidden behind the clouds came out. The brief, stiff shipboard ceremony was all but over when Allied warplanes began passing overhead in vast numbers. Many veterans of the great Tokyo firebomb mission were aboard the B-29s passing overhead, among them radar operator Trip Triplett, who found the surrender event "extraordinary" and "a real moment frozen in time."

About five miles southeast was the spot where a B-29 named *The Merry Mac's* had disappeared five months earlier. The crew of that B-29 Superfortress has never been found. The date of the ceremony aboard the *Missouri*, September 2, 1945, would have been airplane commander Bud McDonald's twenty-fourth birthday.

Acknowledgments

These first-person accounts of pilots and crews in combat are the result of 166 interviews, most of which were conducted in 2010 and 2011. This book would have been impossible without the help of many.

The following combat veterans were interviewed for this book: Gerald Auerbach, Richard C. "Bake" Baker, Carl Barthold, Jim Bury, Leonard W. Carpi, William J. "Reb" Carter, Charles G. Chauncey, Edward W. Cutler, Donald R. Dacier, Andy Doty, Donald F. "Red" Dwyer, Roby Eastridge, Henry E. "Red" Erwin, Philip Guay, James T. Hash, Elmer Jones, Bill Lind, Paul Linden, Joe Majeski, Frank Mann, Chester Marshall, William McKinley, Paul A. Miller, Thomas Moss, Harold L. "Pete" Peterson, Hugh Phillips, Gordon Bennett Robinson Jr., William A. Robinson Jr., Milburn P. Sanders, Roger Sandstedt, George Savage, Walter Sherrell, Hal Simms, Jim B. Smith, Melvin Sonne, Robert Stangland, Le "Trip" Triplett, Frank Underwood, Bob Van Gieson, and George "Laddie" Wale.

Thanks also to family members of veterans, scholars, and veterans of other wars, including: Bobby Baker, Brian Bakshas, Jerome Bakshas, Linda Bakshas, Tom Barthold, Jim Bowman, Walter J. Boyne, John Bybee, Doug Carter, Janet Clement, Bill Copeland, John T. Correll, Carl Curtis, Frank "Bud" Farrell, Rick Feldmann, Leland Fishback, Arline Gilman, Doris J. Goodlett, Frank Grube, Jo Haney, Yukiko Hiragama, Aldora Howard, Kyle Kirby, Clement Kordsmeier, Louis Kordsmeier, Joe Krogman, Mary Kay Krogman, Susan Lind-Kanne, Mike McCaskill, Bryan McCorry, Gary Moncur, Gordon Muster, Colin O'Neill, Joe Queeno, Nancy Reynolds, Terry Tucker Rhodes, Michael Salvini, Holland Simms, Doug Sterner, Bill

Streifer, Dixie Sullivan, Joe Swann, Warren E. Thompson, Barrett Tillman, and Scott Willey.

While working on this book, I formed a strong bond with Doug Carter, the son of B-29 Superfortress gunner William J. "Reb" Carter. The long and rich life of Doug's dad reached its end while this volume was in preparation. Doug and I worked in a productive and meaningful partnership to reconstruct his father's story from journals, documents, and interviews.

Family members of men we lost on March 10, 1945, especially family members of Sam P. Bakshas, Gordon Muster, and Hubert Kordsmeier, were gracious with their time and generous with their memorabilia. The family of B-29 Superfortress veteran Hap Halloran gave me access to many of his writings. Robert Kubieck described his duties as one of the PBM Mariner crewmembers who rescued B-29 crews.

I have a special debt to those who make books: Bryan Trandem, Erik Gilg, Scott Pearson, and Richard Kane; and to those who sell books: Natalya McKinney and Steve Daubenspeck.

Some topics important to the air campaign against Japan, including the prisoner of war experience, are outside the scope of this narrative. Mistakes are inevitable in a story this complex. Any mistakes appearing here are the sole fault of the author.

Robert F. Dorr
Oakton, Virginia

Appendix I

Bombardment Groups in the Marianas

Twentieth Air Force

The Twentieth Air Force was created on April 4, 1944, to carry out bombing missions against Japan. It was commanded from Washington until July 16, 1945, when its headquarters moved to Guam, where this command remained until after the surrender ceremony on September 2, 1945.

XXI Bomber Command

This component of the Twentieth Air Force was constituted as XXI Bomber Command on March 1, 1944. It was moved to the Marianas late in 1944 until this command terminated on July 16, 1945.

Commanders

Brigadier General Haywood S. "Possum" Hansell Jr., August 28, 1944–January 20, 1945.

Major General Curtis E. LeMay, January 20, 1945–July 16, 1945.

With the exception of the 509th Composite Group, B-29 wings, groups, and squadrons bore the description Very Heavy in parentheses following the designation.

58th Bomb Wing**

(West Field, Tinian)
40th Bombardment Group
444th Bombardment Group
462nd Bombardment Group ("Hellbirds")
468th Bombardment Group

73rd Bomb Wing
(Isley Field, Saipan)
497th Bombardment Group
498th Bombardment Group
499th Bombardment Group
500th Bombardment Group

313th Bomb Wing
(North Field, Tinian)
6th Bombardment Group
9th Bombardment Group
504th Bombardment Group
505th Bombardment Group
509th Composite Group

314th Bomb Wing
(North Field, Guam)
19th Bombardment Group
29th Bombardment Group
39th Bombardment Group**
330th Bombardment Group**

315th Bomb Wing**
(Northwest Field, Guam)
16th Bombardment Group
331st Bombardment Group
501st Bombardment Group
502nd Bombardment Group

**Not in the Marianas March 9, 1945

Appendix Two

What Happended to Them?

Henry H. "Hap" Arnold (June 25, 1886–January 15, 1950) was an aviation pioneer before World War II and the leader of America's air arm during the war. Arnold saw the attainment of a lifelong goal on September 18, 1947, when the United States became one of the last nations in the world to make its air force an independent military service branch. Arnold retired the previous year, weakened by his persistent heart ailments, so Gen. Carl M. "Tooey" Spaatz, an Arnold contemporary, became the U.S. Air Force's first chief of staff. On May 7, 1949, Public Law 58-81 changed the designation of Arnold's final rank from General of the Army to General of the Air Force; he is the only person to have held the rank. In retirement Arnold lived in a ranch near Sonoma, California, and wrote an autobiography, *Global Mission*. Arnold was a graduate of the U.S. Military Academy and so, too, were his three sons—Henry (1939), William (June 1943), and David (1949), all of whom reached the rank of colonel. Arnold strongly influenced the creation of the U. S. Air Force Academy but did not live to see the school open its doors.

    Sam P. "Sammy" Bakshas (October 9, 1911–March 10, 1945) is interred at Golden Gate National Cemetery in San Bruno, California. His remains were repatriated four years after the war on July 11, 1949. His wife Aldora lives near Bellingham, Washington, and celebrated her ninety-fourth birthday while being interviewed for this book. Among their son Jerry's prized possessions are a forty-eight-star United States flag, his father's Purple Heart, a long white silk scarf, and a small game board Sammy carried with him to pass the time with a friend when the hours away from home were long. Their loving father-son relationship was cut short when Jerry was four years of age.

Carl H. Barthold left the Army on October 21, 1945. He returned to Washington University in St. Louis where he had studied and met a student named Nancy Davis just before Pearl Harbor. He married her on June 6, 1947, graduated the following year, and went to work as an auditor for Southwestern Bell Company until his retirement on June 30, 1945. The former B-29 Superfortress radio operator is active as a Freemason and Shriner and attends 73rd Wing reunions. He and Nancy are the parents of three grown sons, Charles, Thomas, and Brian. Carl and Nancy Barthold live in Ballwin, Missouri, and are planning a tourist trip to the only U.S. state they haven't visited, Alaska.

William J. "Reb" Carter (December 3, 1923–November 3, 2011), better known as Bill to everyone except his military buddies, ended the war with twenty-seven combat missions. He was discharged as a staff sergeant on November 28, 1945. He returned to Atlanta and became a successful certified public accountant. On December 19, 1946, he wed the love of his life, Phyllis Ewing, in a simple ceremony at her pastor's home. They moved to Tucker, a suburb of Atlanta, where they raised two sons, Doug and Gary, and many dogs. He was an officer in several professional CPA associations and a partner with two CPA firms, his father's Mount & Carter and the international firm Coopers Lybrand. He retired in 1970 and became a real estate investor. Carter also achieved success in his personal life. He and Phyllis enjoyed "a loving and happy marriage," said son Doug. In later years Phyllis fell victim to Alzheimer's. Over a span of twenty years, her health deteriorated. Family and friends often urged Carter to place her in a facility better suited for her care, but he always adamantly refused, replying he promised her long ago they would be together always. He kept his promise. Despite her devastating condition, Bill kept her at home, reading and singing to her, even after she could no longer verbally respond. On November 3, 2008, after nearly sixty-two years of marriage, Bill held her hand, kissed her, and told her how much he loved her as she peacefully slipped away. Exactly three years later to the day, Carter died. At his funeral, his grandson Matt read the letter Bill had written in block letters to Phyllis on July 18, 1945. "There was not a dry eye in the chapel," said Carter's son Doug.

Henry "Red" Erwin (May 8, 1921–January 16, 2002) should never have survived the fiery deed for which he was awarded the Medal of Honor. An Alabama native, Erwin was still receiving medical treatment, including transfusions, skin grafts, internal surgery, and treatment for recurring infections, fully four years and forty-three surgical operations after he saved the Tony Simeral B-29 crew. For thirty-seven years, he served as a Veterans' Benefit Counselor at the Veterans' Hospital in Birmingham, Alabama. In 1951, Hollywood included his story as part of the movie *The Wild Blue Yonder*, starring Forrest Tucker, Wendell Corey, and Vera Ralston. David Sharpe played Erwin. Red Erwin's widow is Martha Erwin. They are the parents of a son and two daughters. In 1997, the U.S. Air Force created the Henry E. Erwin Outstanding Enlisted Aircrew Member of the Year Award, given annually to members of the flight engineering, loadmaster, air surveillance, and related career fields. Active in veterans' affairs, Erwin was affable and well-liked.

Haywood S. "Possum" Hansell Jr. (September 28, 1903– November 14, 1988) returned to the United States in January 1945 and took command of a training wing in Arizona. He served in Air Transport Command and then retired as a brigadier general in 1946 after nineteen years of service. Hansell had gotten a hearing impairment during his earliest flying days and, since it brought an end to his flying status, he used the disability to take early retirement. Hansell tried an airline venture in Peru in the late 1940s and later was vice president of a gas company. Recalled for staff duty during the Korean War, he retired again in 1955 as a major general. Hansell went against custom to take a job with General Electric working in the Netherlands until his civilian retirement in 1966. He later lived in Hilton Head, South Carolina. Most historians today believe Hansell had it right about daylight precision bombing and would have succeeded against Japan given more time. He is interred at the Air Force Academy cemetery.

Hidesaburo Kusama, who wrote of watching the B-29 named *Tall in the Saddle* plummet from the sky, was born January 9, 1937. He graduated from Aoyama Gakuin University in 1959 and was a visiting student at East Carolina University in 1960. He took graduate studies in international relations at the University of North Carolina from 1960 to 1963. He was a visiting scholar at Princeton University in 1970. He was dean of the faculty of foreign studies at Aichi Prefectural University from 1994 to 1997. Kusama built a memorial to the crew of *Tall in the Saddle* at the crash site in 2001. Kusama and his wife Yoko hosted Wilma Cook, sister of the bomber's copilot, 2nd Lt. Eugene Cook, on a visit to Japan in 2006.

Curtis E. LeMay (November 15, 1906–October 1, 1990) had an initial role in organizing the Berlin Airlift in 1948. He commanded the Strategic Air Command (SAC) from 1948 to 1957, shaping and defining the American strategic nuclear deterrent for the Cold War. His successor at SAC was Gen. Thomas S. Power, who led the great Tokyo firebomb mission. LeMay was chief of staff of the U.S. Air Force from 1961 to 1965 and influenced U.S. policy during the Cuban missile crisis and in Vietnam. When he retired in 1965, he had been a four-star general longer than any other (since 1951). He was the vice presidential running mate of American Independent Party candidate George Wallace in 1968. LeMay was always controversial, and many historians feel his brief appearance on the political stage undermined his many achievements. His wife Helen, who died in 1992, survived him.

Robert S. McNamara (June 9, 1916–July 6, 2009), a lieutenant colonel on Maj. Gen. Curtis E. LeMay's staff, was president of the Ford Motor Company before becoming Secretary of Defense under Presidents John F. Kennedy and Lyndon Johnson from 1961 to 1968. In a documentary film, *The Fog of War*, McNamara implies that the firebombing of Tokyo was a war crime. By the time he said this, McNamara was under fire for his role as the Pentagon chief who took the United States into Vietnam. Later president of the

World Bank from 1968 to 1981, McNamara spent his life from 1968 onward analyzing, explaining, and ultimately apologizing for Vietnam. He supported the decision to attack Tokyo with incendiary bombs on the night of March 9–10, 1945.

Yoko Ono, a twelve-year-old child from an upper-class family during the great Tokyo fire raid, resumed the aristocratic lifestyle she disliked after the war when the newly formed Bank of Tokyo hired her banker father. In 1946, she became a school classmate of Akihito, the future emperor of Japan. She immigrated to the United States and enrolled in Sarah Lawrence College in 1952. She became an artist, musician, author, and peace activist, known for her work in avant-garde art, music, and filmmaking. After two marriages, the second of which produced daughter Kyoko Cox, Ono, on March 20, 1969, married Beatles songwriter and musician John Lennon. Interestingly, Lennon's guardian, Mimi Smith, once threw a wet blanket over a sputtering German incendiary bomb in her Liverpool garden during World War II. In the mid-1970s, Ono and Lennon split and then reconciled. After Lennon was murdered on December 8, 1980, Ono continued her artistic and political efforts.

Thomas S. "Tommy" Power (June 18, 1905–December 6, 1970), the on-scene commander of the great Tokyo firebomb mission, was a staff officer for Operation Crossroads, the 1946 atomic bomb tests at Bikini Atoll in the Pacific. Power held several key Air Force postings until 1957, when he was promoted to four-star rank and replaced Curtis E. LeMay as commander in chief of the Strategic Air Command when LeMay became vice chief of staff of the Air Force. When he retired on November 30, 1964, Power was America's last general officer to have no postsecondary education. Power became board chairman of Schick, Inc., with whom he was affiliated for six years. His book, *Design for Survival*, was published in 1965. Power, a bomber advocate and militaristic anticommunist, was caricatured to create the "General Ripper" character in the film *Dr. Strangelove or: How I Learned to Stop Worrying and Love the Bomb* (1964). Power and his wife, Mae Ayre, had no children.

Le Triplett, who was called "Trip" during the war and changed his first name from LeRoy after the war, has stayed closed to his one-eighth Cherokee heritage and his Oklahoma roots. After the war, he attended the University of Northern Colorado, Denver University, and the University of Iowa. He holds several degrees, including a doctorate in education. He spent about forty years in public school administration and teaching at the university level. Triplett and his wife, Nancy Ann Hodge, have three grown sons. Triplett enjoys mountain climbing, backpacking, and writing. He is the author of the novel *American Exodus: A Historical Novel About Indian Removal* (1996). He lives today in Greeley, Colorado.

Percy Usher Tucker (December 21, 1918–February 28, 1991) left the Army Air Forces as a captain on February 14, 1946. After other jobs, he settled into a career with the Metropolitan Life Insurance Company. His wife Annabelle, after whom his B-29 bomber was named, died of cancer on June 3, 1960, at the age of thirty-nine. His second wife, Katie, also predeceased him. Tucker retired from the insurance job on April 14, 1970, at which time he was living in San Diego. He was an avid golfer and won many of the amateur golf tournaments in San Diego. He later married Beverly Reid, with whom he had grown up in Shandon, California. His daughter, Terry Rhodes Tucker, noted that, "both of my stepmoms were great ladies." Tucker and Beverly eventually moved to Mountain View, California, where he died of cancer.

Notes

Chapter 1: Wake-Up

"a wonderful urgency": "A Reporter with the B-29s: I—Possum, Rosy, and the Thousand Kids," by St. Clair McKelway, The New Yorker, June 9, 1945.

Wale-Tucker conversation: Interview with Tucker crewmember Joe Majeski.

Triplett on Tinian: An unpublished memoir by Le Triplett shared with the author.

Hemingway quote: "London Fights the Robots," by Ernest Hemingway, *Collier's*, August 1944.

Love for B-29: Interview with Jo Haney, December 23, 2010.

Barthold and Star Duster: In a dozen interviews over many months, Carl Barthold and the author were unable to reconcile differing information about which B-29 Barthold flew to Tokyo on March 9, 1945. It is clear that Barthold and the J. C. Arnold crew flew *Texas Doll* to Nagoya on December 13, 1944. The Arnold crew was broken up after the death of its bombardier. Barthold changed airplanes and airplane commanders before the Tokyo mission. Documents from the National Archives and recollections from other crewmembers do not identify the aircraft the James M. Campbell crew, including Barthold, flew on the great Tokyo incendiary mission.

The flight engineer was in actual control: William Wolf, *Boeing B-29 Superfortress—The Ultimate Look: From Drawing Board to VJ-Day* (Atglen, Pa.: Schiffer Publishing, Ltd., 2004), p. 331.

Tucker was a man of few words: Interview with Terry Tucker Rhodes, March 11, 2011.

Guam and Saipan: The Sussex descriptions are from a letter of June 26, 1945, written to family members by Lt. James N. Sussex, a medical officer on the seaplane tender USS *Bering Strait* (AVP 34).

Ditching in the Pacific: Statistics on ditching are from The Army Air Forces in World War II, edited by Wesley Frank Craven and James Lea Cate (Washington, DC: Superintendent of Documents, 1950).

Chapter 2: Starting

"On December 7, 1941, one brother took me with him to the country" : Milton P. Sanders, *One Man's World War II: Tending Seaplanes in the Pacific* (Fairfax, Va.: History4All, Inc., 2008), p. 1.

LeMay on Arnold and development of the B-29: Curtis E. LeMay and MacKinlay Kantor, *Mission with LeMay: My Story*, (New York: Doubleday & Company, 1965), pp. 321–322.

Blessing and signing of the cross: Private memoir by B-29 veteran Hap Halloran.

"You knew that every eye on that flight line": Correspondence with Frank "Bud" Farrell.

Chapter 3: Warm-Up

"At Isley field it was common on takeoff": From a memoir by William C. Atkinson posted on the website Wartime Memories (http://www. wartimememories.co.uk/airfields/isleyfield.html).

McKelway on LeMay: "A Reporter with the B-29s: II—The Doldrums, Guam, and Something Coming Up," by St. Clair McKelway, The New Yorker, June 16, 1945.

LeMay lived for an extended period in a tent: Barrett Tillman, *Whirlwind: The War Against Japan, 1942–1945* (New York: Simon & Schuster, 2010), p. 136.

Almost totally lacking in people skills: Ibid, p. 137.

"I believe the drop off the Saipan runway": Interview with Jim Farrell.

Chapter 4: Struggling

Eddie Allen post-crash confusion: William Wolf, *Boeing B-29 Superfortress—The Ultimate Look: From Drawing Board to VJ-Day* (Atglen, Pa.: Schiffer Publishing, Ltd., 2004), p. 47.

"a fire started that blew off a large part . . .": "Superbomber's Achilles Heel," by Stephan Wilkinson, *Aviation History*, September 2011.

". . . 64 contract schools provided primary training: Thomas A. Manning, *History of Air Training Command, 1943–1993* (Randall AFB, Tex.: Office of History and Research, Air Education and Training Command, 1993.

"the biggest S.O.B. I have ever worked for . . .": Kenneth D. Nichols,

The Road to Trinity (New York: William Morrow and Company, 1987.

"not ready for prime time": Interview with Nathan Serenko, held at a pilots' reunion.

"The 462nd Group worked out a standard procedure": Steve Birdsall, F*Saga of the Superfortress: The Dramatic Story of the B-29 and the Twentieth Air Force* (New York: Doubleday & Company, Inc., 1980), p. 44.

"when the cylinder-head temperature gauges were against the stops": Ibid.

"Wild river gorges lay far below, and pillars of clouds sent trickles of moisture across an airplane's windows": Ibid, pp. 45–46.

Wright Aeronautical and the R-3350: "Superbomber's Achilles Heel," by Stephan Wilkinson, *Aviation History*, September 2011.

"the dregs of the workforce": William Wolf, *Boeing B-29 Superfortress—The Ultimate Look: From Drawing Board to VJ-Day* (Atglen, Pa.: Schiffer Publishing, Ltd., 2004), p. 331.

"a little, rural village": Chester Marshall, *B-29 Superfortress* (Osceola, Wisc.: Motorbooks International, 1993), p. 32.

Chapter 5: Way Up

1st Lt. Robert "Bud" McDonald on Guam: Correspondence and telephone interviews wih Nancy Reynolds.

9th group approached at 2,000 feet: "The B-29 Strategic Air Campaign Against Japan," by Henry C. Huglin, November 2004.

Triplett en route: An unpublished memoir by Le Triplett shared with the author.

The weather approaching Japan: Diary of Don Weber provided by Jim Bowman; Triplett memoir; interview with James T. Hash.

". . . he was a wonderful navigator": This quote is from a crewmember interview with the author and relates to a situation the author confirmed with several sources. For obvious reasons, the crewmember did not want to be named and the navigator is not named here either. Incidents of fear, incompetence, or cowardice were relatively rare among B-29 crews, yet they happened more often than might be expected.

Chapter 6: Soldiering

"He had a dead cigar in his mouth": James Gould Cozzens, edited by Matthew J. Bruccoli, *A Time of War: Air Force Diaries and Pentagon Memos 1943–45* (Columbia, SC: Bruccoli-Clark Layman, 1984).

"an interloper with specious claims": Steve Birdsall, *Saga of the Superfortress: The Dramatic Story of the B-29 and the Twentieth Air Force* (New York: Doubleday & Company, Inc., 1980), p. 46.

"The blood ran deep": Leon Uris, *Battle Cry* (New York: G. P. Putnam's Sons, 1953), p. 189.

Chapter 7: The Way In

McKelway on LeMay: "A Reporter with the B-29s: III—The Cigar, the Three Wings, and the Low-Level Attacks," by St. Clair McKelway, *The New Yorker*, June 23, 1945.

"a 'jigsaw puzzle' of antiaircraft installations": Headquarters Army Air Forces Intelligence Summary 45–10 (30 May 1945): 18–25.

Chapter 8: Striving

Carter material: Courtesy of Doug Carter.

Chapter 9: Squabbling

Hansell lost it: Several publications report Hansell's speech to O'Donnell's wing, including *Whirlwind: The War Against Japan, 1942–1945* (New York: Simon & Schuster, 2010), by Barrett Tillman.

Hansell found firebombing repugnant and militarily unnecesssary: Haywood Hansell, *Strategic Air War against Japan* (Maxwell AFB, Ala.: Airpower Research Institute, 1980).

Hansell, Harmon, and Hale: Ibid, p. 208.

Martin Caidin described Hansell's reporting: Martin Caidin, *A Torch to the Enemy* (New York: Ballantine Books, 1960), p. 68.

The 500th Bomb Group suffered its first casualty: Author interview with Jim Bowman, recounting comments by Bill Agee, November 29, 2010.

"I got myself in gear," Barthold said: Author interview with Carl Barthold, November 27, 2010.

"*The entire nose of the* Texas Doll": An unpublished family memoir by Edward W. Cutler.

Chapter 10: To the Target

Col. Henry C. Huglin: Correspondence with Huglin.

Chapter 11: A City Ignited

"*When you have killed enough, they stop fighting*": This quote from Maj. Gen. Curtis E. LeMay was recalled by several veterans interviewed for this book.

"*The only good Jap is a dead Jap*": Author interview with Carl Barthold July 9, 2011. In researching an earlier book, *Mission to Berlin*, the author found some American bomber veterans who had misgivings when Americans began, in February 1945, to target cities in Europe rather than military and industrial facilities. In researching this book, the author found no American crewmembers who felt any concern about bombing cities in Asia.

"*M69s released 100-foot streams of fire*": "1945 Tokyo Firebombing Left Legacy of Terror, Pain," by Joseph Coleman, Associated Press, March 10, 2005.

"*They set to work at once sowing the sky with fire*": Robert Guillain, William Byron (trans.), *I Saw Tokyo Burning: Eyewitness Narrative from Pearl Harbor to Hiroshima* (New York: John Murray Publishers Ltd, 1981).

"*War criminals*": Robert S. McNamara's quotes are from the documentary film *The Fog of War*, a 2003 documentary film directed by Errol Morris.

"*The residents, accustomed to B-29 raids*": *Saga of the Superfortress: The Dramatic Story of the B-29 and the Twentieth Air Force* (New York: Doubleday & Company, Inc., 1980), p. 88.

". . . *more by ritual than by science*": Barrett Tillman, *Whirlwind: The War Against Japan, 1942–1945* (New York: Simon & Schuster, 2010), p. 143.

"*Men were recruited so rapidly*": Ibid.

"*Japanese administrative policy only complicated the situation*": Ibid.

"*In 1943, the Tokyo department had 280 pieces of fire apparatus*": Horatio Bond (ed.), *Fire and the Air War* (Boston: National Fire Protection Association, 1946).

3:37 a.m. (2:37 a.m. Tokyo time) sounding of the all clear: The source for this time is a blog entry, "Fire from the Sky" by Senan James Fox, http://archive.metropolis.co.jp/tokyo/571/lastword.asp. Most other information suggests the bombing continued for about an hour longer.

"*The great city of Tokyo—third largest in the world—is dead*": "Dead City," by Staff Sgt. Bob

Speer, *Brief*, June 19, 1945.

Chapter 12: 30 Seconds over Tokyo

"*George looked to the skies*": The quote is from an informal biography prepared by members of the 7th Bombardment Group, in which George Savage served in the postwar era.

"*The time was 2:05 a.m.*": The time of "Bombs away" is from George Savage's personal account, which he shared with the author of this book and later posted on the Internet.

Chapter 13: The Way Out

How could anyone possibly live through that sea of hell?: An unpublished memoir by Le Triplett shared with the author.

The figure of roughly 100,000 deaths, provided by Japanese and American authorities: "A Forgotten Holocaust: US Bombing Strategy, the Destruction of Japanese Cities and the American Way of War from World War II to Iraq," by Mark Selden, *Japan Focus*, May 2, 2007.

"*a 'red-burning aircraft coming slowly down towards us . . .'*": "US-Japanese Fact-Finding of the B-29 Crash on March 10, 1945 at Itabashi Mura, Japan," by Hidesaburo Kusama, *The Journal of the Faculty of Foreign Studies*, 1999.

"*It was Kordsmeier's tenth mission . . .*": Both an unofficial history of the 873rd Bombardment Squadron published in 1946 and *The B-29 Superfortress Chronology: 1934–1960* by Robert A. Mann (Jefferson, North Carolina: McFarland and Company: 2009)—the latter possibly relying on the former—say that Kordsmeier was flying his first mission on March 9–10. An examination of Kordsmeier's "Overseas Document File" and his flying records make it clear that the mission was indeed his tenth.

"*A blue flame . . .*": The account by Shinichi Kanno is from Japanese language letters provided by Clement Kordsmeier, brother of B-29 pilot Hubert L. Kordsmeier, and translated by the author.

"*Ditching out here . . .*": The quote from Ernie Pyle is from an article attributed to the February 28, 1945, issue of the *Rocky Mountain News*.

Chapter 14: "What's a B-32 Dominator?"

"*He was around a few days, said almost nothing*": "A Reporter with the B-29s: II—The Doldrums, Guam, and Something Coming Up," by St. Clair McKelway, *The New Yorker*, June 16, 1945.

"*Generally, I could understand what he was talking about*": Curtis E. LeMay and MacKinlay Kantor, *Mission with LeMay: My Story*, (New York: Doubleday & Company, 1965), p. 379.

"*A rugged and stable . . . platform.*": Stephen Harding and James I. Long, *Dominator: The*

Story of the Consolidate B-32 Bomber (Missoula, Mont.: Pictorial Histories Publishing Co. Inc., 1984).

Chapter 15: Flexing the Fire

"The assembly was fair": Samuel Russ Harris Jr., Robert A. Mann (ed.), B-29s Over Japan, 1944–1945: A Group Commander's Diary (Jefferson, North Carolina: McFarland and Company, 2011).

"An embattled battalion commander, Major Shelton Scales of the 4th Marine Division": "'Dinah Might' was first bomber to land on Iwo," by Charles A. Jones, Marine Corps Times, June 26, 2006.

"LeMay did not have to take into account": Warren Kozak, LeMay: The Life and Wars of General Curtis LeMay (Washington, DC: Regnery Publishing Inc., 2009), pp. 215–216.

"If this month is successful": Correspondence from Arnold T. Johnson provided by his daughter, Doris Goodlett.

"The effort leading up to the Tokyo raid was immense": Barrett Tillman, Whirlwind: The War Against Japan, 1942–1945 (New York: Simon & Schuster, 2010), p. 136–137.

"Japan was under 10/10 cloud cover": From an unpublished family memoir by Edward W. Cutler.

"local night mission for the specific purpose": Gordon Bennett Robertson, Bringing the Thunder: The Missions of a World War II B-29 Pilot in the Pacific (Mechanicsburg, Pa.: Stackpole Books, 2006).

Chapter 16: The Way Home

Savage quote: Letter to the author.

Black circles around Power's eyes: Wilbur H. Morrison, Point of No Return: The Story of the Twentieth Air Force (New York: Playboy Paperbacks, 1970).

"left B-29s scattered all over the Pacific": From a Savage biography published online by the 7th Bomb Group B-36 Association.

McCaskill crew ditching: The 12:38 p.m. time on March 10 is from the records of the seaplane tender USS Bering Strait (AVP 34), the ship that rescued this B-29 crew.

Chapter 17: The Fire Blitz

"The bomb run went smoothly . . .": Letter dated August 6, 2005, from navigator Alexander L. "Lew" Parry, the only member of the McDonald crew to survive the war.

Arnold like a cadmium battery: Dik Alan Daso, Hap Arnold and the Evolution of American Airpower (Washington, DC: Smithsonian Institution Press, 2000), p. 201.

"Flying above the American formations . . .": "Last Deadly Gale from Japan," by Jon Guttman, Aviation History, May 2006.

"Here we were on another night strike to the Tokyo area": 1st Lt. William C. Atkinson quoted in The Twenty Niner: The Combat Story of the 498th Bombardment Group, by Capt. Michael J. Ogden, 1946.

Truman on April 12, 1945: Harry S Truman, Memoirs, 1945: Year of Decisions (New York: Smithmark, 1995).

Chapter 18: Air Campaign

Atkinson material: Courtesy of the Atkinson family.

Carter material: Courtesy of Doug Carter.

Chapter 19: "Destroyer of Worlds"

Carter material: Courtesy of Doug Carter.

Chapter 20: Mission to Hiroshima

Into the air: The poem by a resentful B-29 crewmember deriding the 509th Composite Group has appeared in several histories of the era including Whirlwind: The War Against Japan, 1942–1945 (New York: Simon & Schuster, 2010), by Barrett Tillman.

"Nobody else was supposed to be in the air during the Hiroshima mission": Correspondence with John Bybee.

Tibbets's crew included four who had flown with him in Europe: "Atomic Mission," by John T. Correll, Airforce Magazine, October 2010.

"It was a shock of course": The quote from Yoko Ono is from "Xeni Jardin Interviews Yoko Ono in Japan" in the online publication Dangerous Minds, http://www.dangerousminds.net/comments/xeni_jardin_interviews_yoko_ono_in_japan. The interview is undated but appears to have taken place in August 2011.

Tibbets had already decided to make use of every inch of the runway: "Atomic Mission," by John T. Correll, Airforce Magazine, October 2010.

As historian John Bybee put it: Interview with John Bybee, November 9, 2010.

B-29 sortie numbers: William Wolf, Boeing B-29 Superfortress—The Ultimate Look: From Drawing Board to VJ-Day (Atglen, Pa.: Schiffer Publishing, Ltd., 2004), p. 331.

"From the symmetrical cigar of a fuselage": "Superbomber's Achilles Heel," by Stephan Wilkinson, Aviation History, September 2011.

Bibliography

Birdsall, Steve. *Saga of the Superfortress: The Dramatic Story of the B-29 and the Twentieth Air Force*. (New York: Doubleday & Company, Inc., 1980).

Bond, Horatio, ed. *Fire and the Air War*. (Boston: National Fire Protection Association, 1946).

Caidin, Martin. *A Torch to the Enemy*. (New York: Ballantine Books, 1960).

Coleman, Joseph. "1945 Tokyo Firebombing Left Legacy of Terror, Pain." *Associated Press*, March 10, 2005.

Correll, John T. "Atomic Mission." *Air Force Magazine*, October 2010.

Cortesi, Lawrence. *Target Tokyo*. (New York: Kensington Publishing, 1983).

Cozzens, James Gould. *A Time of War: Air Force Diaries and Pentagon Memos 1943–45*, edited by Matthew J. Bruccoli. (Boston: Harvard University, 1984).

Craven, Wesley Frank and James Lea Cate. *The Army Air Forces in World War II*. (Washington, DC: Superintendent of Documents, 1950).

Daso, Dik Alan. *Hap Arnold and the Evolution of American Airpower*. (Washington, DC: Smithsonian Institution Press, 2000).

Fukubayashi, Toru. "Allied Aircraft and Airmen lost over the Japanese Mainland." May 20, 2007. http://www.powresearch.jp/en/pdf_e/b29/b29_fukubayashi_e.pdf.

Guillain, Robert, translated by William Byron. *I Saw Tokyo Burning: Eyewitness Narrative from Pearl Harbor to Hiroshima*. (New York: John Murray Publishers Ltd, 1981).

Guttman, Jon. "Last Deadly Gale from Japan." *Aviation History* Vol. 16, No. 5 (2006).

Hansell, Haywood S., Jr. *Strategic Air War Against Japan*. (Maxwell AFB, Ala.: Airpower Research Institute, 1980).

Harding, Stephen and James I. Long. *Dominator: The Story of the Consolidated B-32 Bomber*. (Missoula, Montana: Pictorial Histories Publishing Co. Inc., 1984).

Harris, Samuel Russ Jr. *B-29s Over Japan, 1944–1945: A Group Commander's Diary*, edited by Robert A. Mann. (Jefferson, North Carolina: McFarland and Company, 2011).

Hemingway, Ernest. "London Fights the Robots." *Collier's*, August 1944.

Huglin, Henry C. "The B-29 Strategic Air Campaign Against Japan." He wrote this memoir in November 2004. Publication details are not known. Huglin commanded the 9th Bombardment Group on March 9–10, 1945.

Impact: The Army Air Forces' "Confidential" Picture History of World War II. (Office of the Assistant Chief of Air Staff, Intelligence: Washington DC, 1945).

Jablonski, Edward. *Wings of Fire*. (New York: Doubleday, 1972).

Jones, Charles A. "'Dinah Might' was first bomber to land on Iwo." *Marine Corps Times*, June 26, 2006.

Kozak, Warren. *LeMay: The Life and Wars of General Curtis LeMay*. (Washington, DC: Regnery Publishing, Inc., 2009).

Kusama, Hidesaburo. "US-Japanese Fact-Finding of the B-29 Crash on March 10, 1945 at Itabashi Mura, Japan." *The Journal of the Faculty of Foreign Studies*, Aichi Prefectural University, 1999.

LeMay, Curtis E. and MacKinlay Kantor. *Mission with LeMay: My Story*. (New York: Doubleday & Company, 1965).

Marshall, Chester. *B-29 Superfortress*. (Osceola, Wisc.: Motorbooks International, 1993).

McKelway, St. Clair. "A Reporter with the B-29s: I—Possum, Rosy, and the Thousand Kids." *The New Yorker*, 1945.

———. "A Reporter with the B-29s: II—The Doldrums, Guam, and Something Coming Up." *The New Yorker*, 1945.

———. "A Reporter with the B-29s: III—The Cigar, the Three Wings, and the Low-Level Attacks" *The New Yorker*, 1945.

Morrison, Wilbur H. *Point of No Return: The Story of the Twentieth Air Force*. (New York: Playboy Paperbacks, 1970).

Nichols. Kenneth D. *The Road to Trinity*. (New York: William Morrow and Company, 1987).

Ogden, Capt. Michael J. *The Twenty Niner: The Combat Story of the 498th Bombardment Group*. (Self-published: 1946).

Robertson, Gordon Bennett Jr. *Bringing the Thunder: The Missions of a World War II B-29 Pilot in the Pacific*. (Mechanicsburg, Pa.: Stackpole Books, 2006).

Sanders, Milton P. *One Man's World War II: Tending Seaplanes in the Pacific*. (Fairfax, Va.: History4All, Inc., 2008).

Selden, Mark. "A Forgotten Holocaust: US Bombing Strategy, the Destruction of Japanese Cities and the American Way of War from the Pacific War to Iraq." *Japan Focus* (2007).

Smith, Lawrence. *9th Bombardment Group (VH) History*. (Princeton, N.J.: Ninth Bombardment Group Association, 1995).

Tillman, Barrett. *Whirlwind: The Air War Against Japan, 1942–1945*

(New York: Simon & Schuster, 2010).

Truman, Harry S. *Memoirs, 1945: Year of Decisions* . (New York: Smithmark, 1995).

Uris, Leon. *Battle Cry*. (New York: G. P. Putnam's Sons, 1953).

Wilkinson, Stephan. "Superbomber's Achilles Heel." *Aviation History* Vol. 22, No. 1 (2011).

Whittaker, Wayne. "Here's the B-32—Our Newest Superbomber." *Popular Mechanics*, September 1945.

Wolf, William. *Boeing B-29 Superfortress—The Ultimate Look: From Drawing Board to VJ-Day*. (Atglen, Pa.: Schiffer Publishing, 2005).

Index